LONGING
FOR
COMMUNITY

An excellent presentation of how to achieve a proper balance between sociological and spiritual realities within the challenge of outreach to Muslims. The concept of "Ummah" (community) is explored and suggestions made on how to integrate believers into a new grouping that preserves biblical integrity while not denouncing Muslim culture and life. A valuable resource for practitioners on the front lines.

Phil Parshall
SIM, Missionary at Large

In the present day, sharing the Gospel to Muslims (or to anyone else) is different than the "mission compound" methodologies. I highly recommend this book to be read by readers who are striving to share Christ to anyone, especially to Muslims. It is also a thoughtful reading for general Christ followers (Christians) who are interested in understanding the issues in a mission field context. This book will encourage all of us to pray for those who are involved every day in helping people to understand the *Injil*.

K. Rajendran
World Evangelical Alliance Mission Commission; Global Roundtable

The chapters of this book introduce us to a new way of "bridging" the gap that many make us believe exists between civilizations. We will discover through these pages some explanations to the difficulties a Muslim faces in accepting a "new identity" and how sometimes in spite of our human efforts in "discipling" the new converts, God surprises us in dealing with the Muslim person through keeping their cultural Muslim identity while at the same time being faithful to Jesus in the inner "ego." I found the book very thought provoking in the very issues that many missionaries are facing in the field. Our cultural ways as Latinos or Westerners are sometimes obtrusive of how God sometimes deals in His way with them. We need to be open to the manifold wisdom of God manifested in the East. To miracles, dreams, visions, and allowing the Holy Spirit to apply the revelation of the Scriptures in different homiletical categories that we have learned in Systematic Theology.

Pablo Carrillo
Founder, PM Internacional

LONGING
FOR
COMMUNITY

CHURCH, *UMMAH*, OR SOMEWHERE IN BETWEEN?

EDITOR
DAVID GREENLEE

ASSOCIATE EDITORS
BOB FISH / TIM GREEN / MARY MCVICKER
NICOLE RAVELO-HOËRSON / FARIDA SAIDI / J. DUDLEY WOODBERRY

WILLIAM CAREY
LIBRARY

Published by William Carey Library
1605 E. Elizabeth Street
Pasadena, CA 91104 | www.missionbooks.org

Kelley K. Wolfe, editor
Brad Koenig, copyeditor
Hugh Pindur, graphic designer
Rose Lee-Norman, indexer

William Carey Library is a ministry of the

U.S. Center for World Mission
Pasadena, CA | www.uscwm.org

Printed in the United States of America

17 16 15 14 13   5 4 3 2 1 BP 1000

Library of Congress Cataloging-in-Publication Data

Longing for community : church, *ummah*, or somewhere in between? / edited by David Greenlee.
    pages cm
  ISBN 978-0-87808-533-0
1. Missions to Muslims. 2. Christian converts from Islam. I. Greenlee, David, 1957- editor of compilation.
  BV2625.L66 2013
  266.0088'297--dc23
                        2012044576

CONTENTS

CONTRIBUTORS

Sufyan Baig, an Indian Muslim background believer in Jesus Christ, has been working among Muslim peoples for fifteen years. He is integrated into the mainstream culture through an appealing, secular role in the community. He has a BD in Theology and an MSc in Islamic and Middle Eastern Studies.

Jens Barnett has lived for eighteen years with his family in the Middle East. For much of this time he has been involved in the discipleship and training of believers coming from a Muslim religio-cultural background. He holds a master's degree in Global Issues in Contemporary Mission from Redcliffe College, UK.

Rick Brown, PhD, is a Bible scholar and missiologist. He has been involved in outreach in Africa and Asia since 1977.

James Bultema has lived in Turkey since 1990, serving and seeking to grow the church in that land. He and his wife Renata have led the way in establishing in Antalya the St. Paul Union Church, the St. Paul Cultural Center, and a youth camp called Olive Grove. He is also writing his PhD dissertation on the Turkish Protestant Church and intends to submit it to the Religious Studies Department at Leiden University in 2013.

L. R. Burke has worked in sub-Saharan Africa since 1992. The focus of his work is Bible translation, Bible storying, and training local evangelists. Since 2007 he has collaborated with the Fruitful Practice Research team in researching the ways in which language and cultural issues affect fruitfulness in Muslim ministry.

Mary Davidson worked with her husband in the Middle East for over two decades. She is now involved in teaching and training people in understanding other cultures and faiths, and continues to visit the Middle East. She has a PhD in Education, and is writing another dissertation on Muslim women.

Colin Edwards has worked in South Asia for more than twelve years looking at the growing church there. His PhD research considers the concepts of honor, shame, and patronage and how they impact the beliefs and outworkings of faith in these groups.

Russell Eleazar was born and raised in a Muslim family in the Soviet Union. He came to faith in Jesus in the mid-1990s and later served with OM for about ten years. He received his MA degree from a seminary in North America.

Jean-Marie Gaudeul is a Roman Catholic priest and member of the Missionary Society of the "White Fathers." Ordained in 1963, he worked several years in Tanzania as a parish priest. The author of several books on the history of Christian-Muslim relations, he holds a PhD in Arabic and Islamic studies from the Pontifical Institute of Arabic and Islamic Studies (PISAI) in Rome where he also taught from 1975 to 1984. From 2000 to 2006 he was in charge of the French Bishops' Secretariat for relations with Islam (SRI) and for the past ten years was a member of the Vatican commission for Christian-Muslim dialogue. At the present, he produces, in French, *Se Comprendre*, a bulletin for Christian-Muslim understanding.

Tim Green has enjoyed friendships with believers from Muslim background for thirty years. He has worked in theological education by extension in Pakistan 1988–2003, in Jordan 2003–2005, and more recently from his home in Britain. His particular focus is on discipleship and training in the Muslim world, while also studying for a doctorate at the University of London.

David Greenlee was raised by missionary parents in South America. He has served with OM since 1977, currently in the role of Director of International Ministry Services. Married with three adult children, he holds a PhD in Intercultural Studies from Trinity International University, Deerfield, Illinois, USA. David's publications include *One Cross, One Way, Many Journeys: Thinking Again about Conversion* and the edited *From the Straight Path to the Narrow Way: Journeys of Faith*.

Enoch J. Kim has lived and worked among Chinese house church groups and a Muslim unreached people group for more than fifteen years. He emphasized efforts in training house church leaders to reach Muslims. Enoch received his PhD in Missiology from Fuller Theological Seminary, Pasadena, California, USA, where he currently serves as an adjunct professor.

John Kim has been working among a major unreached people group in Southeast Asia since 1994 along with his wife Yoon and their three children. He now directs INSIDERS, an international mission focusing on biblical and indigenous mission planting movements among Muslim unreached peoples in Asia and is involved in mobilizing and training Asians through the Asian Frontier Mission Initiative and similar networks.

Kathryn Kraft has lived and worked in the Middle East since 2001. She has an MA in Middle Eastern Studies from the American University of Beirut, and a PhD in Sociology from the University of Bristol, England. She has worked in a variety of fields including research, human rights, emergency relief, and social development. Currently she manages programming and advises on social development issues for an international humanitarian agency, and is pursuing publication of her first full-length novel, a coming-of-age love story set in Damascus, Syria.

Ruth Nicholls trained as a teacher before joining an international organization to serve the Lord in a predominantly Muslim country in Asia. Utilizing her gifts in teaching and study of the Scriptures she became a member of a team ministering to Muslims seeking Christ through Bible correspondence courses and radio ministries. Ruth returned to Australia in 2000 and completed her Doctorate of Ministry.

Jihan Paik holds a PhD in Central Asian history from a university in Turkey. He currently works for the Network on the Silk Road, based in China, having earlier served in Turkey and Azerbaijan for seventeen years.

David Radford worked for over twenty-five years in South and Central Asia with Youth With a Mission, much of that time within the context of Muslim peoples and Muslim nations. He has an MA in Religion Studies and is presently completing a PhD in Sociology investigating religious revitalization in post-socialist Kyrgyzstan, focusing on the conversion of the Kyrgyz to Protestant Christianity.

Karen Scott and her family have worked in Bangladesh since 1973. They have ministered primarily through health and community development programs. Karen's interest in women's issues arises from seeing the amazing potential of women during her years working with them in rural health programs. Her interest in women also extends to the family and to the socio-religious structures in which women live. She and her husband currently work under World Mission Prayer League in the Business as Mission paradigm. Out of a holistic perspective, Karen teaches in seminaries in various countries on the role of the church in society and ministry to women in Islam. Karen holds a PhD in Intercultural Studies from Fuller Theological Seminary.

David Smith has lived and worked in various countries of the Middle East for eighteen years and taught in seminaries and mission colleges there and in the UK.

Reinhold Straehler is from Germany and has lived and worked with his family in the Middle East and East Africa for twenty years. His desire is to mobilize and train Christians to encounter people of other faiths and to share the Good News of Christ with them. One of the phenomena that fascinates him is the process of conversion of those who come to faith in Christ from a Muslim background. This was also the area of his research for his MTh and DTh degrees that he received from Unisa, South Africa.

J. Dudley Woodberry is Dean Emeritus and Senior Professor of Islamic Studies at the School of Intercultural Studies at Fuller Theological Seminary in Pasadena, California, USA. He has served with his wife and three sons at the Christian Study Centre in Rawalpindi, Pakistan, and as a pastor in Kabul, Afghanistan and Riyadh, Saudi Arabia. Among his most recent edited work has been *From Seed to Fruit: Global Trends, Fruitful Practices, and Emerging Issues among Muslims*, 2nd edition, Pasadena: William Carey, 2011.

INTRODUCTION: TRANSFORMED IN CHRIST

DAVID GREENLEE

One of the major themes of Paul's letter to the Ephesians is centered on the phrase "in Christ." To list a few of Paul's expressions, we are blessed, chosen, and included *in Christ*. We hope *in Christ* and are marked *in Christ* in accord with God's plan purposed *in Christ* to bring all things in heaven and earth together *under Christ*. We were once far away but now *in Christ* are brought near to God, Gentiles together with Israel sharing in the promise *in Christ*.

How do we live that out? What difference does it make, in comparison to the rest of society, in terms of what we eat, drink, inhale, wear, listen to, believe, value, trust, and hope for?

While editing this book, I made the short journey to Basel, Switzerland to attend a missiological consultation. During the conference, clustered in small groups for prayer, a man involved in youth ministry brought up the concerns of some north German teenagers. They had begun to follow Jesus, but were fearful of being "outed" as Christians. Although their setting is very different from the Muslims described in this book, their core questions seemed to be very similar as their new faith began to work itself out in a transformed identity in Christ (Romans 12:1,2).

For many of us, the normal tendency is to define the faith aspect of our identity in terms of belief. With that frame of reference, Paul Hiebert noted, "We ask people if they 'believe this to be true,' assuming that if they believe this, they are saved. We debate what must be included—should these essentials be few (this leads to cheap grace) or many (who then can enter?)? We spend much time making certain that people's beliefs are set right by preaching and teaching."[1]

In terms of our "in Christ" identity, though, the object of belief is not a set of facts, but a person: Jesus Christ. It is trust in him, not merely assent to truth. As E. Stanley

Jones is reported to have said, "In conversion you are not attached primarily to an order, nor to an institution, nor a movement, nor a set of beliefs, nor a code of action—you are attached primarily to a Person, and secondarily to these other things."

"IDENTITY"—A KEY "COMING TO FAITH CONSULTATION" THEME

As documented in *From the Straight Path to the Narrow Way: Journeys of Faith*,[2] the focus of research and reflection at the 2004 "Coming to Faith Consultation" (CTFC) tended to be on the processes and factors involved in how our Muslim neighbors are coming to faith in Jesus Christ. Three typical factors emerged: they have generally experienced a touch of God's love, seen a sign of his power, and encountered the truth of God's Word.

In February 2010, some sixty who serve among Muslims and missiologists gathered near London for the "Second Coming to Faith Consultation" (CTFC2). Among us were several men and women raised as Muslims who had come to faith in Jesus Christ. There, with no intentional steering of themes by the organizers, we observed a shift in the focus of many research papers as compared to the 2004 consultation. Rather than focusing on *how* people are coming to faith in Christ, many papers centered on issues of identity, seeing believers both as "actors" and "acted upon" in the process and outworking of conversion.

Identity has been a major topic of study elsewhere, and in missiology especially in studies of conversion in India.[3] Until recently, though, this theme has not received sufficient attention in the new but growing body of studies concerning those of a Muslim background who have come to faith in Jesus Christ.[4] While the Indian studies I have read speak of the conversion of individuals, their emphasis tends to be on the shared identity of a group, relevant to questions described by social identity theory,[5] explored in some detail in this book by Jens Barnett and Tim Green, and touched on by many of our other writers. I hope that our combined contribution on this and other topics will help move missiology forward in our shared understanding of conversion and the resulting individual and corporate expressions of new faith and transformed identities in Jesus Christ.

At CTFC2, and in preparing this book, we recognized the need to view conversion through various "lenses" in order to better see the multi-colored tapestry of God's work in our lives. I trust that the value of this multidisciplinary contribution to missiology will be evident in our writing, even though we have not used every "lens" that the social and natural sciences offer us. Yet, whether considering "identity" or any other theme explored, we also affirm that our understanding of conversion must be firmly grounded in the biblical teaching that, through and through, conversion is an act of the triune God (Titus 3:4–6), enabling us to be *in Christ* and part of the new people of God (Eph 2:11–22).

AN OVERVIEW OF THE CHAPTERS

Though there would be many ways to order the chapters of this book, we have chosen to group the contributions in three sections: "Understanding the Complexity of Conversion," "Culture, Community, and Coming to Faith in Christ," and "Lessons to Foster Fruit and Growth."

We begin with contributions from sociologists David Radford and Kathryn Kraft. One reason that we have placed Radford first is his explicit emphasis on the importance of understanding conversion from the perspective of the new believer. Conversion for Radford is a process that combines intentionality and cognitive aspects with the "fuzzy" intuitive side of the conversion process. Kraft, drawing on her doctoral studies in the Middle East, discusses the individual uniqueness yet overall similarity of conversion processes — and the related problem of mutual rejection when believers express a significant difference in their sense of identity and associated lifestyle values, and continuity or discontinuity with the values and practices of their family and society.

Jens Barnett and Tim Green then introduce, through narrative and theory, the complexities of identity and the problems, if not impossibility, of trying to plot anyone's faith expression on a simple grid. The "C Spectrum" description of Christ-centered communities has served a useful purpose; we are indebted to John Travis for his creative contribution.[6] Having only one dimension, however, limiting ourselves to that scale limits our perception of the complexities of individual and corporate identity, and the related missiological discussion. Barnett's and Green's contributions, coupled with others in this book, are an important step forward, not because they offer a "simple, new, and improved model" but because they remind us of the complexity of the issues of conversion and identity.

Sufyan Baig opens our second section, reflecting on the experience he has shared with other Muslims of India who have become followers of Jesus and look for a new *ummah*, a community of faith. Helping them find a welcome in the Christian community, Baig argues, will require that the church leave behind its tendency to suspicion of new believers and be prepared to suffer and sacrifice, following the example of Christ.

Colin Edwards then describes the patron-client, group-oriented society of Bangladesh and the intimately connected relationship between a *pir* and his followers. This strong sense of connectedness to a savior — and a fascinating story of how many Bangladeshis believe end times judgment will be carried out — helps explain how some Bangladeshis understand their own coming to faith and identity in Christ.

In contrast to Edwards' description of people who, in large part, are deeply influenced by traditional values, Enoch Kim has studied the effects of modernization on the Hui of China and their rapidly changing urban social networks. The increased importance of "I" rather than "us" in decision-making and the formation of multiple social identities has changed, and in some cases increased, the receptivity of the Hui to the gospel.

Writing from his native Azerbaijan, Russell Eleazar explores why youth in Baku have not come to faith despite significant exposure to the gospel and experience among believers. In part this can be attributed to the pressure of traditional family ties; however, the greatest challenge Eleazar finds is simply that they do not want to believe the truth about Jesus Christ.

Rick Brown frames his discussion of contextualization around the theme of "courtesy and respect," the natural expression of God's love that should be lived out in our lives and ministry. Larry Burke's chapter, based on his experience in Africa, reflects the attitude that Brown espouses. Both would argue that we must understand different worldview perspectives if we are to fruitfully communicate the gospel message and help our Muslim neighbors understand the gospel as good news. Burke then points to three helpful "gospel roads" appropriate for different individuals and settings, whose perceived needs may center on guilt, shame and defilement, or fear.

In the final chapter of this section, Reinhold Straehler presents insights from his research in Kenya. He describes common stages in the process of conversion, particularly in terms of cognitive and affective changes. Straehler, recognizing typical consequences both within individuals and in their relationship with society, concludes with a section of important missiological implications.

Our final section, "Lessons to Foster Fruit and Growth," is opened by J. Dudley Woodberry who reviews the complementary findings of two tracks of research: his own long-term study, which emphasizes the perspectives of Muslims who have come to faith in Jesus Christ, and the work of Fruitful Practice Research, based largely on the viewpoint of workers serving among Muslims.

Jean-Marie Gaudeul writes from the perspective of recent Roman Catholic history, pointing to a necessary "imitation of Christ" as the church engages in mission: imitation in his hidden life at Nazareth, in his public ministry, and in his suffering and death. Jihan Paik takes us further back in history as he reviews the mission of the Nestorian church whose "spiritual heritage rooted in the Jerusalem church and their role as mediators between East and West on the Silk Road" point to lessons significant today. Despite minority status and great persecution, the Nestorians' cultural rootedness, structure, and involvement of members from all walks of life were key to their success.

John Kim continues his narrative of the community of believers of "Anotoc" told at CTFC in 2004 and presented in *From the Straight Path to the Narrow Way*.[7] Kim provides helpful insights to the story of the growth of this believing community. He examines issues such as disharmony among expatriate workers, discipling the new believers and, in particular, the group dynamics between and among the socio-religious hierarchies, the community being reached, and those he describes as "inbetweeners."

The following two papers focus on what might be termed "women's issues" but are of vital importance for the *whole* church. Karen Scott, based on her research in Bangladesh, highlights the vital importance of discipling women. Women are of inestimable value to their family and community, and key to reaching the children. If the children are not reached, "this movement of the Spirit of God in Bangladesh may very well not make it to the next generation." While Scott points to the importance of change in attitudes and action in the discipling of women, Mary Davidson illustrates multiple ways in which women in Muslim societies already participate and exercise leadership in religious settings that can be better appropriated in witness and discipling among women.

Ruth Nicholls suggests a creative and, in Brown's terms, courteous way to communicate biblical truth: the use of liturgy. Such liturgies fit the ritual nature of faith expression familiar to believers in Christ from a Muslim background. Created for specific individuals and situations, however, they are not effective in themselves but only through the power of the Holy Spirit and the engagement of the individual with the liturgical content.

James Bultema describes the growth of the Turkish Protestant Church over the past half century. Bultema traces three key factors in its growth: the Word of God encountered in various ways, but most often in printed, intelligible form; the witness of believers experienced in myriad ways; and the worship of God's people observed or engaged in at a local church. The narrative style of his chapter, presenting his analysis through the story of Hasan Unutmuş, is a compelling reminder that our work and our writing is not about abstract concepts or projected statistics, but describes the work of God in the lives of precious individuals who often pay a high price as a result of their faith.

To conclude the book David Smith, who participated in both CTFC and CTFC2,[8] offers two brief biblical reflections and then poses important questions based on the content—and the gaps—in these chapters.

EVIDENCE OF GOD AT WORK

One thing I greatly appreciated at both CTFC and CTFC2 was the willingness of the participants to listen, to reflect, and to learn without quickly criticizing those whose theological assumptions or approach in ministry differed from their own. They reflected the attitude of Barnabas who, a Levite and no theological novice, came to Antioch where he found "evidence of the grace of God" (Acts 11:23). Oh, that there would be more of this gracious, humble attitude in the current debates concerning ministry among Muslims and the expressions of faith of the new communities of believers!

At CTFC2 this involved, at one level, simply the call for mutual respect and recognition that would be merited in any serious academic setting. Beyond that, we realized that each of us present deeply longs to see Jesus glorified as Muslims — indeed all peoples — turn in large numbers to saving faith in him.

A WORD ON TERMINOLOGY

The contributors to this volume come from a variety of backgrounds and academic disciplines. Rather than imposing a single definition of words such as "conversion," writers were encouraged to express themselves in their own terms. Radford and Kraft, for example, write as sociologists and, as such, use a sociological definition of conversion. Straehler, in comparison, cites Andrew Walls and uses a definition that may be more familiar to those whose emphasis is on theology or missiology.

Similarly, we have not imposed a single term to describe Muslims who have become believers in Jesus Christ. Whatever term, if any, the contributors have chosen, each of us desired to avoid falling into the trap described by Sufyan Baig, himself such a follower of Jesus, that in the midst of these debates and arguments "the human struggling in his or her search for God is often forgotten and the reality of individual converts' lives is ignored."

We hope that our writing will convey the same attitude that Baig sensed in our consultation, "a refreshing break from that pattern. We gathered from around the world in an attempt to bring those individual lives, with their struggles and joys, to the forefront of attention of those working among Muslims and those developing strategic approaches."

DIVERSITY WITH DEFINITION

We celebrate our diversity, but remember that it is not undefined. Our identity, whatever outward expression is given, is grounded and deeply rooted in Christ that we might be "to the praise of his glory," living carefully and wisely as children of light (Ephesians 1:12–14; 5:15–16).

As Jean-Marie Gaudeul observes in his chapter,

> As we discover the many ways in which Christ, "lifted up from
> the earth, draws everyone to himself" (John 12:32), we are struck
> by the extraordinary variety of ways in which people, finding new
> faith in Him, discover their new identity: they are changed and yet

the same. We know that this diversity is only a small part of God's infinite skill in leading us to His house where Unity will combine with the fulfillment of each person's originality.

A WORD OF APPRECIATION

In conclusion, I want to thank my associate editors for their contribution to this volume: J. Dudley Woodberry, Farida Saidi, Mary McVicker, Tim Green, Bob Fish, and Nicole Ravelo-Hoërson, most of whom were also members of the CTFC2 Steering Committee. Thanks are also due to the various donors who made CTFC2 possible, and those who served us at the event, in particular Laura Adams and Joanne Humphrey. As an editorial team we also express our appreciation to Greg Kernaghan who assisted us in the technical editing of the book, and to Jeff Minard, Melissa Hicks, Kelley Wolfe, Wendy Hayes, and the entire William Carey Library publication team for their vital contribution to making this book a reality.

To God be the glory, for all time and among all the nations!

SECTION 1

UNDERSTANDING THE COMPLEXITY OF CONVERSION

1

FUZZY THINKING AND THE CONVERSION PROCESS

DAVID RADFORD

Sociology has approached religion and religious change in a number of ways. The traditional view is that religion will become privatized and relegated to the point of having a minor, if any, relevant role in modern society.[9] More recently, scholars have challenged this, recognizing that religion continues to have a significant impact on mainstream modern, public society and that new approaches are needed to understand religious life.[10] This paper considers some of these approaches related to religious conversion and addresses how individuals and communities engage in the process of conversion. In particular, I draw on the concepts of "subjective rationality" put forward by Rodney Stark and Roger Finke,[11] and David Smilde's "imaginative rationality,"[12] suggesting that they are helpful tools in explaining an individual's behavior in the context of the social dynamics at work following the collapse of the Soviet Union and, in particular, the conversion process of Muslim Kyrgyz to Protestant[13] Christianity. Following a background description of Kyrgyzstan and the Kyrgyz, I briefly describe these concepts and explore them through the narrative stories of Kyrgyz Christians.[14]

KYRGYZSTAN AND THE KYRGYZ: A BRIEF INTRODUCTION

The Kyrgyz are considered a Muslim people group,[15] despite significant pre-Islamic influences in their religious life including animistic and shamanistic beliefs and practices.[16] The effect of seventy years of Soviet scientific atheism was strongly felt especially in urban centers and was imbibed by many Kyrgyz to a greater or lesser degree, resulting in a very moderate form of Islamic religiosity. Muslim identity, for the Kyrgyz, is viewed primarily as ethnic rather than religious.[17] The collapse of Socialism and independence from Russia in 1991 brought a new sense of freedom for Kyrgyzstan. It also heralded the arrival of a number of foreign missionary groups, both Muslim and Christian. The ensuing years have seen a flourishing religious market resulting in a rise in public Islamic religious observance of and commitment to both orthodox and traditional or popular forms of Islam. Kyrgyzstan also has witnessed the growth of numerous Protestant Christian and non-Christian denominations and sects.[18] The number of Kyrgyz who identify themselves as Protestant Christians has grown from a few in 1991 (at the time of independence) to approximately 20,000.[19]

RELIGIOUS CONVERSION

Religious conversion, from the perspective of sociology, is a social process which includes subjective and rational elements. People both experience and think through religious conversion. Individuals and communities engage in a deliberate, reflective process that inevitably leads to change. The initiative for change and its agents include the person or community themselves as well as external factors such as people, ideas, circumstances and experiences. The way that change occurs and is understood and explained is shaped to a large degree by the tools (concepts and relationships), both conscious and unconscious, with which a person has been socialized. It may also include previously unknown and untested tools that are then adapted and adopted within their existing conceptual framework as individuals and communities find resonance with their experience and their need to find explanatory models.

SUBJECTIVE RATIONALITY

Stark and Finke use the term "subjective rationality" in their analysis of religious decision making, suggesting that Rational Choice Theory describes the idea that people making decisions weigh the costs and benefits in order to maximize gain for the least cost. They suggest that humans are not predictable as to how they make decisions; the process is "fuzzy" and "intuitive." Stark and Finke quote James S. Coleman, "[Much] of what is ordinarily described as non-rational or irrational is merely so because observers have not discovered the point of view of the actor, from which the action is rational."[20] The weighing of costs and benefits is not necessarily a strictly cognitive or linear process but one that involves a healthy dose of subjectivity: it is also what a person feels and experiences as right and true.

IMAGINATIVE RATIONALITY

In a recent publication, David Smilde[21] develops the idea of "imaginative rationality." Smilde sees the instrumentalist perspective which emphasizes the "everyday creative agency involved in cultural practices" as a tool to bring about change by individuals. On the other hand, substantive rationality advocates that culture — values, concepts, and categories — has an autonomous element and acts upon human desires and choices as a moral normative that influences one's beliefs and choices.

Smilde's "imaginative rationality" draws from both traditions. For Smilde, culture is "the product of creative intelligence confronting problematic situations ... People encounter problems, create new projects to address them, and then reflectively evaluate the success of these projects."[22] The reflective process involves the creation of concepts for experiences that people have encountered and are presently walking through. In the specific case of the conversion of Venezuelan men to Evangelicalism, Smilde suggests that "they found a package of meanings and practices that helped them both conceptualize and address their problems."[23]

HOW HAVE KYRGYZ CHRISTIANS EXPERIENCED AND UNDERSTOOD THEIR CONVERSION TO PROTESTANT CHRISTIANITY?

As a framework for this next section, I want to summarize the process that Smilde refers to above in three sections: first, identification of life issues and/or problems; second, how these were addressed in the experience of the Kyrgyz Christians; and, third, measuring the success of this "project" and the interpretation of what has occurred. I then explore these through the lenses of "subjective" and "imaginative" rationality.

LIFE SITUATIONS/PROBLEMS OF KYRGYZ BEFORE CONVERSION

I will illustrate the life experiences of two Kyrgyz who have converted to Protestant Christianity. Nargiza (female) and Rizbek (male)[24] were two of the forty-nine Kyrgyz Christian respondents with whom I conducted in-depth interviews as part of my PhD research in Kyrgyzstan from 2004–2008.[25] Nargiza is a single woman in her mid-30s, a full-time Christian worker who had trained as a nurse. She had experienced recurring health problems for many years identified as epilepsy. Growing up, she was often bedridden and was hospitalized for long periods. Nargiza went to local fortune-tellers (*kozuachyk*),[26] who not only give information about the future but also heal. For one year, she became a disciple of a well-known fortune-teller. Nargiza's health did not improve and she eventually left her home in the village to continue her studies in the capital city.

Married and in his mid-20s, Rizbek was working with a Non-Government Organization (NGO) involved in development work in southern Kyrgyzstan. When Rizbek was about eighteen years of age, he moved to the main city from his village. He wanted to learn English and approached an American man living in the city to teach him, who eventually found him some work. Another Kyrgyz was also working for the American, and Rizbek learned that he was a Christian. Previously Rizbek had heard negative reports by a mullah of how some Kyrgyz had converted to Christianity.

THE "CREATION OF PROJECTS" TO ADDRESS LIFE SITUATIONS

Nargiza: I had lots of questions inside of me. Why am I living? Why was I born? What is the reason for my life? But I could not find my answers. Then I went to the city. When I woke up one night I felt that I needed to read *namaz*, to pray, but my body couldn't do these things. For the whole night I experienced problems with this epilepsy and my body was very tired. After *namaz*, in my soul, something happened. I didn't know what it meant. I believed in God — but what kind of God, where he was, I didn't know. But something in my heart and my soul prayed, "God, do you really exist? If you really exist where is your truth? If you are truth, please show me. If you exist where are you? Why am I sick? Why do I have

lots of difficulties and troubles?" I had these questions. After
praying I went to the medical school, because I needed to take
my documents to apply.

In Nargiza's reflection on what happened to her, she clearly identified specific
life situations. The first was her ongoing health issues which had plagued her for
years. The initial solution to her problem was to seek help from a *kozuachyk,* and
become one herself. As a result of her life situation, she had become a religious
seeker who diligently practiced Muslim rituals. When she failed to find healing,
she attempted to further her studies.

Nargiza identified a specific occasion when a number of things converged
that resulted in her crying out to God for answers. It was at that time that Nargiza
met two Kyrgyz students at the college who shared with her about Christ. In the
course of the conversation, she mentioned her health issues. The girls told her, "If
you want to be healed, God can help you. God loves you." It was the first time she
had heard that. The girls invited her to a church meeting. She went but, when she
saw some Russian old people, she was hesitant.

> *Nargiza*: Some kind of voice [inside me] said, "What kind of place
> is this? You cannot come to this place. How have you come
> to be here? You have sold your faith, your religion. Look
> around you: there are a lot of Russian people." But another
> voice said, "You should come; enter inside." I went inside
> and one Kyrgyz lady and one Russian lady explained about
> God and about Jesus. I felt something. They said, "You are a
> sinful person," but I thought I was a holy person. "If you will
> receive Christ, you will have eternal life. God can heal you
> from your sickness." I just invited him and asked forgiveness
> and received Christ as Savior.

The description and explanation for her "conversion experience" highlight both
the aforementioned "subjective rationality" and "imaginative rationality." Cognitive
processes are at work: Nargiza thinks through her illness and her past and present
religious practices as attempts to find healing. She identified her thought processes
as she "talked" with God to find answers to life. Upon entering the church, she
had to face the cost of her action, including communal and personal accusations of
betrayal and being labeled "Russian."[27] What helped her navigate this process was,
in her own words, another voice—a subjective description of a "rational" process
she was going through. When the Christian message was explained there was not
a "Now I understood it" but rather "I felt something ..." Something intuitively connected with Nargiza. When another solution was offered to her life situation—"If

you will receive Christ ... Christ can heal you" — Nargiza accepted Christ as Savior. If repentance and acceptance of Christ was required to receive healing, Nargiza was prepared to do so.

> *Rizbek*: When I first heard about Christians, a mullah came to the school and told us negative things about "Baptists." He told us, "Do not talk to them and, if they give you books, do not accept them." The mullah said many bad things about Baptists [Christians]. He said that those people lock themselves in a dark room and do wicked [sexual] things with each other. So I started thinking about the information and the [Christian] person I was working with to see if it's true or not. It took me a long time to come to a conclusion. It was a process. As your relationship gets closer, you start seeing the person. So that's how the conclusion came by itself.

> *Interviewer*: What happened?

> *Rizbek*: You cannot express the inside feeling with words. I myself don't understand what happened. I don't know everything. D [a different American] came. He used to live alone in the apartment and I asked if I could share his apartment. I learned a lot from him and he prayed for me a lot. One day I came home and said, "D, I believe in Jesus but I cannot accept Him." Everything was mixed up in my mind and I couldn't explain and express what was in my heart. The next day was a Sunday and I agreed to go to church with him. There was an Uzbek family in the service and the husband shared his testimony with us. When I heard him, some kind of power came to me. When he shared his testimony, he said that he went through many difficulties and he was ready to go to death because of his faith. I have seen that his faith was not just words but he has shown his faith in his deeds. Of course I didn't accept the decision but I started saying I want to be a believer too ... I started searching and reading books with prayers about accepting Christ. But they didn't come out of my mouth. Maybe I wanted proof first, but finally something inside me exploded. And I said I want to believe and accept Christ; please help me with prayer. We sat together and prayed.

Rizbek's narrative, describing the context in which his conversion took place, emphasizes "subjective rationality" at work. Rizbek appeared to have no obvious problems in his life. He appeared to be a level-headed, unemotional, clear-thinking young man. The desire to learn English brought him into relationship with "dreaded" Christians who were not anything like the descriptions he was given by the mullah. In his own words, Rizbek started searching, weighing whether the information he had heard about Christians was correct or not. He came to a conclusion based on his experience of working and living in close relationship with them. Relationships with Kyrgyz, Uzbek, and foreign Christians were instrumental in moving him and convincing him to believe in Christ. Although there was clear evidence of a thinking, searching process, the transforming experience for Rizbek was explained by such subjective phrases as, "You cannot express the inside feeling with words. I myself don't understand what happened ... when I heard him, some kind of power came to me ... Finally something inside me exploded." Those subjective responses seemed to be as instrumental in his acceptance of Christ as the conscious weighing of the issues.

MEASUREMENT OF SUCCESS AND REFLECTIVE INTERPRETATION

Nargiza: From that time, a big peace came into my heart and until today I do not have this sickness. I started to read [the New Testament]. You remember I told you that I had a lot of questions? I felt God was answering me now. The last time I said, "God, if you exist, where are you?" I read from the Gospel of Matthew, "If you will knock I will open; if you ask I will give you; if you seek me I will show you." In John's Gospel Jesus tells his disciples, "I am the way, I am truth and I am the life, only through me can you see God." It was the answer to my questions. I couldn't find the truth and I felt God asking, "You are seeking the truth. I am the truth. Many times you wanted to find where is the life, but I am the life." But the most important thing is this, I took eternal life. I cannot explain it by words, it was just true ... It was like a big miracle in my life; God healed me. After I became a Christian, my family said that now I am like a real fortune-teller (*kozuachyk*) because my eyes were opened now because I found the truth.

The success of the "project" or the proof for Nargiza—that she had done the right thing—was the peace she now felt and the clear evidence of healing (the original goal) as a result of accepting Christ and prayer. Her process did not finish there. She reflects on what has happened and finds answers and explanations (concepts) through both her cultural framework and the introduced Christian framework. Nargiza returns to her experience, remembers her "God questions" and finds answers from the Bible, commenting, "I felt God was answering me now ... I felt God was asking." She would also comment, "I cannot explain/describe it by words; it was just true." Here subjective rationality and imaginative rationality merge. Nargiza realizes that, through both her experience and her reading of the Bible, she has found answers/concepts to explain her life questions. She also sensed that these are not merely right words but that God, who once seemed far away, was personally speaking to her.

When Nargiza reflects on her family's response to her healing and conversion experience, she does so within her cultural framework. Her family apparently said to her, "Now you are a true fortune-teller ... your eyes have been opened and you have found the truth." The Kyrgyz word for fortune-teller, *kozuachyk*, literally means "one whose eyes are opened to see." Her interview indicates that she not only "saw the truth" but, as a Christian, she had prophetic words for different people and engaged in healing. The difference for Nargiza was that previously she lacked proper Biblical knowledge about Satan and God. Concepts for interpreting the past and present gained a new orientation that made sense to her.

> *Interviewer*: And some people say that Christianity is a foreign religion and it doesn't belong to Kyrgyz. As a Kyrgyz and believer what do you think about it?
>
> *Rizbek*: According to God's word, [that's] wrong. Because God's word teaches that God is the God of all peoples. I will quote from Bible. I don't remember the place it was written but it says, "If you were a slave, if you were Greek, if you were Hebrew, stay what you are." So as long as I was created as a Kyrgyz, I should stay as a Kyrgyz. If we come to the practical traditions, many traditions are similar to the traditions in Bible. For example, we have a saying about "the God guest." Where does this come from? In the Old Testament a "God guest" came to Abraham. The way the Jews in the Old Testament used to bring sacrifices is similar to Kyrgyz culture too.

The main problem with believing in Christ was the discrepancy between the mullah's descriptions of Christians and the lives, friendships, and words of Christians with whom Rizbek was involved with daily. Reflecting on his conversion experience to Christianity as a Kyrgyz, Rizbek utilized Biblical concepts to explain his understanding. He had adopted a new reference point: "*According to God's word, it is wrong.* Because *God's word teaches* that God is God of all peoples ... and as long as I was created [by God] a Kyrgyz I should stay a Kyrgyz" [italics mine]. In the same way, Rizbek used the Bible to both criticize and affirm his cultural traditions and identity. "God is the God of all peoples" — therefore he can remain a Kyrgyz. Finding validation and continuity between the new Christian faith and the old culture, community and identity affirms to Rizbek the truth and success of the process of his religious conversion. He can follow Christ and remain true to being Kyrgyz, a legitimate member of his ethnic community. "Imaginative rationality" enabled Rizbek to appropriate language and concepts to bring meaning to and affirm his Kyrgyz Christian identity.

CONCLUSION

This research was done with the view that religious conversion should be investigated from the viewpoint of Kyrgyz Christians. Our understanding of religious conversion grows as we understand the process as seen and understood by converts themselves. This includes not only an analysis of the clearly cognitive process — the thoughtful, calculating, weighing of costs and benefits; "is this good or not good and why" — but also the subjective "feeling," "fuzzy" or "intuitive" process that includes statements such as "I felt God's presence ... I can't explain it but I felt joy ... some kind of power led me ... I had no understanding, but something happened to my soul."

The concepts of "subjective rationality" and "imaginative rationality" are helpful tools in understanding how people choose to engage in religious conversion. We can identify the fuzziness of the conversion process in the Kyrgyz narratives: the Kyrgyz "think and feel" (subjective rationality) their way through the process (before, during, and after) as they test the "projects" they have "created," reflecting on them in the light of "concepts" (imaginative rationality) they have adapted and adopted, within the context of their cultural milieu. At times they are intentional about seeking, thinking about and weighing the "truth" of the Christian faith and how it may affect their lives. At other times, it seems the experience — the fuzziness, the intuitiveness — is what ultimately transforms them and affirms their choices. Both are important parts of the "conversion project" that brings transformation and change to the life situations and problems that respondents experienced.

2

RELATIONSHIPS, EMOTION, DOCTRINE, INTELLECT—AND ALL THAT FOLLOWS

KATHRYN KRAFT

Everyone's spiritual journey is unique. Each person's experience and understanding of God is slightly different from anyone else's. This principle provides an important foundation for understanding what lies behind the decisions made by someone from a Muslim background who comes to a new faith identity. Different people have different needs, and often the root of those needs lies in the path they took to arrive at their faith decision.

In broad strokes, there are three processes that a faith changer will go through, but how and when those processes are experienced varies considerably. They all will at some point involve relationships, which are a part of every conversion[28] story: at the very least, there is a sense of relationship with God through a supernatural experience or strong emotional connection. Beyond this, the question of relationships with people will emerge at some point during or following one's conversion. Religion and faith choices also necessarily involve theology and spiritual understanding. In the three conversion processes outlined below, there is a duality in how these dynamics are experienced which has implications for how a convert will live.

The first process is that of embracing relationships and doctrine. A person is generally drawn to a new faith first by one and then the other. Some people are attracted by relationships and are eventually convinced of the veracity of doctrine. Others study doctrine extensively but are finally pulled to a faith change through significant relationship(s). That which draws first usually remains the strongest binding factor to a convert's new faith identity, while the other takes a secondary or possibly contentious role in the process of forming a new identity.

Within the category of relationships, a second process occurs in which a person considering a faith change develops a sense of relationship that is both spiritual and interpersonal. The spiritual relationship is the essence of faith, while the interpersonal relationship is how faith is lived. Faith changers generally have a strong sense of both, though one likely comes first and has a stronger pull while the other may resemble an afterthought. This influences how life priorities will be set.

Third, within the framework of spiritual relationship, there is an experience of the miraculous, which an extensive body of literature confirms is very frequently a key element of Muslims' religious experience. For some, an experience of the miraculous sparks a search for faith, while for others miracles determine the conclusion of a search. This experience is often held as a badge of honor in a convert's identity. Depending on when a person has this encounter, it can provide an end to an arduous doctrinal search or, alternately, provide a setting in which doctrinal arguments are of secondary importance.

On a faith journey moving toward a decision for Christ/Christianity,[29] some people will follow relationships while some will flee. Some will be attracted to doctrine and others will be somewhat disinterested. These factors then lend themselves to the question of what means they have for living out their new faith, in keeping with their conscience.

While this paper explores the missiological theme of conversion to faith as promoted in the Gospels (Christ/Christianity) it does not seek to evaluate the quality of faith decisions or promote a specific path. Rather, it explores the relationships between processes and subsequent integrity in lifestyle and values. The basic premise is that everyone's path to a new faith is different and, that by following someone's path, it is easier to understand and enable the choices made later on about how to live this new faith to the fullest extent possible.

To illustrate this, I describe some sample paradigms. The characters and names are fictional but are based on models of faith journeys identified through analysis of conversion narratives.[30] My choice of gender is intentional: though there are no fixed rules, some stories are more typical of men and others more typical of women.

1. Ibrahim rejected Islam and everything connected to it before ever hearing about Jesus.

He spent many years thinking and analyzing his options before choosing a "replacement" to Islam. His emotional dislike of what he had rejected never waned. He likely went through a natural teenage rebellion, hating his family and by extension hating Islam. Perhaps he was a communist or marijuana-smoking musician while at university. Yet through reading and study he eventually decided that Christ would "work" for him. He read the Bible — probably multiple times, from cover to cover—and several other theological treatises. As his interest in Jesus grew, he had a dream in which Jesus appeared to him. Or perhaps it was a miraculous healing of a childhood limp that finally convinced him. In any case, he now has a choice: he can have a very personal, intimate love relationship with Jesus, or he can find other people who think like him. He misses his family, so he goes in search of community, thinking a church is the best place. Yet he never feels at home in a church. While it is true that he is not a cultural Christian, at his core he has an aversion to religion and structure and thus has very high expectations of morality and consistency of everyone in the church, which must be entirely devoid of everything he hated about Islam and his family. Since a church is made up of humans, he is disappointed by the experience. He lives frustrated: fully a Christian, but finding it hard to like Christians. If you ever suggest to Ibrahim that "once a Muslim, always a Muslim"—perhaps he might find a more encouraging community among Muslim followers of Jesus—he will be deeply insulted and accuse you of watering down your faith.

2. Samar is a loyal family girl. Her sisters are her best friends and she still lives at home.

She has never thought like the rest of her family, but they are family. She rejected Islam while in high school, and met Jesus as Ibrahim did: through plenty of study, with miracles at key moments. Samar also looks for community in a church and is disappointed yet, accustomed to loving and being loved by people who think differently from her, she continues to attend. She doesn't want to cause conflict at home, or to bring undue shame to her family, so she never tells them about her church activities. However, she starts to share stories with her sisters; perhaps one or two or all of them decide to follow Jesus too. Samar does not think much about whether she is a Christian or a Muslim. In rejecting Islam, she rejected institutional religion (she may or may not realize this) but either way, she does not mind ambivalence. She feels at home in both societies while knowing she is an outsider in each—with the exception of her sisters who now share her faith. As the first in her family to convert, she feels she needs to be a leader to her sisters but, otherwise, she feels very comfortable with them.

3. Aisha grew up in a Muslim family that did not care if she snuck into the back room to eat during Ramadan and never bothered her about prayers or the way she dressed as long as she was not too scandalous.

Yet *Eid* was a big deal and she memorized half the Qur'an during middle school. She was a Muslim, of course, but took her pharmacy studies at university and her appointments at the beauty salon much more seriously than religion. In her third year of university, she met a young man, a fellow student, and fell in love. They never talked about religion; she assumed he was like her and most others at the university: a Muslim, but who cares? Within months, their relationship grew very serious and she expected him to talk about marriage at any point. When he asked to talk about the future, she was shocked to hear first that he was a Christian. As a Muslim, she could never marry a Christian man! Even if her family accepted it — unlikely but not impossible — it was illegal in her country. He then asked her to consider Christianity for herself. He said that while religion was not very important to him, he did love his faith and wanted her to understand. As a girl in love, she agreed; her love for her boyfriend complemented the inspiring stories about Jesus. She was convinced that she wanted this faith for herself. What happened with her boyfriend is irrelevant to this story; maybe they broke up, or found a legal loophole to marry, or even lived in a scandalous secret relationship. Her love for Jesus has stayed strong. She does not want to trouble her family with these details, nor does she feel the need to reject her Muslim identity. Being a Muslim never had much to do with what she believes anyway. Aisha wants the best of both worlds, and will fight to keep both alive as long as she can. She may succeed or she may fail. In stories of women similar to Aisha, their continued loyalty to their Christian faith meant that they moved further and further away from their Muslim identities. Even if Aisha does not reject her Muslim background outright, she never quite figures out how to give equal emphasis to both her Muslim culture and her Christian faith.

4. Mahmoud is from Aisha's city, but his life could not be more different.

His family is very conservative, his sisters all covered and married as teenagers. Mahmoud, his brothers, and his father are among the most faithful attendees at the mosque, and the *imam* is often invited to their house to expound further on how to live as a good Muslim. Mahmoud reads Islamic texts and watches Islamic television exclusively. He feels close to God when he prays. He was always especially fascinated by the Prophet Isa, who spoke as a baby after his virgin mother gave birth to him. Mahmoud loved reading about him. When one of his friends, who also prays regularly at the same mosque, started telling him stories about Prophet Isa, he was fascinated. Some of these stories are not in the Qur'an, others are; but his friend told them with an interesting new twist. Mahmoud read more Islamic texts about Isa and listened to his friend. Eventually he started reading an *Injil* his friend gave him. He fell in love with "the Christ" (*al-Masih*) and decided to follow him. He began telling everyone in his family about this new discovery. Regardless of his family's reaction, Mahmoud is determined to prove his faithfulness to them, while sharing about Christ with other Muslims in a way that they can avoid rejection. He never rejected Islam *per se* even though, as his relationship with Christ grows, his association with, and his need for, Islam dims to what could be labeled a mute rejection. What happens next depends on where Mahmoud finds a supportive community. Coming from a strong family in a strong faith community, he no longer feels the same connection with either, yet wants a community that is also a family. Ideally, he will find other Muslims in love with Isa but, if no such group exists, he may look for Christians.

5. Ghada could be Mahmoud's sister, because of her family's similar social profile.

Ghada never studied Islam but was taught to live it: do not do anything in the bathroom that can be done elsewhere, keep the floors clean for praying, starve herself while preparing feasts every day during Ramadan, do not touch the Qur'an while menstruating. This was the way life was. One day, friends wanted to go to a village with a Christian shrine which they said had magical powers. It was famed for being the place where barren women became fertile, but other illnesses were also healed there. Ghada had a constant earache and so went, hoping for a miraculous healing. Her ear was indeed healed but, more than that, a beautiful feeling took over her entire body. She felt truth enter her heart. She knew it was a Christian thing because she was in a Christian shrine; she knew Jesus was Christian, and that was exciting. She went home and life went back to normal, but she felt different. She was happier, and felt like she was talking with God when she prayed. She knew in her heart that she now knew God and had not before, but her lifestyle did not visibly change. Twenty years later, a Christian family moved in next door. One day, she was visiting with the wife who showed her a Bible. They read a few passages from the book of Luke together, and Ghada started crying. She was reading on paper what she had known for the past twenty years but had never put into words. Generally joyful before, she now brimmed over with contentment and excitement. Ghada never looked for supportive community and never thought of herself as anything but Muslim. This had not bothered her before and, after meeting the Christian family, it still did not: she saw her faith as a spiritual connection shared with the Christian woman and was happy to define it as simply that.

Stories like these illustrate the relationship between a person's background, search for faith, decision, identity, and lifestyle following conversion. Each person's experience of the three processes is slightly different. While the end set of beliefs may be the same, an individual's sense of identity and lifestyle values will vary.

Having presented different paradigms, I will now discuss the theoretical frameworks providing further insight into them as well as a warning about issues that converts face and why, and implications for respecting each individual's unique concerns.

First, when the convert sees his or her faith decision as a careful, well-made choice, questions of identity and community cause more pain. When a convert is ascribed an identity (usually by well-meaning Christians) but is not comfortable with that identity (usually because they feel different), these identity and community struggles are more acute. In contrast, when conversion happens quickly and easily, and/or the convert is not confronted with moving to a new social profile which may not fit, identity and community struggles are much less intense.

All the above stories are of the first person in a family to believe. Generally, the transition is much more gradual and comfortable for the second or third person, who thus has an example to follow from the same background. Adjustment to a new faith identity is most natural when a convert has a sibling's footsteps to follow.

Second, idealism emerges in sociological literature of conversion as a characteristic of many religious converts. As idealistic desires and ambitions are not achieved, people settle into a sense of anomie, which can be defined as a feeling of frustration and loss as one comes to understand that personal expectations are not being met.[31] People joining a new religious community have high expectations which can lead to discontent when the new group fails to deliver.[32] Many people I met in the course of my research expressed a similar idealistic disappointment with all kinds of Christians, including other converts, Christian-background Arabs, and missionaries. They felt like outsiders in every group, a feeling common to many in a variety of contexts,[33] but which many Muslim-background converts believe is unique to their own experience as they regard their families, Christian churches, and other groups where it seems everyone fits in better than they do. This can easily translate to mistrust and even disdain for other believers.

Consider the following quote from one man I interviewed, with a story similar to Ibrahim's: "I'm not welcomed in my new life—maybe by God, but not in the church. I've been going to church for five years but still, there is nothing, no relationship. Through the church I have also attended conferences with children from poor areas. They welcome me, they love me, and I feel like I'm one of them." He sees every slight as yet another indicator that the community of Christians will not live up to his expectations, but he is not as frustrated with poor people. He feels welcomed in a community of people from a lower social class than him.

This anomie to some extent helps explain why some converts place their hopes on something they have never known. Many dream of travelling to the United States or to Europe; some young men hope to marry a woman from the West. Anomie resulting from a strong attraction to the West is hardly unique to converts, but the frustrations they face as outsiders in their own communities strongly exacerbate it, and it is further intensified by the disappointing example they have of Western missionaries, often described as people whom converts wanted as allies and friends, but who had disappointed them deeply. Their expectations of foreign Christians are usually quite idealistic; while some converts could tell me of one or a few missionaries they respected, mostly missionaries failed to meet their standards.[34]

Most people I met in the course of my research lived with a sense of continuous frustration. Some participants told of friends who had returned to Islam because they found the stress too great. Others told of people who saw the potential for problems and decided not to change faith. One young woman, whose story resembles Aisha's, told that she almost committed suicide as she dealt with family pressure, her own desire for freedom, and the challenges in living her new life. Another woman, converted a decade ago, told that despite her unhappiness she feels power to continue living because of her faith. Anomie resulting from idealism and disappointment is an enormous challenge in the narratives of conversion from Islam. However, the degree to which converts experience it, and the nature of their disappointment or frustration, are closely related to the path they took in reaching their faith decision.

My third and final theoretical observation is that there are usually two distinct events in conversion from a Muslim background to a Christian faith: rejection of Islam and embracing of Christian beliefs. Research data on conversions to Islam, usually from a Christian background, suggest that the conversion process is often anticipated by an individual determining that the religion of origin and the values of parents and society are irrelevant. One common path explored in literature on conversion involves a decision to abandon one's heritage (usually Christianity in sociological studies), followed by a period in which the individual avoids any spiritual activity or interest. After several years, this person begins to ask existential questions or has an emotional experience causing renewed interest in religion or spirituality and thus seeks a new religious framework different from what has been already rejected. In the West, it is typically through close contact with Muslims that a person becomes more interested in and considers conversion to Islam.[35]

Similarly, researchers focusing on other religious traditions have found that conversion to a different, mainstream religious group often requires a deliberate renouncing of a previous faith.[36] I have found that a rejection of Islam is generally an essential element in the conversion process for someone from a Muslim background embracing the Christian faith.

Many reported that rejection of Islam was a more straightforward, often easier decision than embracing Christianity, which required considerable time and convincing. Ceasing to practice Islam happens much faster and easier than a wholehearted rejection of Islam. Ibrahim and Samar's stories are typical in this sense.

However, in other stories, contact with Christianity or Christ often sparks the process of rejecting Islam. For people like Mahmoud rejection is not abrupt; it still happens but gradually and naturally. Even if they remain fully culturally Muslim, the importance of rituals they practice fades. They may continue performing them out of family loyalty or love, or as an expression of their devotion to Christ, not because they are essential to their religious faith or identity.

Others, like Aisha and Ghada, can claim they never chose to embrace Islam — although they never doubted Islam either. Though more frequently the case for women, some men also told me that they never rejected Islam because it was only part of their cultural heritage and continues to be so. Unlike Aisha and Ghada, men who experience this still are likely to ruminate about what they are leaving behind doctrinally. Be that as it may, the people for whom rejection is not a part of their faith story are likely those who did not have a sense of owning a faith or doctrine before Christ.

Most converts I met separate this necessary doctrinal rejection from their cultural identity. Many informed me that, upon rejecting Islam as a faith, they were still Muslim; they did not cease to be Muslim until they chose a new faith. In some ways, they say, they have added a Christian faith identity to their Muslim cultural identity. Nonetheless, a firm rejection of the Muslim creed is an essential part of the conversion process for most Muslims who embrace Christianity as a faith system.

The question of rejection may be the most controversial issue facing the emerging church in the Arab world. A debate has led to division with people staking their claims over what might be a deep misunderstanding and variance in terminology with regards to the issue of rejection: the Ibrahims do not recognize the faith of the Mahmouds because they cannot see rejection. The Mahmouds in turn are not interested in the Ibrahims because they seem too obsessed with rejection. If the Ibrahims are right about the Mahmouds — in the sense that the Mahmouds still believe in Islamic doctrine — then perhaps they are right to question their spiritual experience, since a full faith change entails rejection. Meanwhile, if the Mahmouds are right about the Ibrahims — that they are in fact too preoccupied with rejection, bitterly negative in relation to Islam and all things Muslim — then perhaps they are right to question the quality of their new faith, because that would be a terrible indication of character and maturity.

However, it is possible and likely that they are wrong about each other. Mahmoud's spiritual journey has led him to a place of full devotion to his new faith without being distracted by his previous faith. Meanwhile, Ibrahim talks a lot about rejection with Mahmoud because he cares, not because he is bitter. They have developed different priorities for living out their faith, but their core beliefs are actually complementary.

Samar, Aisha, and Ghada are not a part of this debate. Women are often less interested in these issues, only engaging the debate if they have been convinced or inspired by Ibrahim or Mahmoud to take a side. Thus, women may become a bridge between Mahmoud and Ibrahim. Similarly, believers of a different background, such as those born into Christian households, have the potential to bring together converts who have experienced different processes to enjoy together the similarities in the faith they now share.

However, all too often, missionaries and well-meaning people of Christian background develop a theological interpretation of scripture that leads them to believe that either Mahmoud's faith or Ibrahim's faith in Christ is authentic, while the other's is not, thus encouraging further division between these two groups. While sociology and theology investigate different issues in religion, there is much to be learned in cross-disciplinary studies. This study serves to illustrate how social factors inform the nuances of interpretation regarding living out one's new faith, recognizing that various paths can nonetheless cross at the point of a shared faith.

Based on the framework in this paper, people from a Muslim background who have embraced a Christian faith can seek to respect each other's faith path and together build a community of faith. By remembering that each person's faith path is unique — whether from a Muslim or other background — some of the pressure to conform to a pre-defined identity can be relieved as converts work out their own sense of identity using the tools and relationships they find most suited to their situation.

3

REFUSING TO CHOOSE: MULTIPLE BELONGING AMONG ARAB FOLLOWERS OF CHRIST

JENS BARNETT

Visiting with Thani[37] always provides me with food for thought. He has been a follower of Christ for several years, ever since the day his brother lost control of his van while returning from a family holiday. Thani's only son had been in that van.

In his rearview mirror, Thani had seen his brother's van swerve into the median ditch and roll several times. Stopping his car and running back into the huge cloud of dust surrounding the van, he was amazed to meet his nine-year-old son standing there, within the cloud's perimeter.

"How did you get here?" Thani asked.

"You brought me here, Papa," his son replied. "Right after 'Uncle' crashed, I was trapped, but you helped me out. You carried me in your arms though the dust cloud, and told me to wait here. As you carried me, you whispered to me, 'You have to thank Jesus for this.'"

As Thani retells the story, I glance over to his son sitting on the sofa beside him. He rebukes my unbelief with a gentle nod and a grin.

Shortly before the accident, Thani had made the *hajj* (pilgrimage) to Mecca to shore up his slipping faith in the Islamic narratives once so central in his life. However, it was already too late; he had begun to internalize secular and Christian cultural narratives, and in Mecca he was unable to suppress these new ways of seeing and thinking. Instead, Thani found himself as an objective observer, incapable of entering fully into the Muslim symbolism and ceremonies.

"I did the *hajj* hoping to strengthen my faith," he explains, "but as I looked around, I found it to be the peak of paganism ... gripping the black stone and weeping, I cried out over and over, 'God where are you?' ... I came home devastated."

Thani no longer attends local church services run by ethnic Christians.[38] In fact, much of Thani's testimony details his excruciating struggle to live out a faith appropriated by ethnic Christians and their cultural symbols. Sometime after he stopped attending, I came by for a visit and gave him a copy of Wolfgang Simson's *Fifteen Theses*, which outlines a vision for house churches.[39] The phone was ringing as I came in my front door half an hour later.

"Do you mean to tell me that all the things I struggle with most at church are not even essential?" Thani asks incredulously. "You have to give me his book!"

During one visit, the subject of worship comes up. Thani complains about the poor theology in many choruses that portray God as more three than one. He is also distracted by songs and prayers entreating God to "Send your fire upon us!"

"I know what they mean," Thani says, laughing, "but half of me wants to flee for my life ... Fire is a negative thing for us, you see."

Thani's comment and laughter echoes in my mind as I travel home that night. It joins with many other voices and memories that seem to have a similar irony. What does he mean by *half* and *us*?

BLINDED BY THE "C SPECTRUM"

Thani's ambivalence towards the word *fire* and his use of *us* to mean *Muslims* indicate a lingering sense of belonging to his Muslim community. In refusing to choose a single cultural allegiance, Thani's identity cannot be located on the much-debated "C Spectrum."[40] A major flaw in Travis' model is that it is one-dimensional, portraying *Muslim* and *Christian* religio-cultural identities as monolithic and mutually exclusive. That is, every step towards a "Christian" identity is presumed to require a step away from one's Muslim identity. Thani helped me understand that the "C Spectrum" was blinding me to the innovative negotiation of identity that is actually taking place. On this continuum, there is no space for a believer like Thani who expresses belonging to both Christian and Muslim cultural traditions simultaneously, or even for one who has a piecemeal approach of fully belonging in some aspects that do not conflict with his or her faith, while totally rejecting others.

Until recently, most discussion of multiple belonging and cultural hybridity in mission circles has been in relation to *TCKs* or "Third Culture Kids."[41] Yet, after becoming aware of these phenomena in my own home, I also observed them in the lives of my friends.

ISLAM AS A HOMELAND

One such observation comes from several years' involvement in church-run discipleship courses in which believers from a Muslim background have taken part. The observation was twofold:

First, I often witnessed groups of these believers sitting together, competing with each other in their criticism of Islam. These criticisms were sharp at times and would have been highly offensive to other Muslims.

Second, however, these same believers would become upset and defensive if Islam were to be lightly criticized by a lecturer or fellow student who was ethnically Christian. This issue became so problematic that a solution needed to be found.

The solution was to declare Islam as the believers' "homeland." We cautioned visiting lecturers and other students that, although someone may have emigrated and taken on a new nationality, they might still be sensitive to remarks about their homeland — especially comments made by non-natives. This considerably reduced the number of complaints made. However, it was several more years until I realized why this imagery was so successful: it both legitimized the sense of dual belonging felt by these believers, and it did so in terms with which ethnic Christians could empathize.

SEQUENTIAL BELONGING

This lingering sense of belonging to the Muslim *ummah* (community) and of sharing its linguistic and cultural symbols appears difficult to erase. Regardless of how zealous they — or their mentors — may be, the process in which new believers negotiate their identity in Christ can be fraught with ambiguity and ambivalence due to this sense of dual belonging. Forgetting the internalized grammar of their religio-cultural "mother tongue" is a lengthy, if not impossible, process.

Robert Schreiter, a Catholic missiologist who has written extensively on inculturation and identity, calls this sense of dual belonging *sequential*. It occurs when "a person has moved from one religious tradition to another but retains some traces of the earlier belief ... Often this previous belief is so deeply inscribed on the culture of which the person is a member that the new identity can never completely supplant the earlier one."[42]

KHAMIS

Khamis (36) belongs to a well-known Muslim family. He came to faith in 2000 after five years of studying the scriptures. Encouraged by his mentors, Khamis began attending an evangelical fellowship in a nearby town. Although his presence was accepted, building a sense of social belonging with the ethnic Christian believers was difficult. Unable to break into the lively after-service conversations inside, Khamis often found himself outside in the car park, waiting for his ride. After several years of church attendance and discipleship — and against the wishes of his church — Khamis left to attend a nearby seminary, eventually completing a theological degree. He now lives with his wife in his own hometown, among his extended family.

Khamis no longer calls himself *Christian*. "Let me explain," he says, enthusiastically clearing space to plot imaginary lines on our coffee table:

> There are two aspects to my identity: horizontal and vertical. Horizontally, I am a Muslim, you see? This line is my life, my community, my family, my history, my culture, and my tradition ... It is Muslim; it is me. I can't deny it. It is a part of who I am. I am happy to follow these traditions; no problem at all. But don't ask me — or try to force me — to believe it ... And here, this is the vertical aspect to my identity, which is my faith, my relationship with God. This is private. It can't be forced because it is inside ... I just don't believe in what has been sent down to Muhammad. You can't force me to believe this. You would only be forcing me to lie.

THINKING DIALOGICALLY

Khamis' strategy for articulating the Christian and Muslim aspects of his identity avoids language that would elevate one aspect as "primary" or "salient." Instead, he portrays these aspects as being *incommensurable* — belonging somehow to different dimensions — while, at the same time, still interacting with each other. Khamis expresses this as a relationship between *faith identity* and *cultural identity*. Although he presents this dynamic positively, his words also betray real tensions — almost as if these two aspects are arguing with each other.

Several missiologists have noticed something similar to the dynamic Khamis describes. Ridgway, for example, distinguishes between *spiritual* and *physical* identity[43] as does Lewis between *spiritual* and *socio-religious* identity.[44] It would be a mistake to interpret these descriptions as promoting a dualistic isolation of physical from spiritual. Rather, they seek to articulate a lively dialogue between two equally strong but different senses of belonging. To illustrate this relationship, Lewis and other insider movement advocates often use the "Kingdom Circles" diagram.[45] While I find this diagram very helpful, the overlapping rings still seem unable to capture the dynamic interaction and tensions I observed between different belongings, or the strange sense that I was eavesdropping on an argument.

In contrast to traditional Cartesian identity paradigms based on layered hierarchies and the idea of "primary identity,"[46] there is a deep interdependence inherent to dialogical processes. The Russian philosopher, Mikhail Bakhtin, describes how this interdependence works within speech as follows: "Utterances are not indifferent to one another, and are not self-sufficient; they are aware of and mutually reflect one another ... Each utterance is filled with echoes and reverberations of other utterances to which it is related ... Every utterance must be regarded as primarily a response to preceding utterances ... Each utterance refutes, affirms, supplements, and relies upon the others, presupposes them to be known, and somehow takes them into account."[47]

Building on Bakhtin's dialogism above, and Sarbin's work showing that identities are rooted in narratives,[48] Hermans has developed his "dialogical model of the self."[49] Although he primarily applies this model to his field of clinical psychology, Hermans also claims it is vitally important for understanding the increasingly widespread phenomenon of *multiple group belonging* in today's globalized world.[50] He proposes that the self is decentered and consists of

> a dynamic multiplicity of relatively autonomous I-positions. In this conception, the I has the possibility to move from one spatial position to another in accordance with changes in situation and time. The I fluctuates among different and even opposed positions, and has the capacity imaginatively to endow each position with a voice so that dialogical relations between positions can be established. The voices function like interacting characters in a story, involved in a process of question and answer, agreement and disagreement ... As different voices, these characters exchange information about their respective Me's, resulting in a complex, narratively structured self.[51]

In this and the following chapter, I hope to demonstrate that Hermans' paradigm is more suited to capture the complex identity issues my friends are facing than traditional Cartesian models.

AWAL

Awal (50) has been following Christ for two decades. Enduring imprisonment and harassment, his steadfast faith has won him the trust and respect of local pastors. He emigrated recently, but in spite of good career prospects, relationships, and housing, he eventually returned "home." During our interview, Awal particularly focused on identity issues his children were facing:

My concern is for our kids. No one is doing anything for them and they are having an identity crisis ... I call them *MBBKs*, "Muslim Background Believer Kids"[52] ...

A while ago my daughter asked me, "Dad, what am I *really*? Am I a Muslim or a Christian?" ... I said, "You're a Muslim that follows Christ. Our Muslim identity is written on our identity [cards], it's our extended family, our heritage, our people — but we follow Christ as a family. Although it has made life difficult for us, I will never regret my decision to follow Christ" ...

But, that is so hard for them. My daughter — who is now a teenager, you know — asked me, "Dad, what is going to happen to me? Will I ever get married?" It's a very difficult time. They need to find their own way ...

We are not Christians. ... We are Muslims. It is among Muslims we find acceptance and belonging ... We have experienced so much love from Muslim society and so much rejection from Christians. Our children have felt this and it is hard for them to understand ...

I no longer care what Christians think. I care what Muslims think. However, even if our president asked me, "What is Christ to you?" I would tell him my faith. I will not compromise Christ, ever — but I am not a Christian ...

As Awal continues to tell about his life, family, and identity, a relentless internal dialogue is indeed evident. Rehearsing to me his reasons for returning home, Awal appears to contrast Christianity, the West, and freedom, with Islam, home, tribal honor, and morality:

We had emigrated ... but we have moved back to ... our home ... It is better here ... To be honest, if I am — God forbid — going to lose them, I would rather have my children grow up to be Muslims, than to grow up to be gay, drug users, or promiscuous. At least they would be honorable, and have morals and values ...

These stereotypical narratives about the West are commonplace among Muslims here. However, I am surprised to find them prominent in Awal's inner conversation, since at least "half" of him knows they are inaccurate.

While Khamis makes a distinction between *cultural* and *spiritual* identities, the voices of Awal's agonizing dialogue seem to be mainly *cultural*. The narratives, values, and symbols he has internalized from *multiple* cultural systems appear to be irreconcilable. This is comparable to a form of multiple belonging that Schreiter calls *dialogical belonging*, where "two traditions dwell side by side within the life of a person, and there may be greater or less communication between the two ... The self that mediates this duality is ... seen as ... a conversation that actualizes now one tradition and then another."[53]

Awal's emigration and return graphically illustrate the force of this dialogue and the instability it can create. The continual pressure to surrender total allegiance to one "primary" cultural identity is matched by the refusal to choose between them. As I meditate on our conversation, I am reminded of the closing lines in Salman Rushdie's semi-autobiographical story, *The Courter*, in which the narrator says,

> I, too, have ropes around my neck. I have them to this day, pulling me this way and that, East and West, the nooses tightening, commanding, *choose, choose*. I buck, I snort, I whinny, I rear, I kick. Ropes, I do not choose between you. Lassoes, lariats, I choose neither of you, and both. Do you hear? I refuse to choose.[54]

MULTIPLE CULTURAL NARRATIVES

How many identities can one have? William James suggests that a person "has as many different social selves as there are distinct *groups* of persons about whose opinion he cares."[55] A person typically takes on different *roles* within each of these groups, and these roles are appropriated from the cultural narratives he or she has internalized.[56]

On closer examination, I found that my friends are exposed to many more cultural narratives than the public "religious identity" they claim. For example, Khamis, while claiming to be Muslim, is subject to numerous Christian influences through literature, satellite TV, and music. He also has Christian friends with whom he discusses his faith and prays.

To presuppose Awal's inner dialogue involves *only* Christian and Muslim voices is unhelpful. Voices associated with other cultural influences also need consideration. Firstly, from the time of his birth, Awal has internalized Arabic, tribal, and nationalist narratives as *well* as Islamic. Secondly, globalization has brought all manner of cultural narratives into his life and home, through phenomena such as Sri Lankan nannies, Western secularized schooling, satellite TV, and the internet. Thirdly, Awal has needed to internalize Hebrew and Greek scriptural traditions, narratives, and symbolism. Becoming a follower of Christ "involves learning the story of Israel and of Jesus well enough to interpret and experience oneself and one's world in its terms."[57]

Finally, to follow Christ is to be part of a global multicultural movement that "has received from the past a rich inheritance of Christian theology, liturgy, and devotion. No group of believers can disregard this heritage without risking spiritual impoverishment."[58] In Awal's immediate context, this means that access to scripture often involves some form of discipleship or translation mediated by missionaries or ethnic Christians. Thus, no new Arabic believer can — or should — completely avoid exposure to the cultural traditions of Western Evangelical and Eastern Orthodox Christianity.

In practice then, a purely Muslim "insider" identity, free from all other cultural influences, is both an impossible and a misguided ideal. Every believer has internalized a unique combination of narratives from multiple cultural sources. Each of these narratives carries its own scripts, roles, and belongings which in turn can appear as a voice of identity within the dialogical self.

DEPICTING THE DIALOGICAL SELF

It may be helpful at this point to depict some key features of a dialogical paradigm.[59] In Figure 3.1, Awal's self is pictured as a "stage" where the subjectivities of *group belongings* and *personal roles* can be indwelt imaginatively and thus given "voices."[60] The personal identities "Father" and "Christ-follower," and the group identities "Tribe," "Muslim community," and "Local church" are shown "center-stage," indicating they are voices in dialogue. In addition, Awal hears the "voice of scripture" or, in Benedict Anderson's terms, he identifies with an "imagined" scriptural community due to internalization of the biblical narratives.[61]

The two arrows represent two fundamental cultural processes:[62] The first is the *internalization* of *external culture*, through which Awal constructs in his mind a collection of *cognitive models* that "map" or represent the world outside.[63] As noted earlier, external culture is by no means monolithic or pure; Awal is exposed to multiple *cultural systems* and the models of these he constructs in his mind reflect this complexity. The second process is *externalization*, where he draws on these cognitive models in order to take part in society, thereby joining the "conversation" that in turn shapes external culture for the next generation. For example, through sharing his tribe's group identity, Awal is exposed to the narratives, scripts, and symbols that make up his tribe's cultural system, or worldview. As Awal internalizes these, he constructs a cognitive model of what *father* means within the tribal context. He then *appropriates* this model by taking up a father's role and acting it out in society.

Through envisaging himself as *father*, Awal can perceive situations from a father's perspective. In other words, he listens to the father's "voice." Josephs suggests that these voices are "located neither 'in' the person nor 'in' culture, but are born as

... 'borderliners' in the contact zones between culture and person."[64] Thus, I have drawn the "stage" representing the self in the very center of the externalization and internalization processes.

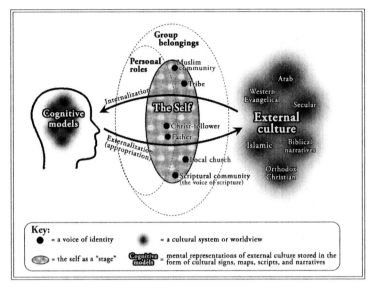

Figure 3.1: A Dialogical Paradigm

We can thus see how Awal can identify himself as a follower of Christ and yet simultaneously feel some sense of identification with his Muslim community. He is simply acknowledging the voice of his "homeland." Such a voice may be weaker, may come from the periphery of the self, or may even be suppressed, but it is still there. In contrast to the West's traditionally individualistic models of self, Hermans argues that, "cultures and cultural oppositions are not outside the self as some kind of "environment" from which the self can exclusively be separated. Instead, culture is in the self ... This implies that collective voices, as represented by groups ... or by significant others ... are constituent parts of the self and organize the self to a significant degree."[65] Hermans' model is thus also applicable cross-culturally to non-Western collectivist societies. Awal's struggles can be understood then as a *dialogue* within the self between many identifications, roles, and belongings.

Additionally, since Awal is influenced by numerous external cultural systems — each one with its own definition of *father* — it is quite possible for *several* distinct "father" voices to be in dialogue with each other. In Awal's explanation of why he returned home one can almost hear the "tribal father" and "Muslim father" standing in close proximity, arguing with a stereotypical "Western Christian father" on the other side of the stage.

This argument should not be presumed to be a binary "win–lose" struggle as to which cultural identity will claim Awal's primary allegiance.[66] Rather, by allowing a healthy dialogue within, believers are able to find creative and synergistic "win–win" solutions to problems that obey the Holy Spirit's voice and are true to scripture while also "hearing," or valuing, voices from multiple cultural identifications. Perhaps this corresponds to Schreiter's third model, *simultaneous belonging*, where "a person has moved through sequential belonging but then chooses to go back and reappropriate earlier belongings on a par with current allegiances. This reappropriation does not entail subsuming one system into another but rather finding a way for them to coexist beyond dialogical belonging."[67]

CONCLUSION

Voices related to ethnicity, geography, religion, and empire often coincide to form singular, sharply-defined identities. However, as globalization, pluralism, and migration continue to unravel and multiply these narrative strands, multiple belonging has become an important issue. While all kinds of hyphenated identities are now commonplace, it is only recently that "multiple religious belonging" has been explored.[68] The phenomenon of multiple religious belonging along the Christian-Muslim border zone, in particular, has had very little attention.[69]

It has not been the purpose of this chapter to argue *for* or *against* multiple religio-cultural belonging. Rather, it is to suggest that it is *already* a factor in my friends' lives, regardless of the "religious identity" they publicly claim. It therefore needs the attention of theologians able to work outside traditional models of identity that are often modern, individualistic, and hierarchical. While multiple belonging is incomprehensible within these Cartesian models, a dialogical paradigm enables these phenomena to be articulated and thus researched. Indeed, quantitative research using this paradigm would be helpful at this point to measure the extent of multiple belonging among believers.

In the next chapter, I will use a dialogical approach to examine several aspects of cultural hybridity linked to multiple belonging and the issues these raise for my friends and others like them.

4

LIVING A PUN: CULTURAL HYBRIDITY AMONG ARAB FOLLOWERS OF CHRIST

JENS BARNETT

The previous chapter began with the story of Thani.[70] At one point in the narrative, my friend describes the ambivalence he feels at church whenever ethnic Christians entreat God to "Send your fire upon us!"[71]

"I know what they mean," he says, laughing, "but half of me wants to flee for my life ... Fire is a negative thing for us, you see."

Thani's urge to flee when the church prays for fire has all the humor of a bilingual *pun*. He does not misunderstand the words as the ethnic Christian worshipers intend them; the humor is there precisely because he *does* understand these symbols, including how different they sound to ethnic Muslim ears. Yet he refuses to either suppress the Muslim meaning, and so enter into the worship, or accept its authority and flee for his life. Caught between Muslim and Christian interpretants for the same symbols, he finds himself as an objective observer, laughing at the irony of his predicament.

This refusal to choose between two internalized systems of meaning—each linked to a different sense of belonging—greatly complicates Thani's life. In fact, sometimes his whole life mirrors Attridge's definition of a *pun*, which, "instead of being designed to suppress latent ambiguity, is deliberately constructed to *enforce* ambiguity, to render impossible the choice between meanings, to leave the reader or hearer endlessly oscillating in semantic space."[72]

THIRD SPACE HYBRIDITY

In Homi Bhabha's terminology, Thani is a cultural hybrid. His identity occupies an ambiguous "third space," where the "incommensurable elements" of multiple belongings are brought into dialogue with each other.[73] *Third space* can be likened to a volatile fault line located between the tectonic plates of older fossilized cultures. Bhabha believes it is here that "newness enters the world" and as such it is the very "location of culture." For Bhabha, *cultural hybridity* does not just mean "mixing"; it is a process that "gives rise to something different, something new and unrecognizable, a new area of negotiation of meaning and representation."[74]

This linking of hybridity to innovation raises an important question: Does the current polarization of opinion over the "C Spectrum" paradigm blind us to something "new and unrecognizable"? That was certainly my experience; only after reading about "third culture kids"[75] living in my own home did I begin to notice similar patterns in the narratives of my friends. In this chapter, I attempt to analyze some of these narratives for signs of hybridity using the "dialogical self" model developed in the previous chapter.

THANI'S SISTER

Thani and I sit in his car, waiting for the traffic to move. Ahead of us, several taxis veer off into the maze of alleyways and side roads on our right, hoping to avoid the congestion on the main road ahead. Thani begins to tell me of his painful struggle a few years ago when he discovered his sister was secretly dating someone, and how torn he felt between the voice of family honor and the apparently very individualistic voice he understood to be Christianity.

Using the imagery of street maps instead of "voices," Thani describes himself as sitting in his car studying two maps. The first shows a main road heading toward honor killing, while the main road depicted on the second map — individualistic freedom — threatens to lead to immorality and family shame. Which map should he follow?

"However, Jesus was in the car with me," explains Thani smiling, "and he showed me a side road." Thani proudly tells me how he solved his dilemma: Realizing his sister was anxious to get married, he introduced her to a friend he thought was suitable, and then helped them wed.

Thani's matchmaking is a good example of synergistic hybridization emanating from the "dialogical self." It is *innovative* in that Thani refuses to choose the main road suggested by *either* map. Instead, by listening to the voice of Jesus and using both maps he possesses, he is able to find "a road less travelled" — a *third* way.

RABI' AND KHAMIS

Rabi' came to faith through a vision he experienced while visiting a church with a friend. The information in the vision was accurate and ended up saving his life; thus, Rabi' gave up all, losing family, friends, riches and status to become a Christian. Yet, for Rabi' the church is a place of both power and powerlessness, of both acceptance and rejection. Although the church is where he experienced supernatural proof of God's personal concern and acceptance, Rabi' complains several years after his conversion that:

> I will always be a second-class Christian ... I will never be given a leadership position over [ethnic] Christians ... and they won't let me marry their daughters ... If I were to stop coming to church they would say, "See, we knew he would backslide." Yet, if someone else were absent, they would rush to visit him, and encourage him to come back to church.

Khamis' feelings about "church" are ambivalent too, having also experienced pressure to perform. While new ethnic Christian believers were readily accepted for baptism, his requests were repeatedly postponed "for another year." It hurt him to see these new believers fast-tracked — especially those who had "no scriptural knowledge" or "worse backgrounds" that presumably involved alcoholism or immorality. Was he under surveillance? Ironically, in his desire to convince them his faith was genuine, he felt pressured to feign an inauthentic spirituality. To be accepted as one of them, he felt he needed to prove he was "more Christian than the Christians."

MIMICRY

Bhabha regards this dynamic as a form of hybridity he calls *mimicry*.[76] It occurs when two cultural systems come into dialogue across a power differential. Mimicry is often observed in colonial situations where a foreign cultural system is forced upon the colonial subject from a position of authority. In order to gain acceptance and success within this system, the subject must appropriate its symbols to send favorable messages to those in power. In doing so, the "mimic man" may become a well-paid and enthusiastic agent of colonialism and therefore a "success story" to be reported about back home.

Mimicry leads to an ambivalent relationship, however; almost regardless of how well-intentioned initial motives are on both sides, the relationship tends to become tainted by a sense of mutual exploitation and mistrust.

> Mimicry is ... a complex strategy of reform, regulation and discipline, which "appropriates" the Other as it visualizes power. Mimicry is also the sign of the inappropriate, however, a difference or recalcitrance which ... intensifies surveillance, and poses an immanent threat to both "normalized" knowledges and disciplinary powers.[77]

The pressure to perform can be especially strong for new believers already experiencing rejection from their own community and who consequently feel their survival depends upon acceptance within the ethnic Christian community. Rabi' and Khamis describe pressure to outperform ethnic Christians in order to receive equal treatment, simultaneously realizing they will always be "second-class." This sense of partial acceptance by the church introduces a hopeless irony into these vulnerable relationships. Although required to act, speak, and dress like a "Christian," the "converted Other" is seldom accepted as such. For most ethnic Christians here, Rabi' and Khamis will forever be a special kind of believer called *min khalfiyah islamiyah* (from an Islamic background). This irony parallels colonial mimicry dynamics that "always require the subordinate to remain at least partially different from the dominant in order to preserve the structures of discrimination on which ... power is based."[78]

Some writers have understood mimicry as a form of neurosis.[79] The biography of Mazhar Mallouhi, a well-known Muslim follower of Christ from Syria, tells of his early days as an apostate and of the high psychological price mimicry exacts: "Feeling the tremendous pressure to be accepted, [he] went overboard in his adoption of this new religious culture. He recalls friends from those times in a similar situation to his own who responded similarly and ended up mentally ill, to this day living in a state of paranoia about Islam."[80] While this is a somewhat subjective report, psychologists using Herman's dialogical paradigm in their research agree that the collapse of internal dialogue caused through suppressing a "voice," or aspect, of identity "could result in behavior or self-experience that parallels schizophrenia."[81]

Conversely, Bhabha's view of mimicry is quite positive. He argues that it is more concerned with *disguising* voices of the self than suppressing them. Thus, for Bhabha, mimicry is a kind of *camouflage*, a potentially subversive survival response to colonial oppression.[82] Nevertheless, this seems to be an undesirable dynamic to foster within the Body of Christ. Not only is it rooted in ethnocentrism and injustice; the camouflage it encourages by prioritizing assimilation of Christian cultural symbols over meaning is likely to become a syncretistic Christian veneer.

Although imitation is an integral aspect of biblical discipleship (1 Thessalonians 1:6–7; Hebrews 13:7) the phenomenon of mimicry raises important issues of power and inequality within cross-cultural mentoring relationships.

KHAMIS AND THALITH

After hearing Khamis tell of the pressure to mimic he experienced at church, I am not surprised when he informs me he no longer attends. However, I am taken aback to learn how he expresses this to his extended family: "I don't go to church," he tells them. "I don't want to bring shame on Christ's name ... I won't take my wife to a place where everyone is half-naked ... My wife is modest."

Unlike Khamis, 25-year-old Thalith is totally "unchurched." Although many in his extended family are devout Muslims, Thalith has good relationships and little fear in sharing his testimony. He has shown Mel Gibson's *The Passion of the Christ* several times to his family, stopping the video every few minutes in his enthusiasm to explain what was happening. Although they occasionally accuse him of being a Christian, he stubbornly maintains he is Muslim and his family, reassured, continues to accept him as such.

Most of my interview with Thalith probes the interaction between the different identities on his ID card — national, ethnic, Arab, tribal, and Muslim — followed by a discussion of how he integrates these as a follower of Christ.

Early on, Thalith appears to express dissonance between his own self-understanding and the standard cultural definitions for *Muslim* he has internalized:

Jens: It says "Muslim" here [on your ID card], right? ... Are you a Muslim?

Thalith: Yes.

Jens: How would you describe the "ideal" Muslim?

Thalith: I am not an *ideal* Muslim.

Later on, as we begin discussing his faith, Thalith begins to use *Muslim* differently:

Jens: How does your faith in Christ affect your identity as a Muslim?

Thalith: My faith makes me a better Muslim.

At first glance, grainier metaphors such as *mix-and-match* seem adequate enough to describe these and many other phenomena celebrated as *hybridity*. Typical clichés such as "Moroccan girls doing Thai boxing in Amsterdam"[83] tend to highlight the outrageous or colorful juxtapositions that hybridity sometimes produces. Khamis' comments are certainly outrageous; both he and Thalith are using Muslim symbols in new combinations and associations. However, the superficial connotations of *mix-and-match* do not capture all that is happening here. An important aspect of experimental hybrid innovation is the idea of *liminality*.

HYBRIDITY AS LIMINALITY

Van Gennep subdivides cultural *rites of passage* into three stages: *separation, transition,* and *incorporation*.[84] The transitional stage is particularly interesting for anthropologists since it involves a threshold or *liminal* point between incommensurable social identities such as child and adult, or single and married.[85]

Building on Van Gennep's work, Victor Turner describes liminal entities as "neither here nor there ... betwixt and between the positions assigned and arrayed by law, custom, convention, and ceremonial ... It is as though they are being reduced or ground down to a uniform condition to be fashioned anew."[86] This stripping away of external symbols allows cultural systems to be drawn into dialogue with each other through "experimental behavior ... In liminality, new ways of acting, new combinations of symbols, are tried out, to be discarded or accepted."[87]

From the perspective of psychology, Hermans believes such dialogical processes are foundational to the self's creativity. Since "new meanings are created on the border zone between different and opposed positions ... contrasts, conflicts, disagreements, and contradictions between components of the self, are ... intrinsic to a well-functioning self in general and to its innovation in particular."[88] Thani's innovative matchmaking solution is just one example of this synergistic potential working in my friends' lives.

Liminal spaces are often spiritual places and can become the site of the *prophetic*, in the sense that a prophet serves as a "gate" between worlds.[89] The liminal voice "crying in the wilderness" (Isaiah 40:3) is like the hybrid migrant who "is empowered to intervene *actively* in the transmission of cultural inheritance ... rather than *passively* accept its venerable customs and pedagogical wisdom. He or she can question, refashion or mobilize received ideas ... [and] is empowered to act as an agent of change."[90] A liminal person, while maintaining the right to speak as an "insider," can thus act as a "bridge" over which outside sources of knowledge may enter into their community.

THIRD SPACE SUBVERSION

As a site of innovative contextualization then, the liminal zone can become a semiotic battlefield. When liminal persons act or speak, their inner dialogue spills out, prophetically engaging their community and culture in the public contestation of meaning. For Bakhtin,

> There are no "neutral" words and forms ... that can belong to "no one," language has been completely taken over, shot through with intentions and accents ... Each word tastes of the ... contexts in which it has lived its socially charged life ... The word in language is half someone else's. It becomes "one's own" only when the speaker populates it with his own intention, his own accent ... Prior to this moment of appropriation, the word does not exist in a neutral and impersonal language (it is not, after all, out of a dictionary that the speaker gets his words!), but rather it exists in other people's mouths, in other people's contexts, serving other people's intentions: it is from there that one must take the word, and make it one's own.[91]

In their "mixing and matching" both Khamis and Thalith are appropriating Muslim symbols in innovative ways. For example, Khamis claims insider status by invoking Muslim interpretants for church and affirming Muslim modesty narratives. Yet he uses these symbols in a context that makes his allegiance to Christ clear. To proclaim his wife to be a "Christ-follower-yet-modest" undermines the simplistic stereotypes held by most in his village.

Although aware of the dissonance between his own self-understanding and his culture's definition of *Muslim*, Thalith does not try to reduce it by rejecting the symbol or minimizing its importance. Instead, he attempts to make it his own by populating it with new meaning. In this way, Thalith takes up a marginal and prophetic position—a *liminal* position.

When talking to other Muslims, Thalith describes himself as a *mu'min* (believer). In appropriating this term, he makes a clear distinction between himself and ordinary Muslims, while at the same time claiming Muslim insider status and even qur'anic sanction.[92]

Mazhar Mallouhi also contests the meaning of *Muslim*. In fact, he boldly claims this label while openly rejecting two pillars of the faith:

> *Interviewer*: Are there any aspects of the practice of Islam that you feel you must leave behind?

> *Mallouhi*: Really only two things: the *shahada* [the Islamic creed —
> "There is no God but God and Muhammad is his Proph-
> et"] and the pilgrimage to Mecca. Often I encourage Muslim
> followers of Jesus to write their own *shahada*.[93]

Mallouhi's interpretant for *Muslim* is highly unorthodox. Indeed, since hybridity is a refusal to choose orthodoxy, it is by definition *heresy*.[94] Yet Mallouhi is loved and accepted as a member of the Muslim *ummah* (community) by many Muslims around the world — including high-profile leaders. Tellingly, his innovative appropriation of *Muslim* differs radically from the textbook-based definitions insisted on by some Western experts that reflect perhaps the Evangelical reification of theology. The problem with such theoretical definitions for *Muslim* though, "is that they predicate the formulation of identity upon a reality that appears abstract and somehow independent of those persons or groups who perceive and participate in it."[95] As Bakhtin reminds us, "it is not, after all, out of a dictionary that the speaker gets his words!"

Taking up this calling to be a liminal prophet, Mallouhi says, "[W]hen one follows Christ, one's own culture and identity should be enriched. Light should be brought into that culture. That is why it is so important for me to stay and live within my Muslim cultural community."[96] Should one complain that Mallouhi is not a "good Muslim," or should he be applauded for making *Muslim* good? According to whose definition of *Muslim* should Mallouhi be judged? How do believers become prophetic bridges of truth without losing their right to speak as "insiders" or straying into syncretism? If dialogical contextualization always involves a messy and local contestation of meaning, is the accusation of "syncretism" only valid in hindsight if appropriation fails? How *should* cultural symbols be taken captive and made obedient to Christ (2 Corinthians 10:5)? Developing a theology of semiotics that is approachable for practitioners on the mission field is an urgent need.

THAMIN'S TWO PERSONALITIES

In the early 1990s, through a chance meeting with a Western pastor visiting the Middle East, Thamin experienced a dramatic revelation of God and simultaneous conversion. Fearing for Thamin's safety and feeling responsible, the pastor managed to bring Thamin back with him to the West. There, he opened his home and discipled Thamin as an adopted son. Over the next year or so, Thamin simultaneously internalized English, Western culture, and Christianity as one integrated system. It was at this point that Thamin attended a discipleship program in which I was involved.

At first, Thamin struggled to express his faith in the context of this course, finding it difficult to worship or pray in Arabic. Indeed, he seemed to have two distinct personalities: although he spoke fluent "Christianese" in English, his Arabic was Islamic, full of Islamic expressions and oaths that those from Coptic, Phoenician, and Assyrian ethnic backgrounds objected to strongly. However, by the end of the course, Thamin had begun to close this gulf between his Arabic and English "selves." By mixing with Arabic-speaking Christians, his Arabic self, although still distinct, became more "Christian" and therefore contrasted less with his "Western evangelical" self.

CHANGING GEARS

Although aspects of mimicry are certainly involved, Thamin's apparent switching between dual personalities more resembles *changing gears* than Bhabha's hybridity. Several observations can be made:

First, it appears Thamin's simultaneous internalization of English, Christian, and Western cultural systems resulted in the voices of these subjectivities being located in close proximity to each other, if not combined, on the stage of his self.

Second, it seems that contradictions between these new cognitive models and the older Arabic, Islamic, and Middle Eastern models were either not perceived to be problematic, or somehow went unnoticed. This indicates that compartmentalization can occur when discipleship is done in isolation from the cultural contexts that have birthed other voices of identity.

Finally, this implies that cognitive cultural models are also linked to contextual information. It was only when Thamin entered an Arabic-speaking Christian context that these conflicting voices were forced into dialogue. The result of this renegotiation appeared to be a separation and movement of the "Christian" voice into a more independent position.

Hong *et al* argue that "internalized cultures are not necessarily blended ... [A]bsorbing a second culture does not always involve replacing the original culture with the new one."[97] Their research into *cultural frame switching* indicates that the mind can represent and integrate multiple cultural models simultaneously. The mind preserves the integrity of each cognitive model and its associated voices by using situational cues as a trigger to switch between them. Thus, a bicultural person's values and behavior — even personality[98] — can change according to context.

Cultural frame shifting therefore appears to be a strategy to *avoid* ambiguity or the hybridization of symbols by managing cross-cultural homonyms and synonyms contextually. Thamin's story is rather extreme, yet clearly illustrates an issue several of my friends struggle with, although the "frame shift" is less observable: If discipleship is not done in a way that brings Christ's voice into dialogue with all voices of the self and all areas of life, compartmentalization of the new believer's faith can occur.

AWAL'S DRIFT

In the previous chapter, Awal calls himself a Muslim and reports coaching his children to do the same. Yet, a decade ago, he publicly proclaimed to his whole extended family that he was a Christian.

Similarly, in our 2008 interview, Awal reports telling his children, "You can believe whatever you like about Muhammad: a good man, a great leader, even a prophet—whatever is easiest ... However, you must know that it is Christ that will get you closer to God."

Thinking back, it is hard to imagine Awal expressing himself in this way eighteen years earlier, when we first met. Although Awal's self-description is somewhat context-dependent, some movement *has* occurred over the years towards reappropriating Muslim elements of his identity.

COMING TO REST

This drift may indicate a later stage of maturity where voices that were once diametrically opposed have resolved their differences. Although one cannot forget one's "cultural mother tongue" (the cognitive models internalized through primary socialization as a child), signifiers can drift if kept in dialogue with other voices.[99] For example, New Testament interpretants for *prophet* and *prophecy* are not as stringent as commonly held Islamic interpretants for these words.[100] Perhaps, as the scriptural narratives become internalized, initially strong judgments made against Muhammad on realizing his fallibility can later be tempered by New Testament concepts of prophecy. Similarly, negative interpretants attached to symbols such as the mosque or *Muslim* may lose the power they once had due to hybridity or reappropriation.

Several of my non-exiled friends exhibit this long-term drift towards, as Mallouhi describes it, "coming to rest in ... [one's] true identity."[101] Interestingly however, my exiled friends often appear to express *less* identity drift. Is it possible that a greater geographic distance between identifications makes frame switching strategies more feasible, which, in turn, enables them to avoid bringing opposing voices into dialogue? More longitudinal research into the strategies of identity construction used by exiles and non-exiles is needed, both to answer these questions and to understand the internal hybridization processes indicated by this drift.

INTERNAL CONVERSION

When the narratives and symbols of external culture are reappropriated and redefined by liminal prophets and then internalized by the next generation, a society's worldview can be transformed from within. Geertz, studying the subconscious infiltration of Western models and narratives into Balinese Hinduism, calls this process *internal conversion*. While externally there may seem to be little change in Balinese culture and identity, the hybridization of Balinese cognitive models has produced something new that Geertz calls *Bali-ism*.[102]

Since internal conversion is subconscious, it cannot be a mode of *Christian* conversion. However, as internal conversion is, in turn, externalized and begins to influence public meanings and narratives, it could set in motion other forms of conversion *within* the tradition. Some examples of conversion within a tradition that *do* have Christian precedents are *intensification*,[103] *reformation*, and *revitalization*.[104] This long-term approach appears to be Mallouhi's strategy, as seen in his innovative appropriation of the label *Muslim*.

Looking at "internal conversion" from another angle, what will happen when my friends' children internalize the frame-switching or mix-and-match behavior of their parents? One imagines that if the children observe their parents "switching" or "mixing" without adequate explanation, a blurring hybridization of their cognitive models will result. According to Awal, many second-generation believers are struggling with identity problems.[105] Perhaps a better understanding of hybridity is needed to face these issues.

CONCLUSION

In this chapter, I have attempted to demonstrate that both hybridization and the "dialogical self" provide useful lenses through which to understand aspects of my friends' lives. Using the dialogical model developed in the previous chapter, three modes of hybridization can be observed occurring at three locations: Firstly, intercultural diffusion occurs between *external cultures* due to globalizing and pluralizing influences. Secondly, third-space innovation emanates from the dialogical processes involving voices of the *self*. Thirdly, drift and blurring of internalized *cognitive models* can occur within the mind.

More research and theological analysis in the areas of multiple belonging, third-space liminality, and hybridity are needed. Are suppression, mimicry, and frame switching the only alternatives to "insider" hybridization? What other strategies exist and which are most fruitful long-term? As globalization continues to accelerate and the number of second-generation believers grows, hybridity will become an increasingly important issue among Muslims who have chosen to follow Christ. While syncretism is a concern, the *fact* of hybridity calls for careful rethinking of this term, recognizing that "since all churches are culture-based, every church is syncretistic."[106] For Lamin Sanneh, who comes from a Muslim background himself, it is precisely these hybridization processes within Christianity that make it a unique and global faith.[107]

5

CONVERSION IN THE LIGHT OF IDENTITY THEORIES

TIM GREEN

I am now waiting for the results of my appeal. I am sick of not having an identity. As an asylum seeker here you have no identity, you are always waiting. I want to be recognized as belonging, to be able to make my contribution.[108]

These words of a 19-year-old in Britain express powerfully the frustration and helplessness of migrants seeking a new identity. Eventually they settle, marry, and have families, yet it can still take decades to integrate their new and old identities fully.

This long-term search is echoed in the experience of "spiritual migrants" who have made the journey from one faith to another. They, too, undergo deep loss and change, especially when family is left behind. They, too, have to find a new community, learn its "language" and unwritten codes of conduct. They, too, struggle with integrating their old and new identities and wonder how many years it will take before they truly feel at home.

In this chapter and the next, I explore these issues. Firstly, I sketch a brief overview of identity theories and propose a three-layered framework to understand them. Secondly, I explore its relevance for believers from a Muslim background as they make identity transitions on all three levels, especially as they try to reconcile two religious identities and live on the "border zone" between two communities. Finally, I apply this to the unnecessarily-polarized debate on the "C Spectrum" and insider movements, proposing ways to move beyond the present impasse.

These two chapters survey a range of theorists from several disciplines and use illustrations from many contexts. Thus they cannot go to the same depths as chapters that focus on a single theory or context. Aware of necessary generalizations, I have written in more depth on those matters elsewhere.

"IN SEARCH OF MEANING AND IDENTITY"

Seppo Syrjänen chose this phrase as the title of his classic study on Pakistani converts to Christianity[109] as it aptly summarizes the lifelong quest which for many believers was intensified rather than resolved after turning to Christ. Take, for example, the story of Mazhar Mallouhi.

Born into a Sunni Muslim family in Syria around 1935, Mazhar as a young man turned to Christ and moved to Lebanon where, in the words of his biographer, he

> aggressively adopted a Christian culture and ended all relationships with Muslims ... Desiring to be accepted in his "new family and community," he even went to extremes in order to please them. The local Christians tried to put upon him all their traditions and views, such as inspiring him toward hating Islam, encouraging him to denigrate his own religious and cultural background, and even to embody Zionism.[110]

This resulted in "a deep internal struggle" and "a profound crisis of identity."

> Regardless of how much Mazhar assimilated himself into a "Christian" culture and appeared to be Christian, he never felt truly at home. He often found himself feeling he was betraying his heritage and people.

> After a long and arduous journey, Mazhar rediscovered his roots, albeit returning to them in a fresh way. It was a process of gradually beginning to see and call himself "culturally" a Muslim and "spiritually" a Christ follower ... For him it is not a means to an end, but rather a "coming to rest in his true identity," discovering who he really is, a finding of his way home. [111]

Mazhar Mallouhi now feels he has reached that place. He says, "Islam is my heritage, Christ is my inheritance."[112] But it took him several decades and the support of a believing spouse to reach this position. Others are not so fortunate. One of my convert friends in Pakistan told me,

> My identity is weak ... I am now bearing the brunt of marrying a
> woman from the community of other faith ... I will have to struggle
> hard to keep my faith alive and dominant in the atmosphere where
> I shall be surrounded by the people of other faith.

Worldwide, believers from Muslim background pursue a long, confusing quest for identity. *"Who are we in Christ?"* was how a group of Afghans in Canada put it to me. My own PhD research is on issues of identity for first-generation believers in Pakistan. Kathryn Kraft entitled her PhD thesis "Community and Identity among Arabs of a Muslim Background Who Choose to Follow a Christian Faith."[113] The field of "identity studies" is highly relevant to believers from Muslim background, and to this we now turn.

"IDENTITY STUDIES," A COMPLEX MINEFIELD

Making sense of identity is notoriously difficult as *different disciplines define identity in different ways*. While psychologists typically use such terms as "the inner self," anthropologists (along with some sociologists) treat identity as a collective label marking out different groups. Social psychologists bridge these opposed notions, by analyzing "identity negotiation" between individuals and groups.[114] In the vast literature on identity there is no universally agreed-upon definition, even before taking theological perspectives into account!

A second cause of complexity is that *identities are shifting and fragmenting* under the impact of globalization. As "waves of transformation crash across virtually the whole of the earth's surface,"[115] old certainties disintegrate. Travel and the internet expose people to new worldviews; migration and intermarriage create new hybrid identities; pluralizing societies challenge assumed alliances of faith, ethnicity, and nationality. Minarets which once dominated the skylines of Muslim cities now compete with forests of TV aerials and satellite dishes. "The days of closed, homogeneous, unchanging societies are rapidly going and they will not come back," comments Jean-Marie Gaudeul.[116]

As identities themselves evolve, *understandings of identity follow suit*—a third cause of complexity. In Western thought, the "Enlightenment definition" of identity was followed by the "sociological definition" and now the "postmodern definition" which delights in "a bewildering, fleeting multiplicity of possible identities."[117] Meanwhile, collectivist understandings of identity ("We are, therefore I am") remain important, especially in non-Western societies.

For the above reasons and others, the field of "identity studies" resembles a minefield. Should we, daunted, simply forgo the attempt to pick our way through it? Should we erect a warning sign: "Abandon Hope All Ye who Enter Here"? I believe not, for this minefield is also a goldmine to those who persevere, yielding treasures of insight on identity issues facing Christ's followers from Muslim background.

IDENTITY AT THREE LEVELS

To make sense of this slippery concept called "identity," we must clarify some concepts and discern overall patterns. In doing so, we find that there is more consensus among theorists than first thought.

Benjamin Beit-Hallahmi surveys definitions of identity from several academic fields and proposes that they be organized in a three-level conceptualization:

> At the top I would place *collective identity*, i.e. identity as defined by the group ... In the middle I would place *social identity* labels as used by the individual and by others to identify him(self). At the bottom or deepest level I would place *ego-identity*, which is privately or even unconsciously experienced by the individual.[118]

Prompted by Beit-Hallahmi's analysis I adapted his scheme in a simple diagram,[119] substituting the more readily understood expression "core identity" for the technical term "ego-identity." This diagram does not reduce a person's composite identity to merely three parts. Rather, it clarifies three complementary layers, or three stories of a building, on each of which the drama of identity development is played out with all its dialogue and action. Of course, identities are neither simple nor static; this diagram merely supplies an introductory framework within which to explore them. For the sake of clarity, I run the risk of over-simplification.

Let us consider each identity layer in turn, especially in relation to Muslim people and societies.

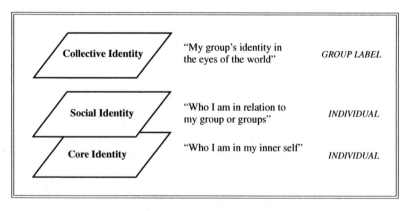

Figure 5.1: Identity at Three Levels

THE "COLLECTIVE IDENTITY" LAYER

From the moment of birth, people are labeled with a collective identity, or rather a set of collective identities. Their nationality, ethnicity, and sometimes religion are entered on their birth certificates before they make any choice for themselves. These are *ascribed* identities. The more collectivist is a culture, the more controlling are such ascribed identities, and the harder it is to change them even in adulthood.

In mono-cultural societies, religion merges with ethnicity as a group identity marker. Assumptions like "all Malays are Muslim" or "I am a Turk; I am a Muslim" run deep. As David Radford shows in this volume, the Kyrgyz in Kyrgyzstan are assumed to be "Muslim" and Russians to be "Christian."

Pathans make the same automatic linkage, and one of the tiny number of Jesus-followers among them told me how he uses this to advantage: "If they ask me 'Are you Muslim?' I reply, 'I am Pathan,' and that is sufficient." This answer saves him from detection without having to deny Christ, perhaps the best that can be expected in a situation where "religion" and "ethnicity" are so strongly fused at the collective level.

In some countries, Islam is deliberately used to provide ideological underpinning for the national identity. My (non-Muslim) son was once required to write in his school notebook, "I am proud to belong to Pakistan because of its Islamic ideology." In such ways a country's educational system can incorporate what Beit-Hallahmi calls "rituals of loyalty."

In pluralist societies, it should in principle be easier to distinguish between ethnicity, religion and nationality, as any Gujarati Muslim Indian would affirm. In practice, however, the religious identity label remains a powerfully controlling factor and loyalty test, especially in times of ethnic tension. Rudolf Heredia, in *Changing Gods in India*, traces in masterly detail the story of how religion has become a symbol and touchstone of identity politics in modern India. "In situations of sharp and hostile religious boundaries between communities, conversion represents the ultimate betrayal," he writes.[120]

In individualistic societies, collective identities loosen up and become less important. It is not that they no longer exist, simply that they exert less dogmatic control over a person's identity and social mobility. A black person is still black, but if she chooses to marry a white man it matters less than in traditional cultures. Collective identities are less likely to be ascribed at birth and more likely to be chosen by the individual. Football supporters have a tribal identity to be sure, but at least it is an identity they are free to choose or to change.

THE "SOCIAL IDENTITY" LAYER

In principle (though this is not always done in the literature), social identity should be distinguished from collective identity. This is because collective identity "is rooted in a symbolic group or a social category"[121] and is *ascribed* to a person at birth as a label, while social identity is *absorbed* gradually by that person through actual relationships with "significant others."

Religious social identity is initially internalized, like other social identities, within the boundaries of the family. Most people are simply born into a religion, rather than choosing one. Islam as a social identity is more often assumed than chosen, at least in traditional Muslim societies, for it is woven into the fabric of daily life. The Muslim creed is whispered into one's ears at birth and recited over one's corpse in death. As Kenneth Cragg points out,[122] an endless interpenetration of religion and society confirms the young in their Islam, and as they grow into adulthood they pass through no ceremony to mark their full, personal, convinced allegiance to the faith. To be Muslim is automatic unless deliberate apostasy is chosen. Arguably it is this "glue" of Muslim social identity, which marks one of the biggest barriers to conversion out of Islam, and perhaps the sharpest cost for converts.

When acting in default mode, Islam provides a secure framework from cradle to grave, a religiously legitimating ordering of society, and a comfortable and comforting backdrop to life. All human societies crave such security, argues sociologist of religion Peter Berger, and religion provides it for them. It acts as a "sacred canopy" and a "shield against terror."[123]

THE "CORE IDENTITY" LAYER

Core identity is shown on the bottom layer of the diagram, the ground floor of the building. It is the inner heart of a person's self-awareness and worldview, first formed as young children subconsciously internalize their parents' values and outlook. According to Erik Erikson's influential theory, "the young individual must learn to be most himself where he means most to others — through others, to be sure, who have come to mean most to him."[124]

As children grow into adolescence and young adulthood, they reach a stage (in Erikson's scheme) where they review their hitherto absorbed values and make their own choices. They may choose to rebel against their parents' faith, adopting an opposing lifestyle and values, or conversely they may claim it deliberately for themselves. Either way it is a personal choice, an *achieved* identity.

James Fowler applied the theories of Erikson and other developmentalists to the particular case of religious identity, marking out "stages of faith" through which people pass. Fowler too believed that a watershed transition occurs when individuals examine critically their prior assumptions and articulate their own, personal faith.[125] Or, as Beit-Hallahmi puts it, "Religion gains its power on the individual level when it becomes tied to one's ego-identity, when it is imbued with high ego-involvement."[126]

However, all these theorists were working in Western contexts, where society and education elevate individual critical choice. What about collectivist cultures where people think more in terms of "we" than "I," and prize conformity more than independence? Would Western theories still apply in Arab cultures, where a proverb says, "Don't tell me who you are; tell me who your friends are"?[127]

Given the propensity in collectivist Muslim cultures to assume faith, with no ritual to mark a transition from "social" to "core" commitment, it is doubtless true that many people function as Muslims primarily on a social level. Sometimes a major challenge such as civil war is needed to disturb social worldviews, or it can come as a stage of maturing. "I was born a muslim; later I became a Muslim" is how one Bangladeshi lady described to me her transition into personal religious commitment as a young woman. (Much later in life, she went through another transition and turned to Christ.)

Nevertheless, it is in non-Muslim contexts that Muslims face the biggest challenge, as they struggle with the cognitive dissonance of trying to reconcile two cultures and two worldviews. "Of all the internal debates that face Muslims in Britain perhaps one of the most vigorous is about identity," writes Dilwar Hussain.[128]

Some second generation British Muslims have chosen to locate their core identity not in the cultural Islam of their parents but in an intensified personal Islam, a standpoint which allows them to critique their parental traditions on the one hand and their British environment on the other. Others have opted to reject Islam and declare themselves as "ex-Muslims."[129] Still others resolve their identity crises through conversion to Christ. "I had always struggled with having two identities; I didn't know what I was," one British Pakistani woman told me. "When I became a Christian, it gave me one united identity. It was astounding!"

The experience of living as Muslims in a non-Muslim society does not generate a uniform outcome. What it does generate, though, is the challenge of having to examine critically the social identity they *absorbed* as Muslims and decide what core identity they want to *achieve* for themselves.

CONVERSION:
A TRANSFORMED IDENTITY AT EACH LEVEL

The field of conversion studies is informed by several disciplines: psychology, sociology, anthropology, history, missiology and, of course, theology. Lewis Rambo sought to integrate insights from all these disciplines except the theological, whose methodology he believes to be incompatible with the rest. His multidisciplinary survey of religious conversion,[130] though more descriptive than prescriptive, has become a benchmark for subsequent studies.

Rambo and many other writers treat religious conversion as a radical form of identity transformation. It has massive implications for a convert at all three levels of identity. Let us consider each of these in turn.

RELIGIOUS CONVERSION AT THE "CORE IDENTITY" LEVEL

Personal faith is closely linked with core values, worldview, and commitments. Therefore "it takes severe biographical shocks to disintegrate the massive reality internalized in early childhood."[131] At the core level, a person changing her faith inevitably undergoes an identity transition.

One formerly Muslim friend from Uganda described to me the excitement he felt at his baptism:

> I felt I have died to my old sinful way, I have given myself to God and am now a new person. I am not the Firaz my friends knew, not the one whom Satan knew, but a new Firaz—forgiven, born again, controlled by the Spirit. The old Firaz is dead, the new one is alive in Christ. I came out of the water feeling I am a new person!

However, to speak of a "new identity" does not mean that that the old is instantly obliterated. According to psychologist Channa Ullman, the identity of religious converts has elements of continuity with the past as well as discontinuity. Heredia agrees that "their old identity is not erased; rather, the new one is overwritten on it."[132]

That is where life gets complicated, for it takes a prolonged internal struggle to change one's worldview—to value humility above honor for example, or forgiveness above revenge. The "voices" of old and new value systems compete to be heard and obeyed, as they argue with each other on the "core identity" layer of the house. Barnett's chapter in this volume analyses this process, with its choices and ambiguities, in the lives of Arab believers from a Muslim background.

Aligning the results if not the methods of the social sciences with biblical theology, we find the same ambivalence in New Testament descriptions of conversion. At times the apostle Paul stresses discontinuity, for "the old has gone, the new has come" (2 Corinthians 5:17).[133] But elsewhere, or even in the same passages, he exhorts converts to keep waging war on the old self which still stubbornly exerts its influence, or to put off old habits and take old thoughts captive, or to keep on being transformed by the renewing of their minds. To internalize and prioritize new values is a kind of ongoing spiritual *jihad*.[134] Whether viewed through secular or theological lenses, there is both continuity and discontinuity in the core identity of converts.

RELIGIOUS CONVERSION AT THE "SOCIAL IDENTITY" LEVEL

Is it possible for a convert to preserve a new, private core identity without receiving social support from other like-minded believers? Will my friend from a Muslim background who put "sheepalone" in his email address be able to survive without joining the flock?

Berger and Luckmann believe the close support of "significant others" to be essential in sustaining religious converts:

> To have a conversion experience is nothing much. The real thing is to be able to keep on taking it seriously; to retain a sense of its plausibility. *This* is where the religious community comes in. It provides the indispensable plausibility structure for the new reality.[135]

This new religious community offers converts not only a "plausibility structure" of affirmation but also a "laboratory of transformation" to try out new roles and patterns of life.[136]

The findings of these sociologists reinforce what we already know theologically and experientially: that the community of believers is of vital importance. It is disappointing but not surprising when, sapped of energy, some isolated believers turn back to Islam (at least at the social identity level, if not in their hearts). We are all the more impressed by those believers who, against the odds, somehow manage to cling on to faith in Christ even when they have almost no access to fellowship.

Another relevant strand in Berger's writing is that of "nomos," or the predictable ordering of worldview and society which comforts followers of a religion. When they forfeit this through conversion or in other ways, they face the disorientation of "anomie" with its "unbearable psychological tensions":

> It is not only that the individual loses emotionally satisfying ties in such cases. He loses his orientation in experience. In extreme cases, he loses his sense of reality and identity.[137]

Kathryn Kraft in this volume applies "anomie" to the experience of Arab believers from a Muslim background. Ziya Meral does the same for Turkish converts like himself:

> Most of the guidelines in life, from what to wear, to what to eat are replaced with a confusing "freedom in Christ." The new convert, devoid of any religious rituals and regulations, often feels lost ... But this anomic state is much more complicated than merely not knowing how to operate under a new system. Conversion from Islam equals a break away from the society ... By leaving Islam, the convert loses his identity totally in relation to his local community and the world of Islam ... Thus church members continually struggle living in such a confusing and emotionally draining state.[138]

Shahid, an African friend, returned to his Muslim home after many years overseas, during which time he had become Christ's follower. His father, instead of welcoming him home, shouted "you are no longer my son" and threw stones to drive him away. "That day was the hardest day of my life," Shahid told me.

Many believers experience social rejection as devastating as Shahid's or even worse. They urgently seek a new social identity, a new "family" to replace the old, a new role model of what being Christ's follower actually looks like in practice, and a new framework of Christian discipleship. Research by Don Little and Tom Walsh shows that personal mentoring was counted as even more important than Bible study in the discipleship of believers from a Muslim background.[139]

For other believers, there is less discontinuity. They continue to relate to their old communities whilst simultaneously embracing the new, through strategies of "dual belonging" to be discussed in the next chapter.

RELIGIOUS CONVERSION ON THE "COLLECTIVE IDENTITY" LEVEL

We saw earlier that traditional societies tend to fuse collective identities of religion, ethnicity, and nationality. Therefore a person who changes one element of these is seen as betraying them all. It means "going over to the other side" or even "going over to the enemy's side."

This attitude runs deep in Muslim societies worldwide, because Islamic history, law, and custom deliver a combined verdict that apostasy spells treason. This "publicly shames their community, as it is seen as an act of hostility toward their culture and social background. Out of a sense of family or community honor, they feel they must respond."[140]

A Saudi believer, Fatima Al-Mutairi, the 26-year-old daughter of a Muslim cleric, had found Christ through the internet. On her blog she wrote anonymously a poignant poem in Arabic, attempting to pry apart religious and national identity. Part of it translates as follows:

Truly, we love our homeland, and we are not traitors
We take pride that we are Saudi citizens
How could we betray our homeland, our dear people?
How could we, when for death — for Saudi Arabia — we stand ready?
The homeland of my grandfathers, their glories, and odes — for it I am writing
And we say, "We are proud, proud, proud to be Saudis"
...
We chose our way, the way of the rightly guided
And every man is free to choose any religion
Be content to leave us to ourselves to be believers in Jesus

Her plea was in vain. In August 2008, her father and brother discovered her Christian allegiance and killed her. Afterwards a female blogger wrote "thousand, thousand congratulations for her death ... and a special thanks to her brother who carried out God's law ... curse upon the apostate Fatima, curse upon the apostate Fatima."[141]

Whether through the courts of community censure or through the courts of law, converts in Muslim lands are likely to face penalties because their decision is seen as a betrayal of the collective identity. Efforts by converts in Malaysia and Egypt to be allowed to change their identity cards have (until the time of writing) been unsuccessful. Official sentences have been passed against believers in Iran, Afghanistan, Jordan, and other countries while unofficial executions (that is, murders) take place occasionally in Somalia, Saudi Arabia (as noted above), and elsewhere. Loss of one's spouse, children, inheritance, or work is not uncommon.

Even in the secular West, conversion out of Islam is nearly always seen as a betrayal of collective identity. "Don't you realize," a British-born Pakistani friend of mine was told by her relative, "that by becoming a Christian you have abandoned your roots, your heritage and your family name?"

However, there are a few signs of change in places where globalization is breaking up the old collectivist assumptions, or where a proportion of the population became at one stage disillusioned with violence or harsh government in the name of Islam (as in Iran, Algeria, and Bangladesh). Moreover, in some countries insider movements seek to combine allegiance to Christ with loyalty to their Muslim communities which may create space for a new collective identity to emerge in due course. This will be discussed further in the next chapter.

6

IDENTITY CHOICES AT THE BORDER ZONE

TIM GREEN

THE DILEMMA OF DUAL BELONGING

My friend Nazir was nearly forty when he came to know Christ. Fifteen years later, his wife and three children are still Muslim. He longs for them to know Jesus. Once, at a Christian camp, very early in the morning, I found Nazir alone, pouring out his heart to God for his family. I came to understand something of his long-term heartache — that dull thud of pain that sometimes grows, sometimes recedes, but never disappears.

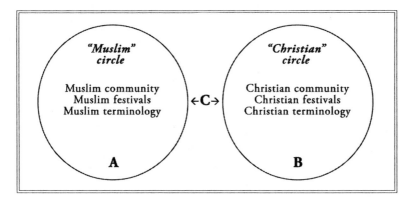

Figure 6.1: Circles Of Identity

Later, during research on issues of identity for believers from a Muslim background in Pakistan, I interviewed Nazir. I showed him this diagram and asked him where he would place himself: Did he belong in the "Muslim circle" (*position A*), the "Christian circle" (*position B*) or somewhere between the two (*position C*)?

Nazir identified readily with this diagram and aligned himself with position C. "I have to show myself in both circles ... I have to show myself as a Muslim [among Muslims] and among Christians as a Christian."[142]

To achieve this, he switches his behavior as required to blend in with his surroundings. Almost everyone in his Muslim community assumes he is a Muslim. At the same time, he states,

> Many Christian people don't know that I'm a convert. They think
> that I was born a Christian; when they do find out, they are amazed
> ... They think I am one of them ... [but] I am a member of two circles.

He sees advantages in this ambiguity, jokingly commenting that "people celebrate two festivals each year, but I celebrate four": two *Eids*, Christmas, and Easter!

As I probed deeper, I found that Nazir is actually not at all content with his circumstances. He does not live at peace with himself. The "dilemma of dual belonging" presses in on him in several ways.

First, he is not free to speak openly of Christ among his Muslim friends and relatives. Initially he had witnessed boldly, but this landed him in serious trouble with his wife who nearly divorced him. He is now much more cautious:

> If I declare openly that I am a Christian and not a Muslim then defi-
> nitely the first thing is that my marriage will be cancelled.

Second, he has to be extremely circumspect in his Christian devotions and worship. He used to read his Bible at home, but once "my wife became very angry and tore up my Bible" so he now only reads it when away from home. When praying at home, he gives his wife the impression he is saying ritual Muslim prayers while in fact praying in Jesus' name. And whenever he wants to go to church, he says:

> I have to say I'm going somewhere else, because if I ever say I'm
> going to church she will never let me ... Suppose you want to go to
> church but your wife doesn't let you go; she says "Here's the wash-
> ing machine, wash these clothes and hang them up" — what will you
> do? That's what happens to me sometimes.

Nazir may appear to be a henpecked husband, but his wife knows she can divorce him any time, for under *sharia* law the marriage of an apostate is automatically dissolved.

Third, Nazir's compromises and deception trouble his conscience. He feels guilty praying the Muslim way at the mosque or at home. He asks God for forgiveness and prays:

> Jesus, you know my problem is my limitations, my hindrances. There's only one way, which is for you to change these people so that I don't have to continue in this double-minded situation.

Finally, Nazir is worried about his children's future. He sees no option but to arrange their marriage with Muslims, much as he would love them to come to Christ and to marry fellow-believers.

Nazir longs to be free to join fully the Christian community and to escape the strain of dual belonging:

> I don't think there will be inner peace by living in two circles. See, it's certainly difficult for me, to live in this situation, in this community. Because of my family problem and in order not to be cut off from my wife and children, I have to stay in this circle [the Muslim one]. I prefer to be in this one [the Christian one], where God's people are.
>
> That situation cannot arise until my wife receives Christ ... The day that happens, it will be for me like celebrating *Eid* or a festival which makes a person happy, or celebrating a child's birth. When my wife comes to Christ I will be so happy! Everything is possible which seems impossible to me today. What seems like a mountain can become just dust.

Nazir has labored under this load for fifteen years. How much longer will it continue? I now realize that his early morning intercession for his wife and family springs not just from his earnest desire for their salvation (genuine though that is), but also to resolve his own dilemma:

> It's just because of one woman I am in a big problem and, if she comes to Christ, all my difficulties will be solved.

DUAL, MULTIPLE, AND HYBRID IDENTITIES

Most Muslim background believers I have interviewed described this dilemma of trying to belong to two communities at the same time. This worldwide problem is exacerbated wherever there is a large cultural gap between Muslim and Christian communities. What options for dual belonging are available at the *social level* of identity? What are the implications for their core identities? Once they grow sufficiently in numbers, how will their group identity be expressed at the *collective level*?

Mixed and Hybrid Identities at the Social Level

In the preceding chapter, I described how individuals absorb a social identity from childhood onwards. In reality, nearly everyone today learns to juggle several social identities. We adopt one role in the workplace and another at home. We learn to move in different social circles, adjusting our vocabulary and dress to blend in with each. Twenty-first century people in pluralist societies are actually quite successful at coping with multiple social identities.

When on occasion a person's identities clash, the inner stress induced depends on several factors, including the closeness of one's relationships with each group, the extent to which both groups tolerate dual belonging, and the degree to which dual belonging requires switching of values at the core identity level.

Coping Strategies

A person holding dual nationality will use whichever passport is more convenient for a particular journey; this makes no difference at the core identity level. However, a dual cultural identity is more problematic, for it impinges on one's inner values. This challenge is faced by children of immigrants or racially mixed parents, and they typically adopt one of three strategies to cope with it.

First strategy: "Switching."

Take the hypothetical example of a British-born Pakistani teenage girl, torn between her traditional Asian family and her rebellious English friends. Her first option is what I call "switching." At home she will speak Urdu, wear a *shalwar-qamiz*[143] and play the part of a dutiful daughter. Away from home with her white peers, she flips over to speak in English, wear jeans, drink alcohol, and date boys. As long as she can keep her two lives physically separate — ensuring they never mix — this switching strategy works well. But eventually the psychological strain catches up with her. The contradiction between her two identities at the social level seeps through to the core level, and she longs for a united identity at peace with herself. Moreover, both of her in-groups may be suspicious or worse at her involvement in the other group. Eventually, her marriage is likely to seal her identity one way or the other.

Second strategy: "Suppression."

Alternatively she may adopt a strategy of "suppression." She totally gravitates to one group and lifestyle, suppressing the other side of her social identity and pretending this makes no difference at the core level. In an extreme case, she may even run away from home and lose contact with her family for years. In their eyes she has betrayed them, and worse still, has shamed them in their community. After several years of suppression, the young woman becomes aware of a yearning which grows at the core of her personality: a yearning to rediscover the suppressed part of her identity.

Third strategy: "Synthesis."

Both "switching" and "suppression," though feasible as partial and interim solutions, prove unsatisfactory in the long run. The third coping strategy is "synthesis," whereby the teenager is able to bring the two halves of her life into a combination that suits her best. She may eat a variety of Western and Asian food, speak a mix of English and Urdu, and bring her white friends home to meet her parents. If she marries a man who is equally willing to blend two cultures, then quite likely their children will grow up with a hybridized identity at peace with themselves and the world.[144]

True hybridization is not merely a mix of two cultures, but a creative "third culture," as "third culture kids" exemplify. New options are created at the "border zone" where cultures meet. This is why hybrid languages (e.g. Swahili) develop a life and literature of their own, and why Islamic cultures have been at their most innovative when rubbing shoulders with other worlds (Abbasid Iraq or Moorish Spain). Hybridization is a long-term outcome which springs from synthesis but takes a creative step further.

Conditions for Successful Hybridization:

Note that synthesis and hybridization are only possible under certain conditions. First, both "in-groups" must allow the individual to live in the border zone between them and relate to both. If either group exerts a veto on this, the person will be forced to choose between them. Second, both groups must allow the individual to experiment with new cultural combinations and meanings, without condemning this as compromise. Third, a marriage partner must be found who is content with this creative ambiguity and dual belonging; otherwise, the individual may be forced to marry into one closed community or the other. Fourth, the real flowering of hybridization will take place in the next generation. If the children are able to form a new hybrid identity and link up with other such families, then their numbers may eventually grow large enough to establish a new collective identity in the public sphere.

This has important implications for insider movements, as we shall see.

SOCIAL IDENTITY OPTIONS FOR BELIEVERS FROM A MUSLIM BACKGROUND (BMBS)

Understanding identity challenges for migrants and their children helps us to understand the parallel problems facing converts ("spiritual migrants") and their children. To what extent might their coping strategies also find a parallel?

BMB Communities at an Early Stage of Development: Pakistan.

In my observations from interviews with believers from a Muslim background in Pakistan, those still living unmarried in Muslim families usually adopt the "switching" strategy. They oscillate between their home circle and their Christian friends. However, this cannot last forever, for the question of marriage looms and will probably require them to crystallize a choice between one community and the other.

For those interviewees who had left home while still unmarried, or who had married into the Christian community, there had been "suppression" of their Muslim cultural identity. Marriage to a Christian served to lock in their identity to their spouse's community. Their children grow up as secure Christians while aware that they were somewhat different from the traditional Christian community.

Of the believers who had married Muslims or went on to marry Muslims, most maintain a "switching" strategy, to the extent their spouse permits it. A few have reassimilated into the Muslim community, thus "suppressing" their Christian identity at the social level, even if they continued to nurture a flickering flame of allegiance to Christ at the core level. Some interviewees saw their Muslim spouse come to Christ, but those who did not have mostly not been able to transmit their faith to their children.

Regarding the "synthesis" option, I found that several mature believers who had married Christians were eventually able to reestablish surprisingly good relationships with their Muslim relatives. Occasional mutual visits take place, as well as some participation in weddings and funerals of the wider Muslim family, and limited social contact for their children with their Muslim cousins. While once visiting Bashir, whose brother years earlier had tried to murder him, I was astonished to meet the teenage daughters of that same brother. They had come on a friendly visit, were eating with Bashir's family and were even staying overnight in the same house as Bashir's teenage sons! Bashir contributed to this remarkable degree of trust by maintaining contact with his family through the years despite their hostility.

True hybridization will depend in part on the community of believers growing sufficiently in size for marriages to take place within it. Until now in Pakistan, the

BMB community is too new and small to allow much of this, and a second-generation hybrid identity has not yet emerged.

A More Mature Community: Bangladesh.

Far more Muslims have turned to Christ in Bangladesh than in Pakistan, in a movement which began nearly forty years ago. For these reasons, and also because the environment seems to be somewhat more tolerant, there are more social identity options for believers from a Muslim background.

One day in 2008, above the buzz of conversation in a crowded Dhaka restaurant and without feeling any need to lower his voice, Abu Taher Chowdhury categorized for me the different groups of Muslim background believers in Bangladesh. He himself had grown up as a Muslim, had turned to Christ nearly thirty years earlier, and is today a respected leader. This is what he told me:

> The first group is made up of the ones we call "Christian." They are completely assimilated in the traditional church with its festivals, language, and social relationships. They no longer have any contact with their Muslim relatives.

> In the second group are the ones called *Isai*.[145] They mostly live in the Christian community but preserve a little contact with their Muslim relatives, visit them at *Eid* and so on. They switch between Christian and Muslim terminology according to the group they are with. The Christians tend to understand the need of *Isais* to compromise in this way; their Muslim relatives view them as heretical but not beyond the bounds of social contact.

> Next we have what I call "*Isai* Muslim." They are mostly in the Muslim community but they preserve a little contact with Christians. They use Muslim terminology. Many in the Christian community view them as "fake Christians." Muslims view them as an odd kind of Muslim, but acceptable within the range of Muslim sects.

> Finally we have those who follow Jesus but are called "Muslim." They remain within the Muslim community, follow Muslim customs, celebrate Muslim festivals, and use only Muslim terminology. They have no contact with Christians. They are considered as Muslim by the Muslim community and also by the Christian community.

Within this last group there are two kinds of people: one kind say they are Muslim but do not attend the mosque or carry out the *Eid* sacrifice. They keep full contact with their Muslim relatives, who would regard them as religiously slack but nevertheless Muslim. Believers in this group meet for fellowship with each other. The other kind observe religious Muslim practices, including prayer at the mosque and the sacrifice at *Eid*. Others around them do not know they are followers of Jesus. And they do not meet up with other Jesus-followers either.

We may map Abu Taher's categories on the two "circles" I used in the Pakistan interviews. This enables us to develop the diagram one step further.[146] Instead of merely plotting how *individuals* can relate to the two circles, as we did for the Pakistani situation, the more developed scenario in Bangladesh allows us to depict *groups* of believers.

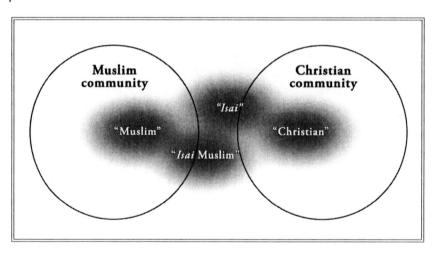

Figure 6.2: Groups of Believers from a Muslim Background in Bangladesh

Two different types of communities are depicted here. The established "Muslim" and "Christian" communities are represented by circles with tightly defined boundaries, for in Paul Hiebert's terms they are "bounded sets."[147] They have their own identity markers and do not intermarry (at least in the Bangladeshi context; I realize that in some other regions of the world, interreligious community boundaries are less tightly drawn).

However, as Abu Taher explained, groups of Muslim background believers in Bangladesh have more ambiguous social identities and more permeable boundaries than do the long-established religious communities. So in this diagram they are shown as "fuzzy" groups, able to merge and overlap with each other and with the traditional communities.

So, in relating to the established religious communities, how do the different groups of believers from Muslim background employ the "coping strategies" described earlier? And what might be the long-term outcomes in each case?

The groups of those who call themselves "Christians" have *suppressed* their Muslim identity and relationships. They have been absorbed into the established Christian community and no longer have a witness among their Muslim relatives. Their children's and grandchildren's identity will be stable but eventually indistinguishable from those "born" Christian.[148] However, if this absorption takes place in sufficient numbers, it might to some extent modify the Hindu-background culture and terminology of the traditional Christian community.

The "*Isai*" and "*Isai* Muslim" groups adopt a *switching* strategy between Christian and Muslim communities, terminology, and festivals. Although viewed with some suspicion from both sides, they apparently manage to oscillate between them, while occupying space in the border zone.

Unlike the individuals in my Pakistan study, the *Isai* community in Bangladesh is large enough to foster its own social identity and arrange its own marriages. To the extent that this community becomes self-sufficient, its degree of contact and frequency of visits with Muslim and Christian communities is likely to lessen gradually. The children of *Isais* still seek a secure identity of their own, which is likely to be a hybridized identity. Some of the children of "*Isai* Muslims" may be reabsorbed into the Muslim community.

The fourth group depicted here is Abu Taher's subgroup who call themselves "Muslim" but who still meet together as followers of Jesus — classic "insiders." They may survive or even grow as a community, so long as they are able to avoid severe persecution, marry fellow believers, and reinterpret Muslim forms with their own Christ-centered meanings. They will need to reinforce those meanings to their children against the flow of majority meanings, and to give their children a very strong sense of inner identity as followers of Christ to compensate for the lack of external identity markers. Will they be able to manage that, and will their Muslim host community allow them to do it?

The final subgroup of believers who call themselves "Muslim" cannot even be depicted on the diagram — they live in total secrecy, with no way to publicly express their faith in Christ. In my opinion, they will find it almost impossible in the long run to sustain the contradiction between their core and social identities. They will be unable to marry fellow believers and will have great difficulty in passing on their faith to their children who, in due course, are bound to be reassimilated into Islam.

BEYOND THE "C SPECTRUM"

The "C Spectrum,"[149] originally proposed as a descriptive tool, has instead been used by missionaries to defend or oppose expressions of faith that maintain a high degree of continuity with Islamic practice. Controversy has especially focused on the so-called great divide between what Travis referred to as C4 and C5 communities of believers.

However, as per John Travis' original definitions, the key issue distinguishing C4 and C5 is not *the degree of contextualization* but *identity*. C4 groups are "Isa-centered communities" while C5 are "communities of Muslims who follow Isa yet remain culturally and officially Muslim."

Similarly, the believers whom I know have more weighty concerns than whether to use a guitar or sitar in worship. What bothers them more are dilemmas of identity such as:

How can I grow strong in Christ while still relating to my Muslim family?
How will I find a believing spouse?
What will be written on the "religion" section of my children's birth certificate?
At school, will they be known as Muslims or Christians or what?
Will I be buried in a Muslim or Christian graveyard?

Such questions reveal a search for identity solutions at all three levels: core, social, and collective. If identity is indeed the watershed issue (not cultural practices), then a one-dimensional spectrum, or a single-point "great divide," cannot possibly depict the multi-dimensional realities of the situation. I therefore believe that Abu Taher's categorization goes one step further than the "C Spectrum" in depicting the realities of identity and community.

His scheme, and our diagrammatic representation of it, belong at the layer of social identity. But what of the other two layers? What options exist for believers from a Muslim background at the core and collective levels? To these we now turn more briefly.

CONFLICTING AND HYBRID IDENTITIES AT THE CORE LEVEL

Recall the three-level diagram of identity developed in the previous chapter. The bottom layer represents "core identity," but is not hermetically sealed from the middle layer of "social identity." Rather, they are like two stories of a building, interconnected with staircases which are busy with movement upwards and downwards.

Any changes or stresses or competing loyalties on the social level of identity will inevitably affect the core identity also. This is why it is virtually impossible, in my opinion, to remain forever a *totally* secret believer[150] — there is simply too much contradiction between the core identity as a follower of Christ and the social identity as a Muslim.

Switching between two social identities is feasible up to a point; switching at the *core* level produces more strain in the long-term because it threatens the inner sense of "who I am." Roland Müller describes this tension as living with "two faces" and believes it can in extreme cases lead to mental instability.[151]

When two or more value systems tug at a believer's heart, a long struggle ensues to integrate a unified identity at the core level. Barnett's chapters in this volume offer hope that this struggle can ultimately lead to a new hybrid identity. His diagram of identity is different from mine, but complementary, and I believe it fits best at the interface between my "social" and "core" identity layers.

MULTIPLE AND EMERGENT IDENTITIES AT THE COLLECTIVE LEVEL

As we have seen at the social and core levels, identities are not static; they flow and develop over time. New combinations emerge and eventually express themselves as new collective labels. How does this process take place, and what are the implications for communities of believers from a Muslim background?

How are New Collective Identities Formed?

As new communities emerge, they create an impetus for new collective identities to be recognized. This impetus has to push against inertia in the host society, which prefers to keep the identity labels static, stereotyped, and simple. Many an incipient new movement has been pushed back into standardized boxes of social prejudice.

Eventually, however, once a critical mass is achieved in terms of numbers or visibility, society grudgingly makes room for the new reality and creates a new label. This can happen when mass *migration* alters the ethnic landscape, or when *intermarriage* creates new hybrid ethnicities. Both these trends are very evident in our pluralizing world.

A third, less common way is through large-scale *religious conversion*. It was by this route that an initially insignificant sect of first-century Jews, functioning as an insider movement and known as "followers of the Way," outgrew its parent community. As this group continued on a creative new trajectory, adopting new identity markers and breaking down old taboos, it eventually emerged as a new collective category reshaping the religious landscape. It reached the point where Judaism cast it out strongly. It acquired the brand new label of "Christian."

New Collective Identities within Islam

From time to time, sects and reform movements have emerged within Islam. Sanctioned by the centuries and secure in their large numbers, some are unquestionably counted as "Muslim" (the Shia, for example). Others survive on the periphery of Islam as deviant but tolerated sects (such as the Druze or the Ismailis). Still others, e.g. the Ahmadiya or the Baha'i, have been forcibly ejected and even persecuted by mainline Muslim communities.

The interesting question is "why?" Why did the Ismailis come to be tolerated and not the Ahmadiya, when both began life as "insider movements" within Islam? Was it more to do with orthodoxy or with orthopraxis? I find it significant that the Ahmadiya are persecuted *despite* retaining Islamic practices and terminology. In fact, the Pakistan Penal Code bans them not from practicing their religion, but from presenting it as a form of Islam! It is their messianic theology that brands them as un-Islamic, not any heterodox practice. It will be interesting to see whether insider movements of Isa-followers, which follow Muslim practices but not Muslim theology, will ultimately be tolerated or ejected.

IDENTITY AND THE INSIDER MOVEMENTS DEBATE

More than fifty years ago, Kenneth Cragg asked what can be done "to encourage in Islam the truth that becoming a Christian is not ceasing to belong with Muslim need, Muslim thought and Muslim kin?"[152] His question is being rephrased today in these terms:

> To what extent can people individually and as a group be faithful in following Jesus Christ while maintaining social, cultural, and even legal identity as adherents of the religion into which they were born?[153]

Supporters of insider movements seek the formation of "culturally appropriate communities of believers who will also continue to live within as much of their culture, including the religious life of the culture, as is biblically faithful."[154] Without here evaluating the arguments for or against this position,[155] I would point out that the terms of the debate itself have been unhelpful in several respects.

First, the debate is *too generalized*. The socio-cultural contexts of such countries as Algeria, Iran, Bangladesh, and Indonesia are very different from each other. Why, then, do we persist in homogenizing them all with the same lines of argument?

Some of the debate has been *theologically shallow*, citing examples from scripture which only partially apply to Jesus-followers from Muslim background. Are they, for example, to be equated with Jewish believers in the early church, or Gentile believers, or with whom?

Both sides in the debate have at times shown a *lack of self-awareness*. Some protagonists appear not to have recognized the ways in which their own field experience (or lack of it) colors their viewpoint.

The debate has not sufficiently taken into account *other fields of knowledge*. For instance, much hinges on whether Islamic terminology can be reinterpreted with new Christ-centered meanings. Has adequate recourse been given to the field of semiotics, or of the social psychology of language?

A serious issue is that the debate is *too short-sighted*. It swirls around the "here and now" of how first-generation believers express their faith, without considering implications for the second generation and beyond. How will the children and grandchildren of today's insider believers identify themselves? We have no crystal ball to gaze into the future, but at least let us learn from analogous movements in the past. How have new streams in world Christianity arisen in history and what has become of them?

The debate has acquired an *imperialistic tone*. Synods and seminaries assume the right to decide, on behalf of Muslim-background believers, what they can and cannot do. The imperialism is obvious when the theological judges are located in the West. A more subtle hierarchy arises whenever national ethnic groups that adopted Christianity before other groups thereby claim a national copyright on "Christian" culture. Whatever happened to the "three self" principle?

Finally, and very obviously, the debate is *too polarized*. Supporters and critics have separated out into two tribal camps that have often talked past each other, made naïve assumptions, and sought to reduce complex issues of culture, theology, and identity into one binary question: "Are you 'for' or 'against' insider movements"?

QUESTIONS OF IDENTITY FOR INSIDER MOVEMENTS

If the debate on insider movements has gotten stuck, perhaps a consideration of identity issues may nudge it forward again in fruitful directions. We might ask the following questions about insider movements at different stages of their development and according to their different local contexts.

At the early stages of an insider movement, it would be helpful to find out how believers are integrating their core identity as Christ's followers with their social identity as Muslims. As they form parallel communities of believers loyal to their Muslim communities, by what strategies do they resolve the dilemma of dual belonging? Does their Muslim community view them as deviant, deceitful, or acceptable?

As an insider movement matures, we will be keen to know how this new community expresses itself in its Muslim context. Is it continuing to grow? What are its identity markers and how permeable are its group boundaries? How is faith in Christ being transmitted to the next generation? Crucially, are the children of believers secure in their personal identity and demonstrating creative hybrid expressions of it? Will they marry Muslims or fellow-believers? What is their public identity in the community?

And on a multi-generational time scale, long after we are dead, will this insider movement still be flourishing? Will it be ejected by the Muslim community, reabsorbed back into it, or retain a tolerated but ambiguous identity long-term? We can be sure that insider movements as we see them today are transitioning into something, but what will that "something" look like in a hundred years' time?

These questions are not intended to argue "for" or "against" insider movements. The answers will in any case vary widely from one case to another.

CONCLUSION

In these two chapters, I have argued that the search for an integrated identity is of urgent importance to many believers from Muslim background. Identity is complex and multi-dimensional, but we can start to understand it through a three-layer conceptualization of "collective," "social," and "core" identities.

This framework, while over-simplified and too static to show how identity evolves over time, at least enables us to explore relationships between different layers of identity. It also sheds light on issues of "multiple identity" within each layer which are highly relevant to believers from a Muslim background.

Finally, considerations of identity may help us develop more multi-dimensional models than the "C Spectrum" and a more nuanced discussion of insider movements.

SECTION 2

CULTURE, COMMUNITY, AND COMING TO FAITH IN CHRIST

7

THE *UMMAH* AND CHRISTIAN COMMUNITY

SUFYAN BAIG

Mission agencies have discussed missions methodology, contextualization, and extraction evangelism among Muslims for decades. There have been struggles between the church and missionaries over theories of evangelism and conversion. Meanwhile, the human struggling in his or her search for God is often forgotten and the reality of individual converts' lives is ignored.

The conference at which I presented this paper was a refreshing break from that pattern. We gathered from around the world in an attempt to bring those individual lives, with their struggles and joys, to the forefront of attention of those working among Muslims and those developing strategic approaches.

Understanding the Islamic concept of *ummah* and identity formation provides essential insights to effectively support Muslim background believers in times of struggle. It is hoped that this research will raise awareness of their struggles, bringing the Christian community to a deeper understanding both of Islam and of its own responsibility and ability to be a place of belonging and true community to Muslim background believers.

I have done research on the *ummah* and identity formation in the United Kingdom and India. In the UK, my research was secular in nature and focused on the identity formation of second-generation immigrants and their understanding of *ummah*. In India, my research was theological and focused on the experience of Muslim background believers with the *ummah* and the Indian church community. In both places, Muslims are a minority, which may impact their understanding of *ummah* and identity formation. However, since in the modern world, up to 40 percent of

Muslims live as minorities, [156] I believe my research is relevant. My research in India is the basis for this paper.

BRIEF EXPLANATION OF *UMMAH* AND IDENTITY FORMATION

Let us begin with a common understanding of the concept of *ummah* in Islam. The term *ummah* is used sixty-four times in the Qur'an. The classical Muslim view, as explained by Aasi, is that the term probably derives from the Arabic word *umm* (mother).[157] However, *The Encyclopaedia of Islam* relates it to Hebrew or Aramaic roots referring to community.[158] Robert Nisbet defines community as "all forms of relationship that are characterized by a high degree of personal intimacy, emotional depth, moral commitment, social cohesion, and continuity in time ... It may be found in ... locality, religion, nation, race, occupation, or (common cause). Its archetype ... is the family."[159] Broom and Selznick have further identified that within a community an individual can share activities and experiences which he values and be bound to others by a shared sense of belonging and feeling of identity.[160] The *ummah* or community of Islam is unique in that it is "not founded on race, nationality, locality, occupation, kinship, or special interests ... It transcends national borders and political boundaries."[161] Ramadan defines the *ummah* as "a community of faith, of feeling, of brotherhood, of destiny."[162] A vivid image of the *ummah* of Islam is found in the Qur'an: "And hold fast all together by the rope which Allah (stretches out for you) and be not divided among yourselves; and remember with gratitude Allah's favor on you; for ye were enemies and He joined your hearts in love so that by His grace ye became brethren; and ye were on the brink of the pit of fire and He saved you from it. Thus doth Allah make his signs clear to you: that ye may be guided" (Surah 3:103).[163] The imagery in this *ayat* (verse) describes people clinging together to the rope of their benevolent Allah. Parshall points out that this ayat shows the believers acting together to form a unified community of faith. The linkage shown is "among the members of the *ummah* as well as between God and the corporate group of believers."[164] The foundation of community is the principle of complete submission to the will of Allah. However, within the *ummah* there is a wide range of diversity according to local cultures and practices.

Eickelman and Piscatori assert, "Muslim communities, like all religious communities, are *imagined* ... the senses of community which derive from faith and practice are necessarily interpreted and shaped in distinct ways in differing times, places, and societies."[165] This imagined community of the *ummah* is composed of individuals who have never met and who cannot communicate even if meeting because of language and cultural barriers; nevertheless, it unites billions of individuals across the world and is a very important part of these individuals' identity formation.

Identity depends not only on the ways in which an individual chooses to define himself but is also formed by how that individual is represented or treated in the society. Tajfel defines social identity as "part of an individual's self-concept which derives from his knowledge of his membership of a social group (or groups) together with the value and emotional significance attached to that membership."[166] According to this explanation, an individual's self-concept or identity is not only dependent on his individual characteristics and quality, but is also made up of an individual's relation to one or more groups, depending on the situation, context, and boundaries. Identity formation involves inclusion in some categories and exclusion from others that creates a sense of an individual's identity in society.

Understanding the strength and unity of the *ummah* and its role in an individual's identity is essential in understanding the struggles that a Muslim seeker will undergo. His life within the *ummah* has been a place of security, acceptance, protection, and identity. For a seeker, it is an enormous sacrifice to lose his place in the *ummah*. As a Muslim seeker moves into fellowship with the Christian community, it is important that his sacrifice should be acknowledged and understood. The community of Christian believers should become a new place of belonging and inclusion.

It is also important to understand the responsibility of the *ummah* regarding those who apostatize. The Qur'an does not give any specific punishment for an apostate but is clear about the place of an apostate in the afterlife. Throughout the Muslim world, execution is commonly understood to be proper punishment for an apostate, based upon Muhammad's example and the *Hadiths*.

In the pluralistic context of India, people coming to Christ from different religious backgrounds often face political as well as religious opposition. Since India's independence, conversion has emerged as a sensitive and politically charged issue. Mahatma Gandhi said, "The idea of conversion, I assure you, is the deadliest poison that ever sapped the fountain of truth."[167] When an individual from a Muslim background chooses to follow Christ, he will be opposed by government structures, ostracized from the *ummah,* and experience suspicion from the church. During the early days of faith, new believers often do not fully understand why they are drawn to follow Christ nor are they able to justify their decision. In response, the Christian community should understand the difficulty of making a decision to change religious identity. However, many times the seeker encounters negative reactions from the Christian community as well.

Let us look into several real life case studies to analyze different areas of struggle for Muslim background believers with the *ummah* and the Christian community.

STRUGGLES WITH THE *UMMAH*

Often Muslim seekers are unaware of the opposition they will face from the *ummah* when they decide to follow Christ. Christian leaders are also unable to prepare them for this persecution. It is common for Muslim background believers to experience physical, mental, and emotional persecution as they become part of the Christian community. We will look at examples from the lives of Indian believers [168] I came to know while doing research for my BD thesis. It has been my privilege to know many of these individuals since the time they came to faith in Christ.

I became a Christian in 1995. My pastor asked me to share with my father about this new faith and get permission for baptism. I sincerely followed these instructions, completely unaware of the possible consequences. My father became very angry and gave me six months to decide whether to follow this new faith or to remain in the *ummah* and enjoy all the pleasures of wealth and family. When I chose the Christian faith, my father asked me to walk out of my home with only the clothes I was wearing. As the youngest son of a wealthy business family, I had no idea how to provide for my needs. After leaving home, I went directly to the church. The pastor was shocked because he did not understand the implications of my conversion. He connected me to an orphanage in Calcutta where I traveled to live. One day I was living as a wealthy businessman; the next day, for the sake of food and shelter, I was cleaning toilets in an orphanage for street children.

Khafil became a Christian in 1972 and began attending a church, where a leader instructed Khafil that he should not tell lies and deceive his father. Eager to follow Christ obediently, Khafil returned home and shared with his father that he wanted to become a Christian. Khafil's father struggled with how he would face the *ummah* and answer the religious leaders' accusations about the apostasy of his son. As Khafil slept that night, his father came to his bed with a gun. Khafil suddenly awoke to see his father holding a gun and ran from the house. As he ran, his father shot him; the bullet missed his heart, passing through his left shoulder. Khafil carries the physical scar of that bullet and the emotional scar of knowing that his own father attempted to end his life.

Yusuf Wahid was nineteen when he decided to follow Christ. After his baptism, the news of his decision spread to his previous *ummah*, and Yusuf was summoned by the religious leaders. They warned him that no one would be allowed to marry his two sisters as long as he remained a follower of Christ. Later, Yusuf was warned that he would be killed within thirty days if he refused to return to Islam. Yusuf contacted the church leaders who assured him of their prayers but said they were unable to provide any physical protection or place of safety. On the twenty-ninth day after this warning, the Muslim leaders returned with a reminder that only one day remained for Yusuf to change his decision. Under this pressure—and with lack of concrete support from his Christian community — Yusuf returned to the *ummah*. As Yusuf completed sharing this story of his journey, the call to prayer was heard and he left quickly to be present for *namaz* (prayer).

When Gulam Mohammed decided to follow Christ, he was excommunicated from his Muslim village. Seven years later, he heard that his father had passed away and so returned to his village for the funeral. He was stopped at the boundary of the village, and his mother and brother were called. They came to Gulam Mohammed, blamed him for his father's death and did not allow him to attend the funeral. He left his village carrying the grief of his father's death along with feelings of rejection and guilt.

Tasleem Ansari decided to follow Christ. Within a year, his father passed away, and the *ummah* did not allow Tasleem to bury his father's body in a Muslim cemetery because of Tasleem's faith in Christ. Since his father was a Muslim at the time of his death, he was also not allowed to use the Christian cemetery. After three days of struggle, Tasleem was forced to dig a grave and bury his father in the courtyard of his own house. In the time of his need, Tasleem was isolated by both the *ummah* and the Christian community.

When Nizamuddin decided to become a Christian, he was forced to leave his home and family. After twenty-six years, he returned to his hometown and was welcomed by a neighbor who poured cow dung on his head. He expected some support from his family, but they shut their doors. As Nizamuddin walked out of his hometown, the street was full of laughter. He left his family and birthplace for the second time, feeling again the pain of rejection and shame.

Muslim background believers endure struggles including fear of physical danger, the grief of rejection from the *ummah*, feelings of isolation and loneliness, and feelings of shame and guilt as they realize the struggles of their family to explain their actions. In addition, they often struggle to find sufficient support and understanding in the Christian community. For the Christian community to be able to nurture and care for Muslim converts, it is essential that it grasps the depth of struggles common in the stories of Muslim background believers.

STRUGGLES WITH THE CHRISTIAN COMMUNITY

India is perhaps the most pluralistic society in the world, with seven major religious communities living side by side. Even though Muslims number more than 120 million they compose only 10 to 15 percent of the population and often are discriminated against as a minority. Christians, composing 3 to 5 percent of the population, often face similar discrimination. Yet Muslims who declare allegiance to Christ undergo intense pressure despite the fact that both Christians and Muslims are minorities.

It is essential for seekers to become rooted in a new community, a new family. Gordon Nickel asserts that there is biblical foundation for the role of the church in providing the security of community for new believers in times of persecution. The early Christians described in Acts 4 and 5 were persecuted yet found encouragement and strength through their new community, the church. In Nickel's understanding, it is part of the calling of the church to become a new community and place of retreat and security for Muslim converts.[169] This corresponds to the observation that fruitful faith communities share meals, practice hospitality, and are committed to one another as extended family.[170]

Unfortunately, the ideal of the church as a new *ummah* and place of security and identity has not become a reality for many Muslim converts, instead presenting another struggle in the early years of their Christian journey. In describing a common experience of a convert, many years ago Bevan Jones wrote,

> He soon comes to feel that many of the Christians look upon him with something uncommonly like suspicion. Here and there particular individuals indicate that he is not wanted, or that he is thought to have changed his faith for the sake of some gain or other. And there are those who are only too ready, unfortunately, to bring charges against converts: they have sensual minds; they bring with them Muslim views of womenfolk; they are arrogant, self-willed, quarrelsome. But surely the unkindest cut of all is the openly-expressed opinion that sooner or later the convert will apostatise.[171]

This suspicion and doubt creates struggles and further feelings of rejection and isolation for the Muslim background believer; having forfeited the security of his old *ummah*, he finds no assurance of acceptance in the Christian community.

Gulam Ahmad was an *imam* and a *haji*. He decided to follow Christ after a believer shared his berth on a train journey, talked with him about Christ and stayed with his family for one week after their journey. At the end of that week, the believer took Gulam Ahmad to the local church to introduce him. The local church leaders bluntly accused the believer and Gulam Ahmad of bringing the church under persecution and suffering by their conversions. The leaders called a worker to show them the way out of the church property. As Gulam Ahmad and the believer walked toward the gate with heads hung in embarrassment and confusion, a 75-year-old widow called out and promised to take care of Gulam Ahmad. Today he is doing his theological training in an Indian seminary.

Abdul was a young businessman when he began seeking Christ. He happened to find a pastor with a Muslim name and thought that this pastor could understand his situation. Abdul went to meet this pastor, but the pastor refused to invite him inside, strictly instructing him that there was "no need to become a Christian. Remain what you are." Abdul was discouraged by this, but eventually found another church where the pastor did encourage him. He was baptized and was forced to give up his business because of family pressure. The church was divided on the issue of accepting Abdul into the church. One morning, news came to the church that Abdul had been burned alive. The church took no initiative for his burial nor claimed any relationship with him; instead, there was talk within the church that he must have done something which caused him to die. Abdul was buried as a Muslim.[172]

Mohammed Ali was a very zealous Muslim. With the help of friends, he burned a truck full of Christian literature. In the evening, they went to see the reaction of the Christians affected and found that they were praying for them. Mohammed was touched and asked, "Why are you praying for us?" They responded that Jesus taught them to love their enemies. Mohammed, drawn toward this love, began to spend time with this team. They introduced him to the local church, but the local church did not trust him. They discouraged Mohammed from attending their Bible studies and were not willing to grant him membership. Yet Mohammed continued attending weekly Sunday services. After almost three years, the local church still refused him baptism, so he was baptized by another pastor in another district. There was tension within the church because of Mohammed's presence, and many members spread rumors that Mohammed had become a Christian for the sake of marriage and a job. On several occasions, Mohammed was in dialogue with Christian families about his marriage but when these families approached the local church, they were discouraged from considering a proposal for Mohammed. Twenty-three years after his conversion, Mohammed is still unmarried and continues to ride his bicycle seventeen kilometers to attend a church in another district.

After coming to faith in Christ, Afzal's business struggled and his wife became seriously ill. Afzal worked hard to balance his failing business, bring his three daughters into a new community and way of life, and care for his sick wife. Last year, his wife's kidneys and liver failed and she was hospitalized. Afzal and his daughters cried out to God for her healing. In the hospital, Afzal had no visitors from their church, even though he had called the pastor many times. He felt isolated and intensely lonely. One day, the doctor told Afzal that his wife was dying. Afzal called an ambulance to take her home, still hoping for her healing. On the way home, Afzal asked the ambulance to stop outside the church and called the pastor to the ambulance to pray for his dying wife, hoping the pastor would be concerned for his family in their time of crisis. Yet no one from the church reached out to him as a caring community.[173]

Gulam Ahmad, Abdul, Mohammed, and Afzal's stories are representative of the struggles many Muslim converts face when they attempt to become part of the Christian community. As Muslim background believers walk away from Islam, they must deal with the pain of rejection and isolation from the *ummah*. It is vitally important that the Christian community realize that to be effective in making disciples from the Muslim community, they must approach these seekers and converts with sensitivity and support.

RESPONSE OF THE CHRISTIAN COMMUNITY

There are legitimate reasons for the negative view of the Christian community towards Islam and Muslim seekers. Many churches have had negative experiences and some have suffered persecution because of the political and social pressure surrounding the conversion issue. Often Christians fail to understand the complexities that Muslim background believers face and therefore lack sufficient wisdom to respond. The church often misses the call to suffer and sacrifice, following the example of Christ—an essential element in becoming more effective in reaching Muslims.

Hassan Dehqani-Tafti was a Muslim convert and former bishop of the Anglican Church in Iran. He understood the church as a community. He states,

> No individual, however saintly, shows the love of God in Christ fully. Its interpretation needs the community of the faithful, the people of God. The church where two or three are gathered together in His name—this is the core of the matter. What a tremendous role is theirs, not least when their gathering together is in the midst of a world where for centuries Islam has prevailed.[174]

In reaching the *ummah*, it is essential that we work as a community in reaching out with the love of God.[175] We are biblically called to live in community, serving each other. Bevan Jones asserts, "No church will ever be prepared to take care of a harvest until it takes part in winning that harvest."[176] When the church has been part of the journey of Muslim seekers, it will be better prepared to embrace and support new believers.

The needs of new Muslim converts are similar to the early church recorded in Acts 2:42. They desire to "devote themselves to the apostles' teaching and to fellowship, to the breaking of bread and to prayer." These needs can be met effectively within the Christian community. As Muslim seekers come to faith, their understanding of fellowship is based on their experience in the *ummah*: a brotherhood where each individual is taken care of by the others, and in which each person has an identity and sense of belonging. During this stage, it is vital that the church shows actions of love and acceptance as well as statements of the love of God. The church must open their homes and lives to the new convert. Howard Snyder defines real community as "shared time, shared meals, shared priorities, and some level of economic sharing. Specific patterns may vary, but New Testament *koinonia* (fellowship) does not exist without this shared life."[177] The new convert will feel accepted and find identity in the community of the church as he experiences the love of God through shared life.

If the convert feels secure in his acceptance and identity within the church community, he will have the confidence needed to face physical or emotional persecution. Acceptance by the church is key to the Muslim convert's ability to grow and mature as a Christian. Even those who have come to faith in Christ through impure or mixed motives can be transformed as they begin to live in true fellowship with Christians. They experience God's power through the love and grace of the church. The Christian community can fill the void of the loss of the *ummah* by listening to converts' struggles, accepting their grief, and encouraging them — they are not alone, but members of a new community which will stand with them. Gordon Nickel states, "After conversion there is a lot of work ahead for both disciple and disciple-maker."[178]

Many Muslim background believers do mature in the Christian community but still long for the intimacy of family relationships. Asif Khan has attended a local church for five years. However, after every Christmas service he struggles with feelings of insecurity and aloneness as various families greet each other warmly, while he stands alone and is greeted formally as "the convert." As they talk of plans for holiday feasting and family time, Asif will return home desiring the joy of celebrating Christ's birth yet feeling empty and lonely — an outsider to others' celebrations.

The church must become sensitive and make intentional efforts to include the convert in family activities, especially during traditional celebrations. As the convert passes through milestones such as marriage, birth of a child, illness or death of a family member, he may feel more acutely the need for family, when it is essential for the Christian community to fill this role.

Another struggle for many Muslim converts is economic survival. Upon their conversion, they are often asked to leave their means of income which is tied to the *ummah*. Converts often then struggle with dignity and independence, while the church struggles with feeling burdened or taken advantage of. Churches must explore solutions to this dilemma, such as partnering with Christian businessmen or working with the convert to find a secular job. It is important for the church to recognize the sacrifice that the convert has made in leaving a livelihood behind and to provide encouragement and support in the ensuing struggle to become financially independent as a Christian.

As Muslim converts grow and mature as Christians, it is essential that they receive consistent spiritual nourishment. Following Christ is a lifetime process of transformation and renewal by his love and power. In the midst of the convert's emotional and financial struggles, the church must focus on meeting the spiritual needs as well. As the Christian community grows spiritually, the emotional and economic needs of its members, including Muslim converts, will be met naturally.

The Christian community plays a vital role in the lives of seekers. When the disciples were caught in a great storm and were filled with fear and anxiety, Christ stood with them and brought peace into their lives. In the same way, the Christian community can be a vehicle of peace in the lives of seekers and new believers who are struggling in great storms of emotional distress, fear, and anxiety.

CONCLUSION

As Christian leaders, we often work to create ways to see a harvest among Muslims. Time is spent with strategies, methodologies, and patterns of evangelism to explore effective ways of reaching out to Muslim brothers and sisters. However, we often fail to invest time or energy in preparing Christians to receive them into community. Our emphasis on "reaping the harvest" often ignores the individuals within that harvest.

As seen in these case studies, Muslim background believers often have as many struggles assimilating into the Christian community as in leaving the *ummah*. Interestingly, the concept of the *ummah* at its best parallels the early church of Acts in many ways, as the believers share faith, hospitality, and daily life together.

I have seen this in my current work: a small business in India where I work with a staff from diverse (mostly Muslim) religious backgrounds. The Hindu lady who cleans our shop needed to take three months off for an operation. The staff, on their own initiative, donated part of their salaries to help her with expenses of the surgery and took turns in cleaning the shop throughout her leave, to prevent the need to replace her. I was touched by their generosity and understanding of community.

This is the cry of Muslim background believers: an intimate community in the body of Christ that meets their practical, social, and spiritual needs. May we be challenged by the example of our brothers and sisters and work together towards building community.

8

PATRONAGE, SALVATION, AND BEING JOINED WITH JESUS: SOCIO-ANTHROPOLOGICAL INSIGHTS FROM SOUTH ASIA

COLIN EDWARDS

Within the stories of South Asian people I have interviewed there are two deeply held perceptions. The first is that of seeing oneself linked with others in a living, dynamic way (a "collectivist" worldview). The second sees the world as hierarchically organized, with particular roles for leaders in this hierarchy. These form two vital facets of the patron-client relationship, a predominant element in relationships in South Asia. In this milieu, concepts of relating to prophets, reconciliation, and salvation are worked out, both in the Islamic setting and in that of Muslim background believers.

NOT AN INDIVIDUAL

People predominantly influenced by philosophical modernity (i.e. Westerners) are strongly individualistic. Descartes' "I think, therefore I am," is not only the core of much philosophy but describes how central the individual is to a Western outlook.

The individual is seen as the core building block in society. Psychiatry and psychology often focus on self-understanding and self-actualization. My English thesaurus lists over seventy-five phrases and words revolving round the word "self." This centrality of the individual is one of the markers of Western society.

This is a far cry from reality in South Asia, where the identity of people is much more defined by group membership. "Who is your family? What social position do they hold? Are you older or younger?" are all key questions. Group belonging defines who one is since the group is the core building block in society. Two African sayings—"You are, therefore I am" and "We are, therefore I am"—accurately reflect the thinking in South Asia.[179, 180]

People here have an ontological sense of interconnectedness which affects how they think and interact and is embraced at the deep level of being. To truly know someone, you must know with whom they are linked. If I know that your family are tradesmen, that you are the oldest son, and that you come from a village called Islampur, then I know who you are as a person. The setting defines you as a person.

That is not to say that people in South Asia see themselves set in a broad, universalistic connectedness. Their belonging is usually curtailed to that of belonging in a small group, or a limited set of groups that interlink where those on the outside are often viewed with negativity and suspicion.

Cross-cultural psychology usefully describes societies in terms of individualism and collectivism. Collectivist outlooks tend to see the person as set in a group (e.g. family or religious identity) and that people find their core sense of identity in the group. Societies where collectivism is strong tend to look to external norms for regulating behavior. Often the leader is considered to exemplify the group's ethos, leading to a marked personalization of authority where power and authority are embodied in a person rather than an impersonal code.

HIERARCHY

Related to individualism and collectivism is the issue of how vertical (hierarchical) or egalitarian (horizontal) a society tends to be. A vertical society expects a ranked order of people from top to bottom, each with different levels of access to resources and power. This is seen as natural and often God-ordained; to tamper with this is to go against the will of God. "God has made them high and lowly, he has ordered their estate," an expunged verse from an old hymn, sums this up well.

Putting these two sets of concepts together, we find societies tending to vertical individualism, vertical collectivism, horizontal individualism, or horizontal collectivism.[181] South Asian countries have a strong tendency to vertical collectivism. In such cultures, the concept of connection is definitely not egalitarian; society is unquestioningly hierarchical. The title of Dumont's book, *Homo Hierarchicus*[182] is deeply descriptive of societies in South Asia which are profoundly affected by views on status, honor and prestige, all bound in a highly developed sense of hierarchy.

Taking cues from others, how people value and rank each other (honor or shame) therefore becomes a matter of extreme importance. Honor is the warp and woof of life in this setting, such that Abecassis describes how "for most villagers, the most important social goal after survival [is] the maintenance or improvement of status."[183] Indeed, honor and shame seem to be the two most important dynamics in most decision-making processes. Many different factors go into ranking. The eldest brother has a special role in the family, and girls are worth much less than boys. Years of experience, age, and date of qualification are important in a working environment, these being more highly considered than a person's skills and ability. Wearing *burqa* is a symbol of status in villages in Bengal, as only the richer classes can afford to sequester their women. All these markers are used in assessing relative status and position as people meet and relate to each other.

LEADERSHIP: HIERARCHY AND LINKAGE

The two themes within vertical collectivism, i.e. hierarchy and interpersonal linkage, find a focus in leadership: my leader represents me and is someone with whom I am linked. His victory is my joy; his shame is my shame. Furthermore, in return, my behavior reflects on him personally. If I fall, I bring shame on the group and on my leader. If I serve, then it is on behalf of my leader.

It is hard to over-stress the importance of the role of a leader and the sense of connectedness with him.[184] He is the focus of many hopes, ambitions, and dreams of advancement. He gives me identity, for I am his man. To pick the right leader is to find a path to provision and benefits, which are often rare commodities in South Asia. A good leader will help provide loans, resources, and good political connections. A follower invests an enormous amount into the person they follow; loyalty to superiors is a key value and the expression of connectedness — the word for "obey" is actually the word "to honor."

PATRONAGE

The patron-client relationship is often the dominant relationship in South Asia. Patronage is an etic model[185] usually set in a political or economic framework. As such, it needs careful application in a different setting, but it can be a helpful model. The crux of the patron-client model is a hierarchical and personal bond between patron and client, rooted in an unequal distribution of resources which facilitates an exchange of differing kinds of resources. The patron offers access to scarce resources (goods, protection, influence, employment) that may be economic, political, or spiritual. Ideally, the patron serves as a father figure who acts with favoritism, faithfulness and loyalty, kindly providing for clients that which they have no access to. The client, on the other hand, offers thanks and honor to the patron, avoids situations that may dishonor him, works to increase his reputation, provides services when requested (rent-a-crowd, labor, etc.), and acts with loyalty and faithfulness. The word "gratitude" sums up the ideal client response.

THE BROKER

In South Asia's multiple extended networks there is a role for a middleman, a broker, who uses his relationships with patron and client to facilitate their relationship. Ideally, the broker is related to the patron and mediates the exchange between client and patron. A person can simultaneously be a patron to a client, a broker between other clients and a more powerful patron, and a client to a patron. The broker continually works on networking and bolstering the relationships needed in order to be trusted by all concerned.

THE SUFI SAINT AS PATRON

The *pir–murid* (Sufi leader–disciple) relationship of Sufism is a prime example of patronage. Abecassis describes the pir's role as that of being an "Arch Patron." [186] The pir fulfills the dual role of broker-patron, whereby he has direct access to limited resources and yet brokers those on behalf of a more distant and unapproachable patron (Allah), or series of patrons (e.g. previous pirs to Muhammad through to Allah). The pir facilitates two main resources:

1. The blessings, protection, and provision of Allah
2. Relationship with Allah

The blessings and provision of Allah include health, children, employment, and victory over adversaries. A relational experience is more about direct spiritual experience and being connected with Allah, lost in his love. The associated notion of *fana* (obliteration or dissolving into; like salt dissolves in water), is therefore intimately linked to the person of the *pir*, where *fana-fi-pir* (loss of self in the *pir*) is the first stage to *fana-fi-Allah* (loss of self in Allah).

The *pir-murid* bond is therefore intensely personal with faith, loyalty, and obedience being major factors. It is also vastly unequal: the *pir* dispenses access to resources and the *murid* can only respond with gratitude and due honor to the *pir*.

SO, WHAT IS SALVATION?

A conversation with a Muslim friend sharpened the meaning of salvation in relation to these worldview themes. I asked him for his view of salvation. This is his
reply: "Ah, well you see, there's what we're taught and what we know." Somewhat
bemused I asked, "And these are different?" "Oh yes," he said. "Let me explain."

> You see, they teach us that, on the last day, we all stand on the field
> of judgment before Allah. We are each judged with our good deeds
> on one side of the scales and our bad deeds on the other. If the good
> deeds outweigh the bad, then we're allowed into heaven. If our
> bad deeds outweigh the good, then we go to hell—maybe for just a
> while, but most people will stay there. That's what we're taught ...
> But no one believes that.

He paused for effect. I obliged, "What do they believe then?"

> Well, you see, it's like this: on the last day, we all stand on the
> field of judgment before Allah. Allah speaks and says "Before we
> begin—Muhammad! Come. Come here. This isn't for you. Come
> stand beside me." So Muhammad stands beside Allah. When he gets
> there, he turns and says "That's my brother. Come, brother. That's
> my cousin, come! He's mine, he's mine and he's mine." Muhammad
> calls out all those that are his. They then enter into heaven, and after
> that judgment for the rest starts.

My friend has fairly broad theology. He belongs to a Sufi *torika* and follows a
pir. He continued his story:

> Not only will Muhammad be called out, but all the holy men of
> history will be called out and will then call to themselves all their
> people. My *pir* will be called too, and because I am *in him* I will be
> saved. [emphasis added]

I sat there for a while, stunned at his turn of phrase, and said, "You know, I believe almost exactly the same thing." Now it was his turn to be somewhat surprised.
I continued "But there is only one person that any of the holy books or scriptures
call holy. Only one." Slowly, almost painfully, he agreed, "Yes. That's the question
really, isn't it?"

This story of salvation through Muhammad is a defining story in understanding dynamics in this culture. I ask my contacts if they have heard it. Almost all say "Yes" and most cheerfully admit to believing it. Most of my contacts, now followers of Jesus, say that they used to believe this. "How else could we be saved? We're certainly not good enough ourselves" is a common response. Most people here view, either tacitly or explicitly, their connectedness with Muhammad's group as the means to salvation.

There are commonly told *hadith* that teach that, on the last day, people will approach other prophets to ask for their intercession, but no prophet will be willing or able to do so (e.g. Al Bukhari 6.3).[187] However, when Muhammad is asked to help he will prostrate himself before Allah, who then will declare that He will give him what he asks for. Naturally, Muhammad will ask for the salvation of all his followers.

I have not heard anyone else use the phrase "in him"; indeed, some people vigorously reject the baldness of this phrase. Many will unreservedly alter it to "I will be saved through him [Muhammad]" or "via him" or something similar. Many of these alternative words have significant overtones of being joined to him.

HOW IS THIS SALVATION ACCOMPLISHED?

This view of salvation acknowledges our connectedness with others, a linkage held at an ontological level, the level of being. I am joined with others in my group, to my leader and my prophet. Thus people can talk about being saved through Muhammad. Allah accepts Muhammad and, consequently, all those linked with him.

This sense of connectedness to a savior is central in understanding how people here are now coming to faith in *Isa al Masih*. In this hierarchical society, where the status of the person you follow and to whom you give allegiance is very important, the position of *Isa* becomes the focus of reconsideration. As we now turn to the shared journey of those that have come to faith in *Isa al Masih,* the point I wish to highlight is the rank that *Isa* comes to occupy.

THE STATION OF JESUS: WHO DO YOU SAY THAT I AM?

When I ask contacts about their journey of faith, most will talk of when they were Muslim and deemed the Prophet Muhammad as most prestigious. They acknowledged *Isa al Masih* as a prophet among many others, but usually with no special place, seldom thought of if at all. However, all informants relate some experience that drew their attention to the person of *Isa al Masih* — usually a piece of literature, someone witnessing to them or a dream — that led them to investigate who *Isa al Masih* is.

A student studying at master's level in a *madrassa* talks of picking up a piece of paper off the road which said "Jesus, the light of the world." That phrase "bit into" him; he could not put it down, and so decided to investigate. He naturally turned to the Qur'an as he understood Arabic (not common here), and saw things he had never noticed before.

The first step is an event that attracts attention to *Isa al Masih*. The second step is to investigate who he is, usually looking to the Qur'an. There they find he is:

- *Kalimatullah,* "Word of God" (Surah 4:169; Surah 3:40)
- *Ruhullah,* "Spirit of God" (Surah 4:169)
- Performer of miracles (Surah 5:110)
- Born of a virgin (This is incredibly important, as this makes Isa one of only two people not conceived by the immensely polluting activity of sexual union. The other was, of course, Adam, who was disobedient.)
- Holy and pure (Surah 19:19–22) (Other than Jesus, the Qur'an describes no one as "most pure.")
- God raised Jesus to himself (Surah 3:40; Surah 4:169)

As they go on to other sources e.g. the *Injil,* they see he is creator, light, powerful, etc. Their search in the *Injil* vitally deepens their understanding. They find the position of *Isa* is higher in the hierarchy than they had originally thought. With each discovery, they reevaluate his position and power. Indeed the very real question they begin to ask is that of his relative status with respect to the prophet Muhammad. In this finely tuned hierarchy, two leaders is one too many; there cannot be equals at the top and so the question arises as to who is more important.

Almost all my informants faced this question, sometimes resolving it in a time of crisis. One man was caught in a dangerous situation and thought he was going to die. He had both the Qur'an and the *Injil* with him. He faced a choice: who was the one powerful to save? Expecting to die, he held the *Injil* against his chest and prayed, "*Isa al Masih*, I know you are the Lord. I commit myself to you." Indeed, he was saved. Those who place their loyalty and faith in *Isa* resolve this crisis by deciding he is the one of most honor. This premier position then means they are joined with him, as leader and patron.

DEATH AND RESURRECTION

In most of my interviews, people here rarely talk about Christ's death in isolation. Most of my informants' discussions concerning Christ's death also include his resurrection, and commonly his ascension. For them, Jesus' death is not a standalone event; rather it is part of a tightly knit package. It is his death, resurrection, and ascension in unity that are brought to the foreground.

Thus, the question was phrased "*Isa* died and rose again, and we are saved. How does his death and resurrection lead to our being saved?" Many of my informants in part or in whole offer the same answer which is profound in its understanding and simplicity. A colleague put it most eloquently with an accompanying descriptive gesture.

> *It's like this. I'm joined with Jesus.* [Here he interlaced the fingers of both hands, both palms facing downwards. As he continued talking, he made a sweeping wave gesture with his interlinked hands, sweeping down and back up]. *Jesus died and rose again. Since I'm joined with him, I am therefore dying with him and have been raised with him.*

How he has used verb tenses is also insightful. As well as talking about being linked with Jesus, he described how he *was* dying, and yet *had been* raised to new life.

This is very Pauline language even though very few of my colleagues have ever read passages such as Romans 6. Still reading the Gospels, most have not moved on to the epistles. Yet many speak of being linked with *Isa al Masih*. They often accompany this explanation with a hand motion (e.g. hooking their two index fingers together or holding their hands together in various ways). The linkage that holds them to him is his death and resurrection. They see themselves in sharing in his death, new life, and salvation.[188]

CONCLUDING THOUGHTS

The paradigm here is of a growing realization of the status of Jesus. Something attracts people's attention to Jesus which leads them to investigate who he is. As his status rises in their estimation, so his potential as a leader is highlighted. The assumption is that, if he is of the highest honor and position, then he is powerful to save. It is also assumed that in giving allegiance to him there is a joining with him. We are linked to others, but this union with the ultimate leader is deeper: being linked with him, his salvation becomes the believer's as well.

Out of this paradigm I would like to draw attention to two points. First, while it is true that the point of theological comparison is between Jesus, the living revealed Word, and the Qur'an as the written revealed word — often the focus in missiological writing[189] — the above paradigm highlights the need to remember the comparison between the lead prophets of honor: Who has the highest honor: Jesus or Muhammad? Despite qur'anic theology, the essence of salvation is tied up with that question for many Muslims. Our missiology needs to allow for this conversation — a dialogue that needs to occur at both the individual and community levels. We cannot force this at the risk of confrontation, nor can we deny it or be blind to it. Anyone bringing the message must allow space for this comparison to occur without invoking a confrontation between "us" and "them."

Second, we recognize that this is not how most Westerners naturally talk about salvation, preferring concepts of moral guilt, judgment, punishment, and price paid. Penal substitution is a core element in much evangelical atonement thinking; in contrast, the sense of debt and price paid, or guilt and expiation, is almost completely lacking from my informants' expression of salvation. Perceived as a serious flaw by many Western missionaries, it is indeed significant. However, I have no desire to undermine the strength of the theological position being expressed here. I have been profoundly touched and greatly instructed by the depth of understanding of union with Christ, participation in his death and resurrection, and joy in new life that my brothers have shared with me.

My hope is that those holding to either viewpoint will realize that we have a lot to learn from each other. We start by recognizing the strength of viewpoints different from ours. Cross-cultural workers can build on those strengths and move people towards a deeper walk with God. Both viewpoints also need to humbly acknowledge their blind spots (e.g. Western Evangelical atonement theory can be weak in the area of stressing relationship in Christ and in the unified body of Christ; the atonement theory expressed in South Asia can be weak on seeing moral guilt and its effects). Dialogue needs to be gentle, understanding, and non-judgmental.

My own walk in Christ has been deepened immensely as my brothers and sisters have shared their journey with me. Believers in South Asia have valid and important things to share with the greater body of Christ. My prayer is that I have spoken on their behalf and that readers can share in their insights.

9

"US" OR "ME"?
MODERNIZATION AND SOCIAL
NETWORKS AMONG CHINA'S URBAN HUI

ENOCH J. KIM

The Hui is a Muslim people group in China with very limited exposure to the Christian message. According to Paul Hattaway, the Hui are "probably the largest people group in the world without a single known Christian fellowship group."[190] Hattaway's report provides a significant motivation for this research.

The purpose of this article is to understand the impact of modernization on Chinese Muslims and to address inherent missiological implications.[191] Several key points are explored in this study with regard to the effect of modernization on the general Chinese lifestyle and, in particular, the lifestyle of Chinese Muslims. Specifically, modernization influences values, behavioral patterns, social stratifications, and social networks resulting in social changes which force Christian workers to seek new mission paradigms to appropriately reach this demographic.

Few missionaries have successfully interacted with this precious, unreached group, even after China's "Open Door Policy" of the 1970s. Furthermore, missionaries are largely unaware of the Hui's social transformation triggered by modernization. However, this impact has prompted several new network models which will be used to explain the current plight of Chinese urban Muslims, and introduce a conceptual framework for categorizing the phenomena of change among their subcultures. Several missiological implications are suggested at the conclusion.

THE HUI: A CHINESE MUSLIM PEOPLE GROUP

The Hui is one Muslim people group among fifty-six Chinese people groups. The Han are the majority; fifty-five other people groups are regarded as minorities including ten Muslim minorities. The Hui is the largest of the ten with a population of 10.7 million[192] and an annual growth of 2.4 percent.[193]

The Hui have lived in China for 1,300 years and have mingled with many different cultures. Their ancestors were not one single group, but represented a variety of people including merchants, nomads, and soldiers. The collective cultural influences on the Hui also originate from a variety of geographic regions including Persia, Pakistan, Turkey, and even Mongolia and Uygur.[194]

During their long history, the Hui have experienced many changes and religious renewals—resulting from external and internal forces—that caused divisions and the creation of new sects. Each of the different Islamic leaders, networks, and areas has the distinguishable colors of different Hui Islamic sects. Most recently, the mosques' relationship with the Communist government has also contributed to this division between sects. Today, Hui Islam is diversified and includes both Sunni and Sufi traditions, as well as Islamic mysticism with indigenous mystical roots.

Notably, in the countryside most Hui are farmers, shop owners, and laborers yet traditionally work as merchants. In the city, many work as laborers, although some run small businesses—mostly Muslim restaurants or shops. Today, the Hui live throughout China, but are highly concentrated in the northwestern provinces.

THE IMPACT OF MODERNIZATION ON CHINA AND CHINESE MUSLIMS

Since the Open Door Policy of the 1970s, China has become dramatically urbanized and modernized. Many young people have moved into cities from rural areas. Muzhi Zho spoke about Chinese urbanization in this way: "China is rapidly advancing towards its goal of being a modernized country, and industrialization is undoubtedly the driving force behind this move."[195] China's urban population has also been growing. The US Library of Congress website reported the dramatic increase of the urban population of China since 1982 thusly, "The pace of urbanization in China from 1949 to 1982 was relatively slow ... According to the 1953 and 1982 censuses, the urban population as a percentage of total population increased from 13.3 to 20.6 percent during that period. From 1982 to 1986, however, the urban population increased dramatically to 37 percent of the total population."[196]

When Chairman Deng Xiaoping became leader in 1978, he campaigned for four modernizations—science and technology, agriculture, industry, and military affairs—with an emphasis on materials-centered modernization.

The Chinese Muslim, including the Hui, faces challenges from modernization as do Muslims in many other regions. Bob Hitching summarized the six main characteristics of modernization commonly faced by urban Muslims: urbanization, secularization, globalization, pluralization, privatization, and anonymity.[197] Modernization forces the Hui to face and to live with many new phenomena in newly formed labor markets, new relationships with non-Muslims, new conflicts with traditional relationships, a new style of consumerism, new media, individualism, privatization and so on.

THE PRIMARY SOCIAL UNITS CHANGED BY MODERNIZATION

Social network theory—a conceptual metaphor that determines and tracks a person's relationships—helps Christian workers understand the dynamics of urbanites' interpersonal relationships, and can provide basal data for mission strategy. William Flanagan defines a social network as "a set of social relationships that encompass the individual's various group memberships (e.g. family, peers, work, and formal group memberships)."[198]

Scholars categorize social networks into primary and secondary networks by densities of relationship. Primary social units are generally predestined and unconditional relationships. Claude Fischer defines primary groups as "social networks that typically do involve individuals intimately, with which they are fully identified, and that are ends in themselves—ethnic groups, friends, and kin."[199] Edwin Eames and Judith Granich Goode limit the primary unit to direct bloodlines such as family, kin, and domestic units.[200]

Compared to the primary unit, secondary units are more extended relationships that go beyond kin and natural relationships. As city size increases, the chances of community being bound by personal ties drop rapidly. In an effort to fill this relational vacancy, urbanites seek and join social clubs or formal associations.[201]

Hui society has a variety of social networks. As urban Muslims experience modernization, their social networks change. Their traditional primary and secondary networks have been influenced by religion and a family-centered, community-centered mentality. Their primary networks seem not to have changed much, but urban Muslims face a revolution in their secondary networks.

With primary networks, China experienced tremendous changes in kinship dynamics after the Cultural Revolution ended in 1976. Martin King Whyte and William Parish summarized three different trends among contemporary Chinese families:

the tendency to form nuclear families, the decline in fertility, and the decreasing power of the aged.[202] Filial obligation is another important issue in family and primary networks in China. In his edited book *China's Revolutions and Intergenerational Relations*, Whyte reports the result of social changes in filial obligation values over the last several decades. He and his coworkers found that filial obligation is still a strong and crucial value in the Chinese family, in spite of the Cultural Revolution and harsh family planning campaigns.[203]

Like other Chinese, the Hui have strong family units and filial piety traditions. I conducted a field research survey with ninety Hui respondents in 2005 and asked, "If you need advice from someone while making an important decision ... with whom do you seek counsel?" This was to learn whom they respect and who influences them the most. The answer was clear: 57 percent answered that their parents influenced them most. The next question asked whom the respondent would least likely inform of a shameful experience. The question was "If you did any shameful act (fail in an exam or business, or a religious or ethical problem), which group would you be most afraid would find out?" This was designed to learn who the real community leader is. Again, the answer was clear: 77 percent of respondents gave their parents as the answer, showing that the status of parents and filial piety remain strong in Hui society.

SECONDARY SOCIAL UNITS CHANGED BY MODERNIZATION

Modernization and government policy have tremendously changed Chinese urbanites' secondary networks. Chairman Mao and his government forcefully led the Chinese to change friendship into ideological comradeship.[204] The government asked people to contribute to comradeship, a special second social network designed by the Communist Party. The general social atmosphere asked people to regard the primary network as negative and inferior in order to advance communist ideology.

Today, the Chinese — especially the Hui — are quickly recovering their normal secondary relationships. Modernization gives more freedom of choice to young Muslims as individuals. A good example is found in Maris Boyd Gillette's book *Between Mecca and Beijing*. A new Hui bride decided to wear a Taiwan-made Western wedding dress in spite of criticism by Islamic leaders that the dress style was not conservative or Islamic. The bride boldly chose what she wanted and her friends and other women in her primary network indirectly supported her — but not openly.[205] Real Hui authorities are influencing young Hui to change from traditional ethnoreligious communities to commercial and extended social networks.

Another type of secondary unit is friends. People form friendships by choice. Some Asian cultures place a higher priority on friendship than on family. Friendship naturally builds peer pressure, and people feel shame and honor based on peer values. Regarding Hui friendship types, the next question in my field research questionnaire asked, "Among your ten closest friends, how many are Muslims?" Amazingly, more than 70 percent of their friends are from different ethnic groups. Thus today's young urban Hui do not strictly limit their friendships within ethnic boundaries. Many Chinese meet their closest friends during school years and most schools are multi-ethnic, thus providing a great chance for building inter-ethnic friendships — a wonderful juncture to communicate the gospel to the Hui.

Eames and Goode summarize three major components of urban secondary social units: common residential territory (neighborhoods), common culture of origin (ethnic groups), and common roles in the division of labor (occupational status communities).[206] These are important for understanding how urban Muslims' networks are formed and changed by the impact of modernization.

If those three components overlap in one individual, the leader of the components and the community will have tremendous power over that person. Individuals would have very limited freedom within the merged zone.[207] In the Hui community, those three components generally overlap. Born into the Hui community, they are raised within an extended family. As teenagers, they usually work in small businesses run by other Muslims. Usually the owners are uncles, brothers, or fathers. Consequently, and especially in traditional communities, for many Hui the three components have overlapped.

With the onset of modernization and urbanization, however, those same components of neighborhoods, ethnicity, and working world are separated and dispersed. Today, an urban Muslim can choose from many different occupations. Added to this mobility, information, new needs and abilities, higher education, and the media all encourage Hui individuals to build new networks and meaningful relationships, even in non-Muslim societies. Thus their secondary networks grow rapidly. Eames describes these phenomena: "In the urban industrial city in developing nations, the three units show less overlap, and therefore barely share common boundaries."[208] As a result, the concept of neighbor refers to more than those in a shared geographical location and includes those with similar concerns and interests. For example, no matter their ethnic background, it is easy to get people together if they have similar hobbies, are fellow PTA members, or are part of an internet community.

Occupational networks are very diversified and extended by the development of personal mobility and ability. Consider a person with incomes from two jobs who studies at school. He or she has at least three kinds of activities — alumni association, internet club, and parents and teachers association — that give him or her many interactions within different networks. Those proximity groups and occupational networks go far beyond their original ethnic network.

MULTI-ID, COLLECTIVE LIFESTYLE, AND MY LIFE MENTALITY

The modernization of society allows Muslim individuals to connect with outside community networks. Depending on the person's ability and situation, secondary networks can be developed cross-ethnically and cross-religiously.

The number of urban multi-ID (multi-identification) holders grows as people identify themselves with more than one set of circumstances. Multi-IDers are similar to people with several different identification cards in their wallet: the person can decide which card to use depending on the situation. These people have the ability to selectively work and share their lives in multiple situations. Some Muslims learn how to meet and act in different situations in order to act appropriately and increase benefits. In this pluralistic world, these multi-ID holders develop several layers of worldview by experiencing multiple societies. In inter-ethnic relationships, which allow for "voluntary membership,"[209] they can easily have multi-ID because their relationships are clearly not limited by their ethnic boundaries.

In this multi-ID concept, one's lifestyle is a collection of several different lifestyles chosen. An individual can choose different networks when dissatisfied with the current group; if one network is deemed not helpful, the person may shift to other networks. Modern secondary networks, characterized by easy entry and leaving, consist of quite weak ties; the relationship is shallow and functional rather than holistic.

Many urban Muslims' collective lifestyle naturally enables them to have multi-faceted relationships. Compared to those of rural people, urban networks are more separated and professional; consequently, members of one facet of a person's relationships know very little about those of other facets.

Having a multi-ID and collective lifestyle gives urban Muslims the ability to achieve, experiment, and make decisions. Though subcultures still heavily influence their decisions, the most important and ultimate decision-maker in the modern world is "I." The Hui used to make decisions by what "we" or "others" want; now, it is what "I" want. This "my life" mentality is slowly forming in modern urbanites and becoming more important than "we and our community." Community pressure that the Muslim individual once felt has lessened because now "I" has more rights and abilities than before. As community pressure lessens, individuals choose what they want. Hopefully, they will choose Jesus who can give what they really want.

PROPOSITION FOR URBAN MUSLIM MISSION

The precedent studies, field data, and analysis of theories have yielded new missiological insights regarding the development of mission strategies for reaching the Hui and other similar groups in the form of three missiological propositions.

Proposition 1.

The impact of modernization creates distinct subculture groups among traditional ethnic Muslim enclaves that challenge cross-cultural workers in two areas: identification of social classes with higher receptivity to the gospel and application of an inter-status mission approach rather than a whole people group approach.

Traditionally, many Christian missionaries have seen people groups as closed systems and homogeneous groups, so many mission strategies are similar, regardless of receptors' social class. However, as expatriates enter into the society, they discover many social classes: the whole people group is a mosaic of subculture groups, each with a different degree of openness to change. Expatriates commencing ministry to an unreached people must determine which social class has a higher receptivity to the gospel.

Secondly, an inter-status mission rather than inter-ethnic or whole people group approach is strategic. A social class approach by expatriate groups to those of similar proximity and background will be more strategic and transferable in reaching proximity Christian social groups among different people.

Proposition 2.

The impact of modernization gives urban middle-class Muslims a new self-consciousness and abilities — resources, opportunities, and mobility — which can create positive circumstances for evangelism.

These abilities have led to the creation of the "my life mentality" allowing individuals to hold a multi-ID in a collective lifestyle. These identities provide great power and energy to the urban Muslim middle class.

Urban secondary networks generally have weak ties that keep relationships functional and business-centered. These ties ask for limited contribution and sacrifice to the network, and guarantee individuals significant freedom of choice and self. The newly formed "my life mentality" enables urban Muslim individuals to make choices according to personal preference without much community pressure. As characteristically objective thinkers, this freedom has important implications for evangelism. Traditional social hurdles to reaching Chinese Muslims are now relatively lower.

Proposition 3.

In cities, family-oriented Muslims' unbalanced development between primary and secondary networks will be a major challenge when hearing the gospel. Recognizing this, Christians need to understand Asian values and relationships when introducing the gospel.

The impact of modernization causes urban Muslims' secondary networks to grow faster but their primary networks remain relatively tied to tradition. This differentiation may create inter-network and intergenerational conflicts. The primary network will be a major challenge to receiving the gospel. Opportunities for urban Muslims to hear the gospel may increase, but religious and ethnic persecution from kin will remain. In order for them to consistently grow in the gospel, mission workers need to understand Asian values and styles of communication.

10

KNOWING BUT NOT CONFESSING: ATTITUDES OF YOUTH IN BAKU WHO HAVE HEARD THE GOOD NEWS

RUSSELL ELEAZAR

Azerbaijan is an oil-exporting republic bordering Turkey, Russia, Iran, Armenia, and Georgia. Some 2.1 million of its population of nine million reside in the capital, Baku, which lies on the Caspian Sea. Throughout its history, Azerbaijan has been influenced by Zoroastrianism, Judaism, and Christianity, with the first Orthodox church in Baku opening in 1815 under Russian influence. For many centuries, however, Islam has been the dominant religion.[210]

Despite the continuous presence of Christians in Azerbaijan during the Soviet era—Orthodox as well as some Lutherans, Baptists and Pentecostals—few from a Muslim background were known to have become believers in Jesus Christ. However, since its independence from the USSR in 1991, the number of followers of Jesus in Azerbaijan has grown to some 10,000. I myself am one of them.

This return to democracy (Azerbaijan had been independent and democratic from 1918–1920) brought increased freedom and a heightened interest in the gospel. In response, a ministry I will refer to as the "Baku Students Network" (BSN) was formed in 1998. Years of relentless investment of time, energy, commitment, and love for God by the staff and leaders of the BSN movement resulted in leading several local students to Christ since then. However, most students involved with the BSN in this period rejected Christianity and Christ's claims, holding to their own beliefs and convictions. As for many Muslims of Azerbaijan, Jesus Christ is considered to be the "God of Russians."

Concerned about this lack of response, I carried out a study to discover the main hindrances preventing evangelized youth in Baku from confessing Jesus as the Christ and, in response, to identify possible ways of more fruitful outreach among them. Supplemented by interviews of BSN staff members, I interviewed ten university students who, despite a long-standing relationship with believers in Jesus, had not themselves professed faith in Christ. Since the sample of students interviewed was small, I am cautious about extending the application of my findings to other settings. However, the candid responses of the ten students provide important insights.

I will center my discussion of the findings around seven principal topics raised in interviews with these non-believing evangelized students, all of whom were already my friends or acquaintances. Intending to create an honest, loving, and relaxed atmosphere, I deliberately did not make a long list of questions but instead drew upon a shorter list tackling the basic and, in my opinion, most important issues which centered on the following themes:

1. Differences observed in the lives of fellow Christian students
2. Attitudes toward their life-changing stories and blessings from God
3. The central message of the gospel
4. Attitudes toward the gospel as a revelation of God's love for humankind and his plan of redemption through Jesus
5. The person of Jesus Christ
6. Attitudes toward John 14:6
7. Jesus' being the Savior of all humankind — including you

I have separated my analysis of responses into four types of hindrances: issues surrounding Christians and their impact, the message of the gospel, the person of Jesus Christ, and sin and salvation. Further, I present other hindrances as described by BSN staff members that complement findings from the interviews of the evangelized-but-not-believing youth.

HINDRANCES SURROUNDING CHRISTIANS AND THEIR IMPACT

Do you have any Christian friends/relatives? If yes, are there any differences between their lives and those of non-Christians?

What kind of feelings do you have when you hear of their powerful life-changing stories and blessings that come from God?

The differences in the lives of Christian youth — as observed by the respondents — are mainly in terms of their relationship with God and each other and less so in their relationships with others, i.e. non-Christians. Some even claim that, apart from their "speaking about God, reading the Bible and praying, everything else is not much different from others." However, the core of their indifference or apathy is found in such areas as:

- unbelief
- important things taken for granted
- carnal security
- love of sin
- habits
- company kept

The differences in the lives of Christian youth that the interviewees observed can be summarized by the response of Natiq Mehraliyev (a university student of construction and architecture) and Nazilia Zakirova (a student at the Azerbaijan State Art University).[211] They are their "strong faith and trust in God, through worship, prayer, Bible reading and various other ministries" (Natiq). The leaders are "very friendly, tend to uphold and glorify God and refer to his name very often when they speak. They connect everything in their lives (daily matters, decisions) to God and thank him for everything and have total reliance on him" (Nazilia). Ramin Hamidov (a student at Baku State Economics University) observed that "they have a clear and right perspective of life, are confident even though they live in this corrupt world, are mature, and possess healthy worldviews."

A main strategy of the BSN ministry is to share one's life with a non-believing peer over the long-term. Leaders try to identify with their friends in as many areas of life as possible, e.g., fun, recreation, sports, sharing a meal, travelling. Naturally, in constant long-term substantial relationships, the ups and downs, strengths and weaknesses of one's life are revealed. Making a wholehearted commitment to others, with the purpose of mentoring and winning them for Christ, causes a believer to become completely exposed and open with the unbeliever. The believer should not hide this vulnerability. However, these weaknesses should be prayed for, brought before God and overcome by his Spirit. The leaders present themselves to their Muslim-background and non-religious friends just as they are, with their shortcomings as well as their newfound identity[212] which ultimately permeates and surpasses everything in their lives.

HINDRANCES RELATED TO THE MESSAGE OF THE GOSPEL

What is the central and most important message of the gospel?

Do you believe that the gospel is God's Good News of his deep love to humankind, and of his sending Jesus to die for our sins and reconcile us with God?

In our dealings with evangelized youth, they are well aware of the central claims of the gospel. Most of the youth interviewed understood and could discuss the fact that, according to the Bible, God sent Jesus to lay down his life for the sake of saving all sinners; everyone who comes to know Jesus and accepts him will be forgiven and given eternal life. The gospel calls people to turn away from sin, and presents a right and true way of living.

Ramin pointed out what he thought was outstanding from the gospel that "Jesus preferred forgiving instead of [stoning as required by] the Law of Moses."

Nazilia, in addition to common answers, commented that the gospel calls "to trust God and not only in hardship, praise him, devote time to him, pray and surrender all areas of life to him." The gospel shows "how sinful we are and how perfect God is. Thus there is a gap between him and us and Jesus is a mediator."

Orxan Mehraliyev (a student at Baku State University) in turn added that according to the gospel "this world is not as important as the one to come and we need to strive in this earthly life to earn the one to come."

Sadly, knowing these claims does not necessarily mean that they believe that the gospel is absolutely true and unchanged. This is a key argument used by Muslims to resist the gospel. This concept has been inherited from previous generations of Azeris—a huge obstacle resulting in reluctance and unwillingness to confess Christ. Although we respond that the *Injil* (Gospel) is a book permeated with God's Spirit and truth, the students consider it a distant and irrelevant book for Muslims.

HINDRANCES RELATED TO THE PERSON OF JESUS CHRIST

Who is the person of Jesus Christ to you?

Do Jesus' words "I am the way, the truth and the life" give you any hope and comfort in a world of despair, evil and violence?

As with all Muslims, the person of Jesus Christ remains largely a mere prophet for evangelized youth in Baku, although they recognize very distinctive and vividly outstanding characteristics in Jesus. He had power and authority to heal the sick, perform great miracles, and even to raise people from the dead.

These students believe that Jesus would always forgive, correct, and change lives. But, in (unemployed) Fariz Makmudhov's opinion, "there are so many things he is not able to deal with. How can he allow so many wars and such violence and terrorism to take place? Why does he not intervene in these terrible global disasters? He must not be the Supreme Being powerful enough to stop or prevent these devastating events."

However, Nazilia, who is more open, shares that before her contact with students in the BSN, "he had been just a prophet for me, but now I know he is greater than a prophet; he must be a Savior."

Jesus' death on the cross for our sins appears to be true to the youth, but for others it is irrelevant or completely ridiculous. The latter question how it is possible to die for the sins of the whole world. Are we ourselves not going to deal with and give account for our own mistakes and sins? If we commit sins, we ourselves will be held accountable.

Such skeptical attitudes to Jesus' person and mission cause most of the students to take Jesus' words in John 14:6 lightly, which reveals their belief about the authenticity of Scripture. Only Nazilia found those words encouraging and assuring.

One major fact concerning the person of Christ that the youth categorically reject is Jesus' incarnation as the Son of God. The claim that God has a Son is considered utter scandal and blasphemy. Since students come from different backgrounds and worldviews, their attitudes toward certain spiritual topics tend to vary:

- Jesus cannot pay for the sins of all; everybody should and will pay for himself.
- One should confess his/her own sins and change. This is the way our wickedness will be resolved.
- I am a sinner and there naturally must be a way out.

- The only hope is that good deeds by living righteously would outweigh bad ones.
- A righteous life, in turn, would lead to paradise.
- God is merciful and just; with His right judgment, He will justly send men where he resolves.
- The goal in life therefore is to strive to be merciful and good in order to inherit the best result.

HINDRANCES REGARDING SIN AND SALVATION

The New Testament says that Jesus Christ is the Savior of all peoples. Do you consider yourself among them? Why?

As Christians, we are well aware of sin and receive the joy of forgiveness through the atonement of Christ. Muslims are also aware of their sinfulness, but have no clear understanding of how to overcome it.

Jesus claims to be the Savior of the world and the New Testament bears witness to this. Natiq agrees that "based on the New Testament, it is true" and, moreover, "every prophet has come with the same mission of preaching the ways of God and drawing people to him."

Ramin also consents that "as far as the gospel is concerned, I am a part of this picture but I am not [in terms of actually believing]." Furthermore, Farkhad Namazov (a student at the Construction and Architecture University) pointed out "Jesus cannot pay for the sins of all; everybody should and will pay himself," furthermore, "One should confess his/her own sins and change. This is the way our wickedness will be resolved." Thus, Jesus is the Savior only according to the New Testament, which the youths do not find relevant. In general, every student I interviewed has these opinions.

OTHER HINDRANCES

Through interviews with BSN staff workers, I identified other hindrances that deter students from embracing Christianity. The most common of which related to loyalty to their religion and traditions, and fear of being ridiculed and scorned by families, friends, and fellow students. Persistent factors included:

- reluctance to change
- poor awareness of their lost condition
- material instability
- "it is impossible to be a Christian in such a wicked world"

- wrong image of Christianity (Orthodox Christianity or the religion of Russians)
- divisions in Christianity
- Armenian aggression (twenty years of war and hostility with neighboring Armenia, a "Christian" nation)

CHRISTIAN BEHAVIOR THAT OVERCOMES HINDRANCES

Christians committed to serve and reach Muslim youth should understand the principles presented in this study as they face different ministry challenges. The study touches on several crucial topics, and its analysis can help equip effective ministers among Muslims. This research presents helpful material and knowledge from various reliable sources. It is hoped that this awareness will lead to seeing more Muslim youth achieve a correct perspective of the essence of Christianity and the Lord Jesus Christ.

Observations from interviews reveal how Islam, as a predominant religion in the country, has influenced the minds of young people to create an unreceptive spirit (which is true of any committed Muslim). Identifying their beliefs and values within the framework of this Muslim mentality and worldview will reveal their convictions and greatest longings. The students know and understand the main aspects of Christianity through their interaction with BSN staff and involvement in other evangelistic activities. When it comes to the message of the gospel, the person of Christ and the concept of salvation they are well acquainted with the claims of Christianity, but deliberately do not want to agree with or respond to them by stating what they believe — knowing but not confessing Jesus as their Lord.

In Azerbaijan, many religious observances are not usually practiced by nominal Muslims. However, young people would not be completely independent when it comes to commitment and accountability to the family and others. Traditions of strong family bonds and respect for parents and elders, as a part of local culture, make embracing Christianity costly and troublesome for Azeri youth.

Other non-theological hindrances are their indifference, their love of secular and sinful lifestyles, and a belief in their own security. In this study, we have dealt with the main challenges and responses. The greatest challenge is that they do not want to believe some facts in the Qur'an and the *Injil* regarding Christ, the message and authenticity of the Bible, rather interpreting them as it suits them.

BSN staff members mentioned that acceptance, long-term quality friendships and relationships, transparency, and a sense of worth have been powerful in winning students for Christ. These are fundamental in working with Muslim background students (as with everyone else). Our ministry to them should be not only as God's messengers but as people who truly care.

Of the several characteristics listed by all BSN leaders as essential to attract students, sincerity is key. The people we try to influence will usually want to discern our true motives, wondering if we really care for them as persons. A sudden approach could well put them on guard, whereas a gentle approach is more effective. Naturally, if they know that someone will challenge their beliefs, they will erect barriers and not listen. We thus should be transparent, with our motives open for all to see. Our friendship should not be based on a desire to win them to our way of thinking. True love and care for people means we continue to appreciate them, even if they do not respond to our message as we want.

A personal testimony of one's salvation can make a profound impact on any hearer. Believers must be able to verbalize their own dramatic change in life and experience of salvation received by the grace of God. The personal testimony has been called our "fifth gospel" with power to challenge and make an unsaved person desirous of the same kind of crucial transition.

A practical Christianity will consistently integrate our words and deeds. Especially in a Muslim context, deeds and life generally speak much louder than words; in fact, spoken words become futile if not supported by deeds and attitudes.

It was encouraging to hear in July 2006 that the long-term ultimate vision of the BSN movement, in the words of their team leader, is "changing the future of the country through evangelism and discipleship of local students and raising them as leaders to impact both the church and society." The BSN team envisions sharing the gospel with as many unbelieving students as possible, seeing them come to know Jesus Christ as Lord and Savior. Further, the team's vision for saved students is to become faithful members of a local church, reaching fellow students and peers in their workplaces.

Most people are initially reluctant to give up their attitudes and behavior, and will react if pushed. In Azerbaijan, people react according to the traditional saying "Qara meni basinca men qarani basim," which translated means: "I'd better suppress ghosts before I start seeing them." We should prayerfully consider how we can approach and minister in a winsome manner.

CONCLUSION

As we consider our ministry among Muslims and our fellow citizens, our motivation comes from knowing that he will strengthen and empower us for this task, and accomplish his plans through us. We understand this from the following Scriptures:

> For the eyes of the Lord range throughout the earth to strengthen
> those whose hearts are fully committed to Him. (2 Chronicles 16:9)

Go up and down the streets of Jerusalem, look around and consider, search through her squares. If you can find but one person who deals honestly and seeks the truth, I will forgive this city. (Jeremiah 5:1)

I looked for a man among them who would build up the wall and stand before me in the gap on behalf of the land so I would not have to destroy it, but I found none. (Ezekiel 22:30)

For if you remain silent at this time, relief and deliverance for the Jews will arise from another place, but you and your father's family will perish. And who knows but that you have come to royal position for such a time as this? (Esther 4:14)

We should never doubt that God works through ordinary individuals in practical and powerful ways. The journey of spiritual impact can start with a cup of tea while compassionately listening to an acquaintance. It may require going the extra mile, doing something beyond normal for the person. Small acts, attention, simple ways of service can accomplish much more than the "spiritual intrusions" we tend to employ.

The early church was not comprised of professional evangelists. They did not even call themselves evangelists; rather they were nameless loyal followers of Jesus whose passion had no bounds. They were ordinary, street-level people who lived regular lives, surrounded by like-minded people with the same daily cares. Yet their faith and simple acts of dedication made them biblical heroes as they went beyond themselves and their fears.

Because of such devotion and allegiance, the church grew enormously during the first century. If we take our call seriously and seize every opportunity to reach out to others by going public with our faith, God will indeed bless these efforts. Who knows what he can do in and through ordinary and apparently unpromising moments we have with others who do not share our faith? [213] He will accomplish his plans through us!

11

SHARING THE TRUTH WITH COURTESY AND RESPECT FOR ALL CULTURES[214]

RICK BROWN

The world exhibits a diversity of ethnic groups, each with its own particularities of language and culture. Paul wrote that God is the Father of every clan in heaven and earth (Ephesians 3:15–16). It is not surprising, therefore, that Jesus commissioned his followers to disciple people from every ethnic group, and said he would not return until the gospel had been proclaimed to all:

> Go therefore and make disciples of all nations [all ethnic groups].
> (Matthew 28:19 ESV)

> And this gospel of the kingdom will be proclaimed throughout the whole world as a testimony to all nations, and then the end will come. (Matthew 24:14 ESV)

Revelation 5:9 reports a future date at which Jesus will have successfully "ransomed people for God from every tribe and language and people and nation." In Revelation 7:9 when John the Apostle reports his vision of the redeemed in heaven, he could "see" that they were "from every nation, from all tribes and peoples and languages," indicating a recognizable cultural diversity in God's Kingdom community. These passages indicate that God values ethnic diversity and wants to save representatives of every culture.

If God loves people and values every ethnic group, then they deserve our courtesy and respect. Peter said we should "honor all people" and share the gospel hope "with courtesy and respect" (1 Peter 2:17; 3:16 NET). Paul said we should "not give offense to Jews or Greeks" (1 Corinthians 10:32 NET). He described how he did this:

> When I was with the Jews, I lived like a Jew to bring the Jews to Christ. When I was with those who follow the Jewish law, I too lived under that law. When I am with the Gentiles who do not follow the Jewish law, I too live apart from that law so I can bring them to Christ. But I do not ignore the law of God; I obey the law of Christ. (1 Corinthians 9:20–21 NLT)

Paul does not say he became a Jew or Gentile but that he lived like those among whom he lived, insofar as he could without violating the law of Christ. Actually, this is what we expect foreigners to do when they come to our own countries and communities: we expect them to speak a language we know, respect our customs, obey our laws, and fit in as best they can, but we do not demand that they convert to our own ethnicities and religions.

The world exhibits a diversity of conflicting worldviews — the set of core values and beliefs that any person holds.[215] God is not the father of all those. God has revealed a set of core values and beliefs that he calls all people to accept and follow, calling them in effect to bring their worldviews into accord with the Bible. This call to realign worldviews is evident in the Great Commission, when Jesus told his followers to teach every ethnic group to obey everything he had commanded his disciples (Matthew 28:20). So while God values cultural diversity and plans to preserve aspects of every culture, he also aims to reform their worldviews by instilling in all people the core values and beliefs revealed in the Bible. The Kingdom of God, therefore, includes and values ethnolinguistic diversity, but aims for worldviews to be aligned with all that Jesus has commanded.

We therefore need to distinguish carefully between culture and worldview. A culture consists of the normal patterns of behavior shared among members of a society and transmitted to their children usually through stories, examples, and laws. Examples include driving on the left (or the right), shaking hands (or bowing), giving thanks before a meal (or afterwards), praying on one's knees (or while sitting), and praying with hands and eyes lifted heavenward (or downward). A worldview, on the other hand, consists of a network of core values and beliefs by which a person interprets the world and decides what is best to do. A biblical worldview usually includes the following beliefs:

> There is one God. He is good. He created all things. He is sovereign over all things.

The world was created good, but has fallen into evil.

There is a purpose for life. There is life after death. There is a new age to come.

There is good and evil. There is right and wrong. There is honor and shame.

A biblical worldview usually includes the following values (beliefs about goodness):

It is good to love and serve God with all one's heart.

It is good to love others and show them respect.

It is good to honor one's parents.

It is good to obey those in authority (insofar as this is compatible with "the law of Christ").

It is good to be kind to others.

It is good to think, speak, and act in accord with what God has revealed in the Bible.

It is not good to divide one's loyalty between God and other things.

It is not good to think, say, or do anything that God dislikes.

While in the past traditional, homogenous societies transmitted particular worldviews along with their cultures, in today's world it is common for different individuals in a society to have different worldviews though they share the same culture. For example, they might drive on the same side of the road, and greet people in the same way, reflecting commonalities of their culture, yet have different beliefs about authority and different values regarding compliance with traffic laws or courtesy in personal relations. Similarly, people in different cultures can share the same basic worldview though their customs differ. For example, one can find humanists, Reformed Christians, or Marxists in diverse cultures. It is more helpful, therefore, to use the term "culture" to refer to the shared and transmitted social conventions of an ethnic community, and "worldview" to refer to the framework of core values and beliefs that individuals have, including core elements of theology, whether others in their society share them or not.

People in the *same* culture can have *different* worldviews (core values and beliefs), and people in *different* cultures can have the *same* core values and beliefs. Therefore, a person's worldview can become biblical without that person moving to a different culture.

It is clear in the Bible that God wants everyone in his Kingdom to adopt the core values and beliefs revealed in it. The Bible is a record of revelations urging people to change their values and beliefs — their worldview — to align with what it calls "the faith" and "the truth." Paul wrote that "God our Savior ... desires all people to be saved and to come to the knowledge of the truth" (1 Timothy 2:3–4 ESV). The biblical authors communicated these true beliefs through the assertion of propositions and the narration of meaningful events. They communicated true values by revealing the causes, consequences, and purposes of historical events and by recording commandments such as the Ten Commandments, the Greatest Commandment, and the Great Commission. Thus one of the chief functions of the Bible is to transform people's worldviews into alignment with what God has revealed. Jesus said, "For this reason I was born, and for this reason I came into the world — to testify to the truth. Everyone who belongs to the truth listens to my voice" (John 18:37 NET).

THE BIBLE MANDATES CULTURAL DIVERSITY AND HENCE CONTEXTUALIZATION

Jesus affirmed cultural diversity, yet he transformed worldviews through the values and beliefs that he taught. He clearly aimed to promote a unity of core values and beliefs amidst a diversity of cultures. Jesus demonstrated this when he preached the gospel to the Samaritans in Samaria (Luke 17:11–19; John 4:5–42), to Gentiles in Lebanon and Decapolis (Mark 5:1–20; 7:24–8:10), and to Romans in Galilee (Matthew 8:5–13) without demanding that they convert to Jewish customs and identity. He emphasized the value of cultural diversity in God's plan when he said the gospel must be preached to every ethnic group before he returns (Matthew 24:14). He gave John a vision of the end-time fulfillment of this goal, in which people of every tribe and tongue will praise God (Revelation 5:9–10; 7:9–10). A preview of this goal was demonstrated at Pentecost, when the Holy Spirit enabled the disciples to praise God in a multitude of languages (Acts 2:4–11). The implication is that *God's Kingdom will not be complete until it includes people representing the full diversity of races, cultures, and languages!*

Most of the disciples remained reluctant to invite Gentiles to follow Christ (Acts 11:19–20), but the Lord showed Peter in a vision and by the outpouring of His Spirit that He grants faith and salvation to Gentiles, even if they are not converts to Jewish religious customs (Acts 10:1–11:18). More importantly, He showed James and the Apostles, through key Scriptures and the manifest evidence of the Holy Spirit, that Gentile believers everywhere should follow the customs of their own cultural norms rather than adopting Jewish religious practices, although they would need to shun some practices common to their indigenous communities (Acts 15:1-35). Paul modeled this policy by establishing house churches that maintained or adapted local customs rather than requiring them to adopt the customs of his own Jewish background (Acts 17-28). He insisted on this in spite of severe criticism from Christians who wanted him to enforce uniformity of custom and Jewish tradition in the churches.

Paul's ministry team modeled cultural diversity by including people from a variety of ethnic groups (Acts 20:4). In his letters, Paul emphasized spiritual unity amidst cultural diversity (Colossians 3:11; Romans 10:12; 1 Corinthians 12:13; Galatians 5:6). He modeled respect for different cultures by adapting his lifestyle (1 Corinthians 9:20-23) and preaching style[216] to fit the customs of the people to whom he was ministering.

The result of this was that believers in different cultural contexts had different ways of worshipping and living out their faith in community with one another, presumably appropriate for each culture. Yet they shared the same biblical faith. In other words, the outward expression of their evangelism, discipleship, fellowship, and worship was *contextualized* to their local cultures, while they shared a common faith in Christ. They continued to have differences of culture and ethnic identity, but this no longer constituted a barrier preventing fellowship among them because they shared a common spiritual identity as disciples of Christ and members of God's Kingdom.

The Apostle Peter said we should share our hope in Christ "with courtesy and respect keeping a good conscience" (1 Peter 3:1 NET). One way an outsider to a culture can show courtesy and respect is to contextualize their own approach to fit the customs and language of the people. This has not always been the practice. Some Christians have insisted that believers in other cultures use the same kinds of music, dress, and style of worship used in their own culture, or even worship in their own language. Some Christians have learned to speak the language of a Muslim people group, yet have rejected the group's names for prophets of the Bible and their terms for religious concepts, insisting on using imported terms. This conveys disrespect for the people by pointedly rejecting their authentic mother tongue. *When Christians present the message with disrespect for their audience, by ignoring their sensitivities of language and custom, this often provokes the audience to reject the message.*

Another reason for contextualization is to communicate biblical meaning and worldview more accurately within people's own cultural and linguistic context. If a Christian is speaking with a Muslim and refers to the Spirit of God as the Holy Spirit, the Muslim will generally think of the angel Gabriel, since Muslims call him the holy spirit. To contextualize his statement, the Christian may need to say "the Spirit of God." Jesus used the term "son of man" to identify himself as the heavenly ruler foretold in Daniel 7:13, but in many languages it means a bastard. To convey the intended meaning in another language, a different expression may be needed.

A biblical mandate for contextualization is to maintain both the biblical faith and the diversity of cultures by ensuring that, in each language and culture, the faith is expressed in forms that preserve its meaning and integrity.

Recent research in mission fruitfulness highlights the importance of using linguistic expressions that are natural to the authentic mother tongue of the audience.[217] In a study cited by Adams, Allen, and Fish,[218] practitioners from one agency who focus on establishing fellowships among Muslims were asked whether, when communicating the gospel, they intentionally use terms that local Muslims will understand from their own culture, language, or religious background. Their responses showed a positive relationship between the frequency of use of terms they judge Muslims to understand and their self-reported fruitfulness in church planting. Ministries in that study that always use authentic heart-language terminology saw four to six times more churches emerge from their work than ministries that never, rarely, or only occasionally use heart terminology.[219] The correlation is probably not with the terminology alone but with a positive attitude towards the culture, in which the use of the people's heart language was one of several ways in which courtesy and respect was shown.

Western Christianity has been contextualized to Western culture. When imported into Asian cultures without fresh contextualization, it can result in misunderstanding and syncretism. In other words, insufficient contextualization breeds syncretism.[220] An example is the practice of wearing shoes into a place of worship, letting people put Bibles on the ground, and letting unrelated men and women sit next to one another, with women bareheaded. In some cultures, these practices are understood as acts of impiety and lewdness which leads visitors and even new believers to think that piety and purity are unimportant in the life of Christians. When Western Christians publish Bibles on pure white paper, with no border around the sacred text, with pictures in the text, and with plain black covers or even paperback, Muslims interpret this to mean either the book is not holy or Christians treat it disrespectfully. If Muslim background believers do the same, they seem impious and their testimony lacks credibility. The need is for these believers to practice "critical contextualization" as described by Paul Hiebert,[221] so they can express their faith and practice their discipleship in culturally appropriate ways that nevertheless conform to the "law of Christ" as revealed in the Bible. This requires a careful assessment of each custom in their culture to see if it is

> (1) compatible with what the Bible teaches about mature Christian behavior, in which case it should be retained
>
> (2) capable of being adapted to biblical standards of behavior, in which case it should be retained in a modified form, or

(3) irredeemably incompatible with the Bible, in which case that custom should be abandoned or replaced.

For example, (1) marriage is compatible with what the Bible teaches, but (2) the local customs regarding the marriage relationship might need to be revised for believers, while (3) customs like wife-beating should be abandoned. Indigenization alone will not lead to these conclusions because it lacks a criterion for deciding what to retain or reject. Critical biblical contextualization, which shows respect for both the biblical faith and local cultures — thus safeguarding both of them — is needed.

MISSIONARIES CAN FOSTER CRITICAL CONTEXTUALIZATION

Since Scripture calls for people to realign their worldview with the Bible in a way that retains customs compatible with the Bible, it obliges missionaries to foster critical contextualization as well. Darrell Whiteman describes this missionary task as follows:

> Contextualization attempts to communicate the gospel in word and deed and to establish the church in ways that make sense to people within their local cultural context, presenting Christianity in such a way that it meets people's deepest needs and penetrates their worldview, thus allowing them to follow Christ and remain within their own culture.[222]

Contextualization makes the meaning of the believer's words and practices clear while showing courteous respect for all that is good or redeemable in their native culture and identity. This can lead to greater fruitfulness. Beyond that, it complies with God's plan to redeem every culture. Thus critical contextualization is a duty to God, as Whiteman also notes:

> Contextualization is not something we pursue motivated by an agenda of pragmatic efficiency. Rather, it must be followed because of our faithfulness to God, who sent God's son as a servant to die so that we all may live.[223]

Whiteman presents the incarnational ministry of Jesus as the chief mandate for appropriately adapting the behaviors of believers to local customs. As noted above, however, the Scriptures make it clear in many places that God calls peoples and communities to be transformed into the moral and mental likeness of His Son in contextualized ways that maintain their cultural identity.[224] A first step, Whiteman notes, is for the Word to "penetrate their worldview," but it seems to me that the ideal goal cannot be less than full alignment of the audience's worldview with the Bible.

Although the Bible as a whole does not endorse a particular culture or dictate a full set of cultural customs, the biblical worldview does require certain beliefs and values while excluding others. Faith communities need to work out, with the leading of the Holy Spirit, how to apply these to their culture. The New Testament, for example, does not dictate any particular mode of dress, but it does command modesty; different cultures have different perceptions of what is modest. The NT does not dictate any particular political system but does call for servant leadership; societies might work that out in different ways. The NT does not mandate any particular economic system, but does condemn greed and advocate generosity. It does not dictate certain postures for prayer, but does call for people to pray often to God.[225] It does not dictate particular forms of music and instrumentation, but does call for one to sing praises to the Lord.

Part of God's program and purpose, then, is to save and sanctify His people in the context of a community of faith. Ideally, these Christ-centered communities learn and practice a biblical worldview that brings out the best in their local cultures, while shunning practices that conflict with biblical standards. In this way, they can achieve an expression of God's Kingdom in their society that shows "courtesy and respect" for their culture and identity, while honoring Christ from the heart as Lord (1 Peter 3:15–16).

12

GETTING TO THE SOURCE OF GUILT, FEAR, AND SHAME: INNOCENCE, SECURITY, AND HONOR IN THE MUSLIM CONTEXT

L. R. BURKE

Consider the following stories based upon actual experiences of believers from a Muslim background in three different countries:

> A young man living on the southern edge of the Sahara desert professed faith in Christ. Coming from a Muslim background, he was persecuted for his faith but persevered and grew, showing potential as a leader. Then something happened that shook his faith and caused him to consider reverting to Islam.

> In central Asia, a group of believers from a Muslim background began to meet. The group was growing and the future seemed optimistic. However, in time, they were confronted with an obstacle to their continued development. A worker familiar with the situation reported, "Unless they find a way to solve this problem, their future is uncertain."

In the lake region of Southeast Africa, a group of believers from a Muslim background came to Christ and began learning more about their new faith. While working through a series of oral Bible stories, they concluded that they needed to be baptized. Before doing so, however, another issue needed to be addressed.

In each of these stories, the obstacle holding these new believers back was the same. They were ready to face persecution for their faith but they struggled with the prospect that, upon their death, there would be no one to mourn their passing. The prospect of dying in isolation and shame was a huge obstacle to their continued development.

The group of African believers did eventually decide to be baptized. By that time, there were enough of them that they felt comforted by the prospect that at least their fellow believers would mourn their deaths.

For the young man, however, it was different. When his infant daughter died, virtually no one came to share his grief. As a result, he asked himself, "What will happen when I die? Will anyone come to pay respect? Will they just bury me like a dog in the bush?" He could not face the potential shame, and abandoned his newfound faith.

The issue is yet to be determined for the Central Asians. Will they find a way to overcome this obstacle? Will they be willing to face the potential shame? Their struggle continues.

Hebrews 13:12–13 says, "Jesus also suffered outside the city gate. He suffered to make the people holy by spilling his blood. So let us go to him outside the camp. Let us be willing to suffer the shame he suffered" [NIrv]. To many Christians in the West, these words have little meaning. Our brothers and sisters from a Muslim background, however, face the real, tangible prospect of experiencing "shame outside the camp" if they continue to follow Christ.

It is thus crucial for those working in Muslim contexts to understand the differences between a shame orientation versus a guilt and/or fear orientation. Those distinctions form the foundation of people's worldview everywhere. Understanding these distinctions is essential in learning to effectively communicate the gospel and in helping believers from a Muslim background to overcome obstacles to ongoing development.

The purpose of this chapter is to discuss shame and honor in the Muslim context, together with the parallel concepts of guilt and innocence, and fear and power. I will propose a modification and extension to Roland Müller's original classification[226] and explore how these concepts can be helpful in communicating the gospel in a Muslim context.

THREE PRIMARY CONTROL EMOTIONS

Compare the following stories of two young boys, "Johnny" from North America and "Abakar" from an Arab country:

> Johnny sees a model car that he really wants at the local store. He knows that if he asks his mother to buy it she will say no, so he slips it into his pocket. When they return home, his mother sees him playing with the toy car and confronts Johnny. Realizing that Johnny stole the car, she shakes her finger at Johnny and says, "Johnny, stealing is wrong! You're going to take the toy car right back to the man at the store and apologize. And you're going to be grounded for a week so that you will learn your lesson." Despite his protests, Johnny and his mother go back to the store. Johnny apologizes. The storekeeper tells him that he was very courageous to come back and apologize. After a week of being grounded, life returns to normal. Johnny has learned his lesson.

> Abakar goes to the local market and finds a model airplane that captures his attention. While the owner of the boutique isn't watching, he slips it into his pocket. Later his father sees him playing with the airplane and realizes Abakar stole it. The father grabs the airplane and, shaking his finger at Abakar, he says, "Shame on you! Don't you know what would happen if the shopkeeper saw you playing with this! You're being way too careless. You could bring shame to the whole family!" Then Abakar's father takes the toy airplane and disposes of it so that no one will ever know. Abakar has learned his lesson.

In the hypothetical stories above, Johnny and Abakar each learned a very different lesson. Johnny learned that it is wrong to steal; if he does something wrong, there will be consequences. He may feel a measure of shame whenever he sees the shopkeeper, but the shopkeeper respects him and is convinced that Johnny's parents are doing a good job of raising their son. On the other hand, Abakar learned that what he does potentially affects everyone in his family. He has begun to understand how important it is to maintain the family's honor in the community. He was sorry to disappoint his father, but at least no one else knows of his shame. If Abakar ever steals something again, he will be much more careful. Johnny and Abakar have both learned their lessons.

Johnny and Abakar come from two different parts of the world. From child-hood, they learn to respond differently to the world around them. According to psychologist David Augsburger, "Unquestionably, the most common opinion about the emerging psyche is the sequence of the three primary control emotions. Anxiety intimidates, shame suppresses, guilt obligates. The three function together, although the intensity of each influence varies significantly from culture to culture" (1986:126). He states elsewhere that,

> Anxiety, shame, and guilt are the normal and sequential control processes that emerge in the first, second, and third years of a child's development in every culture. Each culture has its own bal-ance and its own integrative hierarchy of these internal controls ... Tribalistic cultures often are dominated by the fear/anxiety motive. Individualistic cultures generally seek to minimize anxiety and shame while socializing the child to have more of a guilt orienta-tion, while many collectivistic cultures generally tend to encourage a shame orientation.[227]

Augsburger argues that the three controlling emotions exist side-by-side in all cultures but to varying degrees.[228] In individual-oriented societies, for example, guilt is the normal process of shaping and directing its members' behavior, while both anxiety and shame remain more "primitive and diffuse," operating largely at the subconscious level.

In his book, *Shame and Honor*, Roland Müller builds upon the work of Augsburger and others[229] in proposing three continuums, with shame and honor on one con-tinuum, guilt and innocence on another, and finally, fear and power on a third. He builds his model upon what he sees as the three results of sin evidenced in Genesis chapter three. He argues that after Adam and Eve sinned, they experienced three emotions that they had never had reason to experience before. First of all, they felt guilt when "they *realized* they were naked." Second, they felt shame evidenced when they "*hid* themselves from the Lord." And third, they "were *afraid*" when they heard the Lord walking in the garden. Based upon this exegesis, Müller argues that guilt, shame and fear are therefore all results of the Fall. He writes,

> In the Garden of Eden, Adam and Eve experienced guilt, shame, and fear. I believe that these three responses to sin make up the basic building blocks of worldview. It is similar to the three basic colors that an artist mixes to make all the colors of the universe. On my computer, I can mix the three primary colors to make up 64 million other colors. That's the way it is with worldview. There are many different kinds of worldviews but, when carefully examined, they

can be better understood when looking at them in the light of man's response to guilt, shame and fear.[230]

Müller agrees with Augsburger that we must not try and make cultures and worldviews fit into one of the three categories. Rather, "all cultures are made up of a mixture of all three, and individual families and even individuals in the west identify with different worldviews."[231]

EXTENDING R. MÜLLER'S THREE "MEGA WORLDVIEWS"

According to Müller's model, the three continuums are foundational to the world-views of people everywhere. Müller argues further that guilt, shame, and fear are all the effects of sin. Before the Fall, Adam and Eve would have had no occasion to experience these emotions, living in complete innocence (without guilt) and unquestionable honor (without shame). Since God himself provided for all of their needs and was their protector, they had absolutely nothing to fear. In Müller's analysis, innocence is rightly understood as the absence of guilt and honor as the absence of shame. At this point, however, his comparison seems to break down. Is power best understood as the absence of fear? Furthermore, whereas in Müller's model innocence and honor are understood as part of Adam and Eve's pre-Fall condition (reflecting God's ideal), it is questionable whether power belongs alongside innocence and honor as a godly virtue. If power is not the best parallel for innocence and honor, what might be?

In an earlier paper, I argued that a better equivalent to "innocence" and "honor" would be "security."[232] People who feel secure have neither fear nor do they feel threatened in any way. Certainly this fits in well with the pre-Fall condition of Adam and Eve. Not only did they enjoy complete innocence and unquestionable honor, but also total security. In the Garden of Eden, their physical security was under no threat. God himself was their protector. He provided for all of their needs. Just as shame, guilt, and fear are effects of sin, so also honor, innocence, and security can be understood as part of God's original plan for mankind. God created man in his image (Genesis 1:26). He was honored over all creation, he was innocent of any taint of sin and he lived in perfect security. Therefore, I propose modifying Müller's model to replace power with security as the parallel to innocence and honor.

Even if it is accepted that power is not the best parallel to honor and innocence, it is a useful concept that belongs somewhere in the analysis. Both fear and power can be understood as deviations from the ideal of security. When our security is threatened we feel fear but, when a person is in a position of power and influence, he or she may feel that sufficient wealth, political influence, and/or family connections will protect them from any perceived threat. Taken to the extreme, this can result in self-satisfaction and pride.

Understood in this way, fear and power are both related to security, albeit in different ways. In the Garden of Eden, Adam and Eve lived in perfect security, relying on God to meet all of their needs. Fear entered the world as a result of sin. When people are in a position of power, however, they may feel no need for God. This self-satisfaction or independence is a manifestation of pride. Both fear and power are therefore results of the Fall and fall short of God's ideal for mankind. Our security should be based upon our relationship to God and our dependence on him, not on our own efforts or status.

God's ideal is for men and women to live in total security which, ultimately, is only available through our reliance on Him. Failure to do so may result either in fear from a perceived threat or an unhealthy reliance on our own power and influence.

In the same way, Müller's guilt-innocence and shame-honor continuums can be extended to include corresponding manifestations of pride. Honor is the ideal; shame results when a person does something which dishonors him or her before God. Arrogance results when people are overly impressed with their own status or abilities—self-glorification which, along with power and legalism are manifestations of pride. Both shame and self-glorification dishonor God and are results of the Fall.

Finally, on the guilt-innocence continuum, guilt is on one end and legalism or self-righteousness is on the other. God created man in perfect innocence; guilt is the result of sin. Self-righteousness and legalism, however, are manifestations of pride in one's own ability to attain holiness apart from God. The Bible is clear that our only hope of regaining innocence is through our identification with the death and resurrection of Jesus Christ.

Innocence, honor, and security were all part of God's original design and will continue to exist after Christ's return. Guilt, fear, and shame, on the other hand, entered the world as the result of sin. Christ came to free us both from the guilt of sin and the fear of death while cleansing us from the source of our shame.

While guilt, fear, and shame were not part of God's original design, they do have a crucial role to play in bringing people to Christ. Understanding the significance of what Christ did for us on the cross means recognizing our need of a savior. Guilt, shame, and fear can play a crucial role in this process. Only as we recognize our guilt before God can we fully appreciate the forgiveness offered in Jesus' name. Only as people acknowledge their shame before God can they fully understand the significance of reconciliation through Christ's work on the cross. And only those who fear God's judgment will find true comfort in the promise of salvation through Jesus Christ.

Augsburger refers to guilt, fear, and shame as "self-controlling emotions" which keep us from doing things that lead to negative consequences. In the region of Africa where we live, for example, it is not unusual for a young mother to hold a small child with one hand while holding a glass of sweet tea in the other. At a certain age, the child will take an interest in the tea and try to grab the glass, thus risking serious injury. A wise mother therefore waits until her child shows an interest in the tea. Then, in a controlled manner, she will touch the child's hand to the hot glass. The child will scream and cry out, but will not be seriously injured. In the process, the child will have learned a healthy fear of the hot tea glass and will not try to touch it again.

Similarly, through acknowledging guilt, fear, and shame people can recognize their need for a savior and fully appreciate what God has done for us in Jesus Christ. At the other end of the continuum, power, arrogance, and legalism have the opposite effect: these manifestations of pride lead people to rely on their own efforts. Legalism may lead to a self-righteousness that sees no need for forgiveness. The arrogant are self-satisfied, impressed with their own status and accomplishments, thereby denying any cause for shame. Consequently, they spurn the cleansing offered through Jesus' blood. Those in positions of power may not be conscious of any threat to their personal well-being and hence see no need of a savior. Such self-confidence taken to the extreme becomes self-glorification which, along with self-righteousness and self-satisfaction—all manifestations of pride—constitute crucial barriers to the acceptance of the gospel.

How can these barriers be overcome? How can we help the self-righteous acknowledge their guilt and their need for forgiveness? How can we help the proud to acknowledge their need for reconciliation with God? How can we help those secure in their own power and resources to appreciate their need of a savior? How can an understanding of these three self-controlling emotions and three manifestations of pride help us more effectively communicate the gospel?

UNDERSTANDING HOW THE GOSPEL MEETS OUR DEEPEST NEEDS

In order for Muslims to truly appreciate the gospel as good news, two things are necessary. First, they need to understand the pre-existing problem. Second, they need to understand how Christ's death and resurrection resolves this problem. Understanding both man's separation from God and God's solution (Christ's work on the cross) reveals the gospel as truly good news.

With this in mind, it is important to understand the Muslim perspective of the Fall and then to reflect on how to help lead them to a more biblical understanding. In many ways, there are remarkable parallels between the quranic story of Adam and Eve and the biblical account. However, there are also important differences. In the quranic account, God states: "We gave a commandment to Adam before, *but he forgot* and We did not find in him any determination" (Surah 20:115).[233] The words "he forgot" are important, suggesting that Adam did not deliberately disobey—he just forgot. Based on this, Muslims argue that surely the original sin could not be that significant. Yes, Adam and Eve sinned. Yes, they were expelled from the garden, but God is merciful. He readily forgave Adam and gave him guidance, saying: "whoever follows My guidance, no fear shall come upon them, nor shall they grieve" (Surah 2:37). Muslims believe that whoever follows Allah's guidance—says his prayers, gives tithes to the poor, fasts during Ramadan—need not fear the judgment of God. They believe that Adam and Eve "were absolved of their sin, and their descendants made immune from its effects."[234] As a result, Adam's sin is understood to be nothing more than a bad example: man can do better than this!

The difference between Muslims' interpretation of quranic teaching regarding the Fall and biblical teaching creates a significant barrier to understanding the problem of sin. As Martin Lomen states, "Islam is talking just about a headache while in truth there is a tumor growing on the brain."[235] As a result, "nobody is allowed to ask the tough questions and man's face is saved. There is no need for washing away shame or defilement, not to mention transformation or new birth."[236] In minimizing the importance of the Fall, Muslims misdiagnose the problem. Not surprisingly, their proposed cure is inadequate as well.

How can Christian workers help Muslims understand the consequences of the Fall from a biblical perspective? Müller argues that, by focusing almost exclusively on a guilt-innocence perspective, Christian workers from the West have cheated both themselves and those to whom they have sought to minister.[237] Lomen concurs saying, "Guilt is too limited and partly too superficial a concept to convey the whole biblical message."[238] It focuses mainly on our misdeeds and subsequent rather legal consequences. Shame, on the other hand, goes beyond our misdeeds to our identity: who we really are. Rick Brown wrote to me in February 2010 that "Muslims think it absurd that Adam's children should suffer for the guilt of his one misdeed, but when this is put in terms of him shaming God by his distrust, his disobedience, and his connivance with the devil, then they understand why relations were broken and why the shame of this makes Adam's offspring outcasts as well. In Arab/Muslim society, one bears the shame and reproach of one's ancestors. If they fell from their social position, then their descendants fall with them." Lomen concludes, guilt normally only concerns "the person who committed the trespass; shame spreads to the whole family, tribe, nation—yes, even to all mankind."[239]

Roland Müller, Lomen, and others have done us a great service in developing the theme of shame. Perhaps we need to go one step further back, however, and ask the question: What is the cause of shame? What is the cause of guilt? What is the cause of fear? Might it be more effective to address the cause of the problem rather than the problem itself?

Just as sin can lead to guilt, a common cause of shame is defilement. Fear, in turn, can result from a threat to our well-being (physical harm, spiritual attack, or even the threat of eternal judgment). The link between sin and guilt, defilement and shame, and threats which lead to fear suggest three parallel gospel roads. On the first road, sin leads to guilt which longs for forgiveness — the restoration of innocence. On the second road, impurity leads to shame which longs for cleansing — the restoration of honor. Finally, on the third road, threats lead to fear which longs for comfort — the restoration of security. Each road begins in a different place (felt need), but all roads, though differing in focus, lead to restoration.

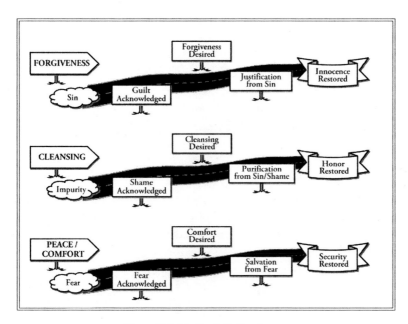

Figure 12.1: The Roads To Forgiveness

It is no secret that Muslims tend to be obsessed with the idea of purity. The Prophet Muhammad himself is commonly reported to have said, "Purity is half the faith." For a Muslim, ritual washings are repeated throughout the day as a prerequisite to prayer. Certain foods are considered to be clean (*halal*), while others are unclean (*haram*). The idea of purity/impurity is a daily reality for the vast majority of Muslims. What might a presentation of the gospel look like that begins with the idea of defilement or impurity? How might it differ from more traditional approaches?[240]

In areas where folk Islam is prevalent, the focus on fear and power may be more relevant. Here the road of peace/comfort might speak more to the felt needs of the people. In the part of Africa where we work, for example, many Muslims wear talismans for protection. The perceived need for spiritual protection signals an underlying fear that could provide a key for presenting the gospel. The crucial thing is to seek to understand the *cause* of the fear which then makes it possible to tailor the gospel presentation to help them understand how Christ's death and resurrection can free us from any fear.

In other settings, both approaches might be used side-by-side. The crucial thing is to seek out the cause be it shame, fear or even guilt. Beginning with the cause of the problem, it is easier to demonstrate in a meaningful way why the Good News is truly good news.

CONCLUSION

Understanding different worldview perspectives can be crucial in communicating the gospel message. Jesus did not come to save only those with a guilt-innocence orientation but also those with a worldview dominated by a shame-honor orientation or a fear-security orientation. Understanding these differences in worldview can help us both anticipate potential barriers to the gospel and understand how we can help our Muslim neighbors truly see it as good news.

It can also be useful in helping believers from a Muslim background to overcome inevitable obstacles to their faith. Just as Christ "faced shame outside the camp" (Hebrews 13:5), in many cases our brothers and sisters from a Muslim background face the prospect of similar treatment both in life and death. Understanding the emotions involved helps us to encourage our fellow believers and find ways to overcome the obstacles as much as possible.

Of course, no strategy for presenting the gospel to Muslims can succeed apart from the work of the Holy Spirit. By understanding the source of their fears, we can lead them to passages of God's word addressing those fears. Through understanding the origin of their shame and/or guilt, we can help them understand how God has met their need in Jesus Christ. The words of Lomen provide a fitting conclusion:

> Millions of Muslims who try to honor God so sincerely do not understand how much we dishonored God and ourselves and are encouraged to encounter the Holy One with the fig leaves of their own accomplishments! What a tragedy! May God give mercy that we [might] learn to communicate His message more accurately to our Muslim friends and neighbors, so that ... one day [they might stand] together with us before the Lamb of God in honor and dignity for all eternity![241]

13

AREAS OF CHANGE IN THE CONVERSION PROCESSES OF EAST AFRICAN MUSLIMS

REINHOLD STRAEHLER

By analyzing the conversion stories of Muslims who become followers of Christ, a number of commonalities can be observed. Such spiritual journeys develop over time through different phases, eventually leading to a new faith allegiance. In this development we can identify a cognitive and an affective dimension, each with specific layers or properties. On each of these layers, changes take place simultaneously with regard to convictions and attitudes. The transition from one phase to another is caused by specific factors acting as catalysts to move the person forward.

This paper is based on research of conversions of Kenyan Muslims.[242] In-depth interviews were conducted with nine men and eight women who grew up as Muslims and had decided to follow Christ in an urban environment. Coming from different socio-economic levels, some are oral communicators and others well-educated. Six come from a Muslim-majority community (Somali, Digo, Duruma, Gabra, and Borana) whereas eleven are from communities in which Muslims are a minority among mainly Christians (Luhya, Luo, Kikuyu, Kisii). The interviews were analyzed using principles of grounded theory, where new theory is developed by interaction between data from reality, analysis, and existing theories.

The understanding of specific aspects of conversion processes of Muslims is crucial for the missionary activity of the church. It helps Christians to adapt their approach in sharing the gospel with Muslims and encourages such conversion processes. Whereas certain features of the processes analyzed in Kenya are specific to converts' particular background, the main findings seem to be relevant to the conversion of Muslims in general.

WHAT IS CONVERSION?

Conversion is a fascinating phenomenon studied from the perspectives of sociology, psychology, anthropology, theology, and missiology with each field contributing specific insights. For Christians, the biblical-theological understanding is of particular interest and therefore some crucial aspects are briefly explained.

The basic meaning of the word "conversion" in this context is the idea of turning in response to God's saving activity.[243] The biblical concept of conversion centers around two aspects: the negative being repentance from sin, and the positive being faith in Christ.[244] The New Testament uses two Greek words to express these aspects:

- Repentance from sin is expressed mainly with the word *metanoeo*, literally "to think differently about something" or "to have a change of mind."[245] Together with the noun *metanoia* it expresses the idea of repentance as an alteration in the total moral attitude, a profound change in life's direction affecting the whole of a person's conduct.[246]
- The main word to express faith is *pisteuo*, meaning "to believe what someone says, to accept a statement as true." It also has the meaning "to have personal trust as distinct from mere credence or belief." The type of faith necessary for salvation involves both *believing that* and *believing in*, or assenting to facts and trusting in a person.[247]

From these keywords, conversion in the biblical understanding refers to a person accepting a new set of beliefs and switching religious allegiance to Jesus Christ as supreme authority or *Lord*. It means to repent from sin and to put one's faith in Christ as *Savior*. These two titles — Savior and Lord — were used by the early church to express this understanding of conversion.

DIFFERENT APPROACHES TO DESCRIBING CONVERSION PROCESSES

The process of conversion has been described by missiologists in different ways. The best-known model is the *Engel Scale*.[248] This one-dimensional model has been expanded by Viggo Søgaard who added to the cognitive dimension an affective dimension which describes attitudes and feelings.[249] In the *Gray Matrix*,[250] the cognitive axis of knowledge crosses the affective axis of attitudes and feelings, indicating that the convert needs to cross a certain point on both axes. In Hiebert's model of "centered sets" conversion is seen mainly as a change of direction towards the center, Christ, not so much as an issue of what a person knows about Christ or a specific behavior.[251]

All these describe the process of conversion insufficiently by either concentrating on one dimension (not defining individual steps in the process) or describing a momentary situation. Previously I developed a *Spiritual Decision Matrix* to describe individual steps in the process of conversion of Muslims in the Sudan.[252] Based on thorough analysis during recent research in Kenya, this matrix was revised and refined. The insights gained into the process of conversion and as presented in this paper therefore constitute an important addition to existing models.

CHANGES OCCURRING DURING CONVERSION PROCESSES

Understanding conversion from this biblical-theological perspective is important when looking at the conversion of Muslims to Christ. Even though Muslims already accept Jesus as a prophet, when they decide to follow him they believe in him in a new way as Savior and Lord. In the process of conversion, a Muslim gradually understands that the biblical claims of who Jesus Christ is and what he has done are true. He is God's Son and the Savior of the world — the "believing that" aspect. At the same time, he or she will put his or her trust in this Jesus, following him as Lord — the "believing in" aspect. During this process, a Muslim experiences changes on two dimensions: cognitively dealing with changes in knowledge and understanding, and affectively relating to changes in attitude.

Before looking into these dimensions in detail, the chronological phases of the conversion process need brief consideration.

CHRONOLOGICAL PHASES IN THE CONVERSION PROCESS

In the conversion process of Muslims five chronological phases can be identified:

- before an interest in Christian faith is present
- when an awareness of the Christian faith begins
- interaction with the new ideas
- making a decision, and
- incorporation into the new faith community.

In some conversion processes, an additional phase of "early awareness" can be found. For some converts in Kenya, this often occurred during the school years. Not all converts experience this particular phase; for others, it does not usually lead straight to interaction but rather to a fuller awareness.

THE AFFECTIVE DIMENSION IN THE CONVERSION PROCESS

During the conversion process, a Muslim typically experiences changes in four particular attitudes: (a) the attitude to Islam, (b) the attitude to Christ and the gospel, (c) the attitude to Christians, and (d) the intensity of spiritual interest. These four changes in attitudes make up the affective dimension and occur in step with the five chronological phases noted above.

The first change takes place with regard to the attitude to Islam which, typically, Muslims are positive towards. Even if religious duties are not practiced, the person still views Islam as the normal course of life. As the person begins to interact with the Christian faith, this positive attitude towards Islam gradually turns negative, culminating in the decision to no longer accept Islam or its claims but to follow Jesus Christ.

A second change takes place in attitudes to Christ and the gospel. Whereas a Muslim respects Jesus as a prophet, this gradually changes to attraction as the person becomes aware of the life and teaching of Jesus and begins to interact with the gospel. Eventually the person accepts the claims of Christ as Savior and Lord and decides to follow him.

In the course of conversion, the attitude towards Christians also changes. A Muslim, often with no firsthand contact with Christians, may have a negative attitude towards them but, upon getting to know a follower of Christ, the realization comes that these people are not as bad as previously thought. Reconciling assumptions with actual experience may cause unease initially, but will give way to a growing sympathy and the convert will eventually join a group of other followers of Christ.

A fourth change regards the intensity of spiritual interest. Awareness of the Christian faith arouses spiritual interest, which may be a new experience or the culmination of a longing unmet within Islam. As the person interacts with the Christian faith, worry may ensue over which is the right way or possible consequences of conversion. These worries differ from struggles experienced later as a follower of Christ. As the convert matures, the relationship with Christ becomes more intensive.

These four developments take place simultaneously during the conversion process (Figure 13.1). As the spiritual journey progresses, the person experiences these attitude changes chronologically, although changes in one attitude do not necessarily occur at the same time as in others. For example, during a period of intensive interaction with the Christian faith, a young Somali in Kenya maintained a positive attitude to Islam, respecting Jesus as a prophet, but was strongly attracted to Christians he was in contact with.

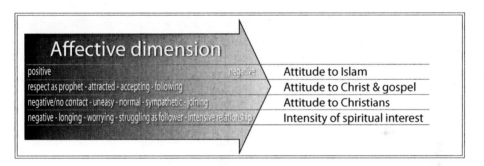

Figure 13.1: Changes In The Affective Dimension

THE COGNITIVE DIMENSION IN THE CONVERSION PROCESS

The changes that take place in the cognitive dimension relate to an increase in knowledge. They are made up of (a) a conviction about Islam, (b) knowledge about the Christian faith, (c) knowledge about Christ, and (d) acceptance of the Christian faith.

Muslims usually have a strong conviction that Islam is the only true religion. Many study it, and some of the converts in Kenya were involved in spreading their religion. As Muslims become aware of the Christian faith, they compare their own religion to these new thoughts. As interaction increases, they question Islamic convictions and eventually reject them to follow Christ. They do not necessarily discard all Islamic religious forms (like prayer or fasting), but reject specific teachings of Islam that are in contradiction to the Bible.

A second change has to do with knowledge of the Christian faith. Most Muslims are either ignorant about what Christians believe or have misconceptions. As a person becomes aware of and begins to interact with the Christian faith, knowledge of this faith increases and misconceptions give way to a clearer understanding—a process that continues as a follower of Christ.

The change in knowledge about Christ is particularly important. A Muslim understands Christ in the framework of Islamic teaching of Jesus as a prophet. As interest in the Christian faith develops and the person interacts with these new ideas, eventually the knowledge about Christ will be informed by biblical teaching.

The fourth change regards acceptance of the Christian faith. Whereas a Muslim will normally be indifferent about the Christian faith or reject it outright, interaction with this faith leads to struggles with various issues, such as who Christ really is or how God can be three in one. Eventually the person will come to grips with these issues, decide to accept this new faith, and be incorporated into a fellowship of other believers, where growth in understanding of this faith will continue.

In similar pattern to the affective dimension, these four developments on the cognitive dimension take place simultaneously, but not necessarily at the same speed, during the conversion process (Figure 13.2). For example, a woman in Kenya who faced serious troubles in her marriage had given up her Islamic convictions and followed Christ, but accepted the divinity of Jesus only years later.

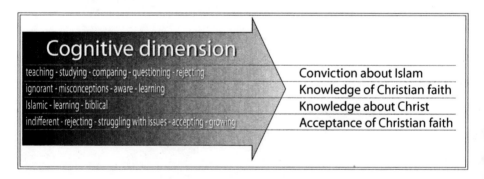

Figure 13.2: Changes In The Cognitive Dimension

What is important is that if a person becomes a follower of Christ, there will be a change with regard to all four areas of the cognitive dimension. If these changes do not take place, the person would not want to become a follower of Christ and we cannot speak of conversion.

A MATRIX FOR CONVERSION PROCESSES

In order to understand the conversion process of a Muslim, it is necessary to visually combine the two dimensions to clarify how the different changes on the affective and the cognitive dimension relate to each other (Figure 13.3).

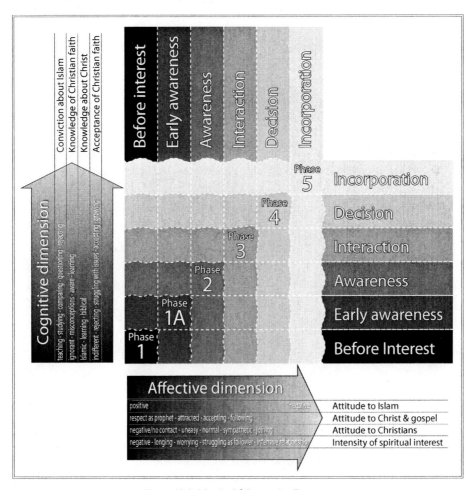

Figure 13.3: Matrix Of Conversion Processes

This matrix is made up of two dimensions, each consisting of six chronological phases. As a person moves forward in the process of conversion, changes occur in the four areas of both the affective and cognitive dimensions — a complex development that takes place on different layers at the same time.

In order to illustrate the development of a person undergoing the conversion process, two cases are presented as examples: conversion process A which initially has a stronger emphasis on cognitive elements, and conversion process B in which affective elements play a stronger role, at least in the early phases (Figure 13.4). In both processes it is essential that progress continues at least to Phase 4, the time of decision. If this stage is not reached, one cannot really speak of conversion because the person has not yet accepted Christ nor decided who is to be followed. This is indicated by the dividing line on both dimensions between Phases 3 and 4.

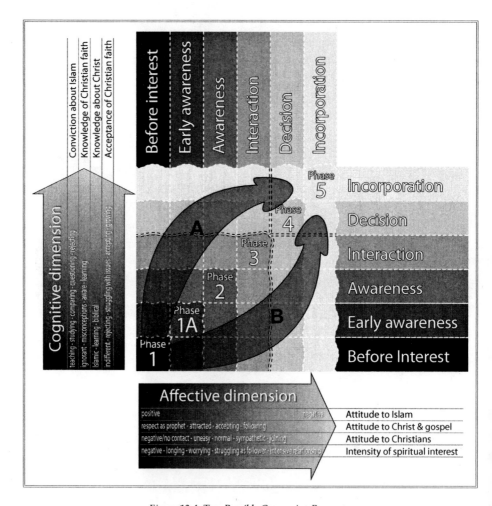

Figure 13.4: Two Possible Conversion Processes

In each conversion process, both dimensions play an important role. If conversion in a biblical understanding occurs, it is not possible for a person to progress on one dimension yet hardly on the other. A young woman with little education in a slum area in Nairobi understood clearly some basic content of the Christian faith, particularly that Jesus helps people who are heavily burdened and that he died for her. If at least some knowledge about the Christian gospel is not given, a person will not express faith in Jesus. The matrix does not indicate the level of intellectual capacity or the amount of in-depth theological knowledge; it simply indicates that the person acquires some knowledge, however basic, about the Christian faith.

A highly intellectual person who pursues studies about the Christian faith will progress rapidly on the cognitive dimension. However, unless there is concomitant progress on the affective dimension, no conversion has taken place. There can be reverse movement in some areas of change but, when a conversion takes place, progress can be seen in all areas. A person remaining in Phase 1 or 2 on the affective dimension would still respect Jesus only as prophet, have a negative attitude towards Christians, and not have a relationship with Christ. A well-educated Muslim scholar in Kenya interacted with the Christian faith intellectually for several years. However, when he finally was convinced of its truth, his attitude changed and he willingly decided to follow Christ. In theological terms, a person needs to believe *that* Jesus is the only way to God and, at the same time, needs to believe *in* Jesus Christ in the sense of trusting him. This biblical principle is true for all people, regardless of their intellectual insight or developed emotions.[253]

CONSEQUENCES OF CONVERSION PROCESSES

Conversion processes have particular consequences. The converts interviewed in Kenya experienced changes in their attitude and behavior towards others as well as in their understanding of God. They had to deal with a negative reaction from the community, even though relationships often improved after some years. It is apparent that a significant transformation takes place in the life of a Muslim who decides to follow Christ. The biblical metaphors about conversion, such as a new birth or a radical change, are visible. Conversion to Christ creates a new identity that ruptures an Islamic identity.[254] The conversion process is a dramatic experience that does not happen in isolation from the rest of life but affects all areas of life.

When evaluating conversion processes, it is possible to distinguish between who is and is not a follower of Christ. The idea of identifying those who are "in" and those who are "out" is not popular. However, if people want to be called followers of Jesus (or traditionally "Christians"), they need to know something about him and have a positive attitude toward him. Obviously some people are followers of Christ whereas others are not, an observation that is basic to the biblical understanding of the spiritual condition of human beings. What criteria do we then apply in differentiating between who is and who is not a follower of Christ? Rather than outward "correct" behavior or doctrinal convictions, a better criterion is following Jesus Christ, a concept centered on a relationship with him.[255] The question really should be: "Does the person, who claims to have converted to the Christian faith, follow Jesus Christ as Savior and Lord?" Following Jesus implies changes on the cognitive, affective, and evaluative level.[256] Charles Kraft's suggestion to think in terms of a "starting point plus process" is helpful here.[257] The behavior of a new convert changes gradually after a time of teaching (discipleship) and spiritual growth. It takes place in a culturally appropriate way and not necessarily in line with the behavior of the change agent. The converts in Kenya developed different models of expressing their identity as followers of Christ. They were encouraged in their personal development by Christians who accepted them and helped them on their way as disciples.

PRACTICAL IMPLICATIONS FOR MISSION

A thorough understanding of the conversion process of Muslims is an important contribution to the evangelistic outreach of the church. There are several practical implications resulting from the insights into conversion processes of Muslims as described in this paper.

- Christians may assume that conversion is a spontaneous event after a one-time explanation of the gospel. If a Muslim does not respond positively, it is assumed that the person is not interested and therefore further discussions are futile. In reality, Muslims on a journey to encounter Christ need time and, in most cases, only gradually grow in their understanding of the Christian faith. It is important to keep patient contact and to continue to communicate truth appropriately.
- There is a need to communicate truth in order to facilitate growth in the cognitive dimension of a conversion process. Interested Muslims need the opportunity to learn new information about Jesus Christ so that they arrive at their own decision regarding this alternative. Christians should not be afraid to share their own convictions and faith experiences with Muslims wherever possible.
- In addition to sharing information about the Christian faith, there is a need for personal relationships to facilitate growth in the affective dimension of a conversion process. The personal lifestyle of Christians, how they relate to other people in love, and their personal verbal witness often make a deep impact on Muslims.
- Conversions of Muslims occur in a variety of different settings and with different dynamics, but can only happen by interplay of the willingness of the convert, the presence of significant factors, and God's hidden activity. When these three

aspects come together, changes can take place on different layers of the affective and cognitive dimension that will lead to a transformation of the person.

- As Christians are in contact with Muslims who have embarked on such a spiritual journey, the matrix of conversion processes as described in this paper can be used in order to evaluate progress. The description of the different layers of development helps to determine where change has already taken place. Based on this evaluation, appropriate measures can be created to facilitate growth in areas where it is lacking.

- Finally, Christians should not be afraid to invite Muslims to join Christ and to encourage them to express their new identity clearly. Even though conversion has to do with changes inside a person and is therefore a spiritual matter, it has consequences in the life of the convert and leads to a transformation observable by others. The biblical understanding of conversion as a "turning from" and "believing in" clearly indicates an obvious and observable change in the life of the convert.

SECTION 3

LESSONS TO FOSTER FRUIT AND GROWTH

14

FRUITFULNESS FROM THE PERSPECTIVE OF THE FRUIT AND THE FARMER

J. DUDLEY WOODBERRY

I planted, Apollos watered, but God gave the growth. (1 Corinthians 3:6)

The *New York Times* recently published an article comparing foreign visitors to the Louvre and other European museums today and in previous generations.[258] It noted that today many visitors stop only to take a snapshot of a work of art with their cell phones and move on, while those in previous generations would take time to study and perhaps sketch it from various angles, seeking to learn all they could from the different perspectives. The present study is an attempt at the latter — to learn by comparing different perspectives.

Recently, we have seen two global studies of factors identified as influencing the conversion of Muslims to Christian faith — one from the perspective of individual converts (the fruit)[259] and another from the perspective of church planters (the farmers who plant, water, and harvest).[260] These provide us with an opportunity to compare and learn from the two perspectives. The study of individual converts included 750 (now 1000) from 30 countries and 50 ethnic groups, while the study of practitioners was from 46 nationalities working among 149 Muslim people groups and representing 78 organizations. This study continues by the Fruitful Practice Research network.

In the first study, individual converts were asked to distinguish between factors that had some influence and those that had much influence in their conversion; twice the weight was given to the latter. In the second study, 280 practitioners involved in the planting of at least one church in a Muslim context were asked to indicate which church planting practices—identified over a four-year period by agencies comprised of some 5000 practitioners—they believed were important and were actually used. In this chapter, the results of the studies are compared with respect to the evangelists or church planters involved, the medium used, the influence of converts' experiences, the spiritual needs better answered by the Christian faith, the obstacles encountered, and the influence of circumstances.

THE EVANGELISTS OR CHURCH PLANTERS INVOLVED

As would be expected, most evangelists were of the same ethnicity, and many were friends of the new believers. This reinforces the church planters' emphasis on the importance of planting the gospel in social networks (families, neighbors, community groups, etc.)[261] where there is already trust. Next, converts noted evangelists of a different ethnicity; however, research shows that there was considerably greater fruitfulness when church planters had fluency and used the heart language rather than the trade language.[262] A significant number came to faith through family members—so important to the growth and stability of home churches that one South Asian movement delayed baptism of new believers until the head of the household was ready for baptism.

THE MEDIUMS USED

The precise ranking ascribed by believers of Muslim background (BMBs)[263] to the means God used to lead them to faith was not of primary importance, since the ranking order of some mediums changed as new groups were researched and conditions changed within countries. What is significant is the wide spectrum of mediums that God blessed, thus reinforcing the practitioners' recognition of the need to sow widely.[264]

The highest ranking medium by the BMBs was personal witness, as would be expected with an incarnational gospel. The practitioners added to this the importance of being bold but not foolish, and the need for intentional reproduction so that individuals and groups were encouraged to share what they had received as they were coming to faith or growing in faith.[265]

Bible study ranked high among the BMBs as would be expected but the means varied with the context. Where mail is more secure and there is more freedom, Bible correspondence courses have been important—with increased enrolment in Pakistan after President Zia al-Haq tried to introduce elements of *sharia*.[266] Even instructors in a terrorist training facility came to faith partly through a Bible correspondence course. In more restrictive contexts radio was mentioned, and now in the Middle East *satellite TV* is having a larger role. Audio cassettes were not prominent until we surveyed a region in South Asia with high illiteracy in a movement based largely on inductive Bible study. Then they became very significant.

The importance of Bible study was echoed by practitioners who stressed the use of Muslim-friendly translations and the value of "storying" the Bible among people who prefer oral communication, even if they can read — even if the Bible had been translated into the language of a people group, it was sometimes not distributed until people had gotten into the practice of sharing its stories with others. [267]

Depending on the context, BMBs identified literature, evangelistic meetings (often restricted in size), even dialogue and debate (though cordiality of participants proved important) as factors. In regions of human need and in those prohibiting proselytism, they mentioned educational programs (such as language for refugees), relief and development and medical programs (which showed the wholeness of Christian concern). Church planters in turn stressed the importance of addressing tangible needs and using mediums reproducible by local people, since an ultimate goal is to plant reproducing fellowships.[268]

THE INFLUENCE OF EXPERIENCES

The greatest influence of experiences that the BMBs identified was the lifestyle of Christians, which they did not expect, commenting, "What they say is what they do," and "They treat their wives with respect and love." This is mirrored by the church planters highlighting the importance of an exemplary lifestyle or reputation.[269]

Next, the BMBs indicated a cluster of answered prayer, miracles and the power of Christ, and healing. In one case, a crippled Muslim girl went on *hajj* for healing but was not healed. When her *imam* prayed for her and she was not healed, he sent her to the Christians, who prayed for her and she was healed. Christians following a suffering Messiah have a more developed theology of suffering for the times God chooses not to heal.[270] The practitioners also emphasized the importance of prayer, including it among their most important practices. One recounted how Christian workers in an NGO listed their prayer requests each day and then noted when they were answered. A Muslim looked through the pages and said, "These people are the ones God is listening to. It's their prayers in Christ's name. Our people's prayers are rarely answered. The truth is in Jesus."[271] Practitioners also sought opportunities to pray for the needs of their friends in their presence[272] and to pray for healing and deliverance.[273]

BMBs subsequently listed their dissatisfaction with Islam, which increased as they experienced the imposition of forms of *sharia* in Iran and Pakistan or the militancy of the Taliban in Afghanistan. Church planters in turn sought to offer an alternative: an exemplary lifestyle, communities of trust, and the study of Scripture and prayer.

Finally, BMBs mentioned visions and dreams, a frequent component of the influences that lead to conversion. Commonly these included a figure understood to be Jesus inviting them to come. Understanding this, practitioners often pray that seekers will experience dreams and visions to support the gospel message.[274]

SPIRITUAL NEEDS ANSWERED BETTER BY CHRISTIAN FAITH

BMBs listed as the greatest attractions of the gospel a cluster of inner peace, assurance of forgiveness, assurance of salvation, and freedom from fear. An Indonesian spoke of a *hadith* about people having to walk on a bridge the thickness of a hair over the fires of hell to get into Paradise. God forgives whom he wills but does not forgive whom he wills — there is no assurance of salvation (Surah 2:284). An Egyptian called this assurance the "greatest attraction" of the gospel. These and others were emphasized by practitioners who made getting Muslims engaged with the Bible among their highest priorities.

Along with the cluster of attractions related to the assurance of forgiveness, new believers listed the love of God which, as we have seen, was reinforced by the love experienced from Christians. As one Muslim saw that love expressed in Jesus, he was attracted to Jesus even before he was attracted to Christians. Next, BMBs listed the guidance of spiritual truth found in the Bible. A Javanese Muslim, after reading the Sermon on the Mount said, "If Christianity is like that, I want it." Subsequently, new believers listed a desire for spiritual fellowship, met by practitioners' attempts to transform social networks as a bridge for the formation of fellowships or churches.[275] BMBs then listed freedom from sorrow and loneliness since, in their adversities, they could cling to Christ's promise "Lo, I am with you always." Finally, BMBs listed freedom from demonic oppression which many had experienced, especially in beliefs and practices of popular piety.[276] To deal with these beliefs and practices, practitioners emphasized biblical assurance that the most powerful being, God, is a loving Father.

In light of the attractions that BMBs saw in the Christian faith, it is instructive to compare these with the attractions that converts to Islam in North America have identified.[277] Some are quite similar to factors that drew BMBs in the opposite direction. These attractions included Islam's social laws, morality, and practices which focus on Islam's formal teaching. The testimony of the lifestyle of some Muslims was also mentioned, similar to the exemplary lifestyle that BMBs had not expected to find but did in the lives of Christian workers among them. The new Muslims mentioned the brotherhood of Islam, comparable with both the love BMBs found among Christians and the attempts among Christian practitioners to transform social networks and build believing communities. New Muslims mentioned the Qur'an's beauty, applicability, and theology which can be compared with the truth Muslim seekers found instead in the Bible. New Muslims then mentioned the attraction of Islam's spirituality in formal prayers, somewhat in parallel to the discovery by Muslim seekers that God answered the prayers of Christians. Lastly, converts to Islam mentioned the simplicity and rationality of Islam's teaching with its emphasis on the unity of God, without mind-boggling teaching like the Trinity and Incarnation, which leads us to our next section.

THEOLOGICAL, SOCIAL, AND POLITICAL OBSTACLES ENCOUNTERED

As could be expected, BMBs encountered difficulty with the theological concepts of the Trinity and Incarnation. Practitioners who encouraged inductive Bible study, under the guidance of the Holy Spirit, found that new believers were able to grasp biblical descriptions such as "God was in Christ reconciling the world to himself" (2 Corinthians 5:18) better than later contextualization of biblical materials with Greek questions and concepts by later theologians.

The BMBs highlighted the obstacles to Christian faith: community and family opposition. Some who did not want Zia, a blind leader among Afghans, to speak about Jesus before he died reportedly cut out his tongue. Another Afghan was poisoned, apparently by his family. A Muslim who saw him die said, "I have never seen a Christian die. He must have something real." The practitioners in turn saw a role for suffering in Christian witness.[278] The majority of BMBs sampled did not indicate that laws forbidding conversion were a major barrier for them to convert. In like manner, the majority did not think that non-welcoming churches were a barrier. Church planters in fact encouraged the discipling of seekers as part of the process of coming to faith.

THE INFLUENCE OF CIRCUMSTANCES

The BMBs recognized very little influence by political conditions in their conversions, yet recent political conditions certainly have caused a climate for Muslim disillusionment with the expression of Islam now becoming prominent. Consequently, increased receptivity to the gospel occurred in Bangladesh after the war with West Pakistan, in Iran after the Khomeini revolution, and among Afghan refugees after the fighting among mujahidin and the Taliban.

Likewise, the BMBs recognized very little influence by economic conditions on conversion, but the plight of people as a result of droughts, tsunamis, earthquakes, or conflicts has given Christian workers occasions to address tangible needs[279] by giving "cups of cold water" in Christ's name. Muslims wanted to know the source of that motivation.

A Christian organization imported thousands of sandals for children in a very primitive Afghan refugee camp in Peshawar. However, they decided not just to hand out the sandals, but first to wash the feet and dress the wounds of the children. Months later, a local grade school teacher asked her class, "Who are the best Muslims?" A girl raised her hand and said, "the *kafirs*." When the shocked teacher asked why, the girl responded "The *mujahidin* killed my father, but the *kafirs* washed my feet."

Returning to our original image, it would seem that many of the orchards that have the most potential of bearing fruit are those that have been laid waste by disaster and conflict. As we enter them to serve, let us learn both from the fruit and the farmers that have been there before.

15

MISSION: IMITATION OF CHRIST

JEAN-MARIE GAUDEUL

As we consider how people from all walks of life and religious backgrounds come to faith in Jesus Christ, our response may find new depth as we reflect on the teaching of three men which, for the sake of clarity and brevity, we have stripped of many important nuances, rewording when necessary in a more modern vocabulary.

In the past eighty years, through various people, the same message has apparently been given to the church. In her mission to non-Christians, the church must imitate Christ in all the stages of his earthly life: his hidden life at Nazareth, his public life with its preaching and healing ministry, and in his death on the Cross as priest and victim.

Strangely enough, this message has reached the church through people with firsthand experience of mission life and inter-religious dialogue with Islam. It is this encounter with Muslims — with its beauty and difficulty — which led these Christians to a new understanding of God's will for the church.

THE MYSTERY OF NAZARETH:
CHARLES DE FOUCAULD (1858-1916)

After a rather dissipated life which almost caused his dismissal from the French army, Charles de Foucauld mended his ways, resigned his commission and became an explorer in North Africa. Disguised as a Jewish trader, he explored Morocco in 1883 and 1884. In 1886, de Foucald returned to the Christian faith and, four years later, joined the Trappist order, serving in Nazareth, Syria, and Algeria, eventually being ordained as a priest in 1901. The last twenty years of his life were spent as a hermit, first in Nazareth (1896-1900), then in the Sahara where he was killed by Sanusi raiders in Tamanrasset, Algeria in 1916.

Among the various themes developed in his writings and actions, the mystery of Jesus' life at Nazareth seems the most important. De Foucauld's vocation was to imitate this way of life:

- a life of poverty: the "last place," that of a servant
- a silent presence in the midst of a human group
- love expressed in daily occupations: to be a "universal brother"
- adopting the way of life of a certain people as Christ adopted our human nature in his Incarnation
- winning the esteem and friendship of this people ("s'apprivoiser")

THE RESPONSE OF THE CHURCH

Many times in the past, the church reflected on the need for missionaries to become one with the people to whom they were proclaiming the gospel.[280] With de Foucauld, the church was called to go beyond the practical, functional idea of inculturation for the sake of some ulterior efficiency, continuing the movement of Christ's incarnation into this world as a part of the church's very life.

A mystique of incarnation has spread throughout the whole church, in confirmation of C. de Foucauld's intuitions, but not necessarily in connection with them.[281] In particular, four religious groups have been founded in line with de Foucauld's spirituality:

- Two excluding any organized apostolate, in imitation of Jesus at Nazareth:
  - The Little Brothers of Jesus (1933)
  - The Little Sisters of Jesus (1936)

- Two reintroducing this apostolic dimension into the same
  type of life:
  - The Little Brothers of the Gospel (1956)
  - The Little Sisters of the Gospel (1963)

This response, and that of countless militants and religious who have chosen to contemplate and imitate this way of life, is a reminder to all missionaries. That such spirituality was born and developed in a Muslim environment is probably not an accident. After centuries of mutual hostility between Christians and Muslims, Christ seems to be calling Christians to make the Muslim world and its culture their home as He made our world his home.

What are the dimensions of such a move? The Spirit will show us progressively. Already one can discern:

- a *physical* dimension: a proximity, both geographical and social
- a *cultural* dimension: language, art, lifestyle
- a *religious* dimension: common elements of faith and devotions[282]

It may be important to realize that this call is addressed to the church as a whole. No single individual can ever hope to bring about the perfect integration of Christ into a new human group, whether a foreigner or a member of that particular group, for our union with Christ and our solidarity with the world at large are always limited. Yet progressively, through imperfect steps, the presence of Christ will reach a particular group and culture to reveal His love, to bless and transfigure the particular richness of that culture. This entails establishing a certain distinction between Islam as an orthodoxy incompatible with Christianity and Islam as a culture, even though the two aspects are not separate.

It is not possible to know the times and the moments when this incarnation of Christ will be manifested in Islamic and other cultures, but the call is there to begin now to be missionary in the way Jesus was at Nazareth.[283]

A FEW REMARKS

This "Nazareth" vocation in the Christian approach to Muslims comes at a time when such an encounter has become possible. It was not so in centuries past:

- Christians and Muslims formed two worlds, indifferent or hostile, but in any case estranged from each other.

- Political structures kept the two groups apart. In the Muslim world, Christians were dhimmi, protected but restricted in their cultic and political roles.[284]
- Missionaries were foreigners and bound to remain strangers, even if they knew the languages. There was no place for them in Muslim society except as subjects of a foreign power, protected by their consuls.
- Moreover, the emphasis on preaching a message made it difficult to conceive that a life of friendly encounters could be anything but a waste of time.

Nowadays, a number of changes have occurred in the political and economic spheres and new possibilities have opened up.

- Our societies are becoming pluralistic.
- Muslim immigrants live in "Christian" Europe or America.
- Christian immigrants work in Arabia, the Gulf, and many other Muslim countries.
- Confessionalism, a heritage of the Millet System, appears as outdated to more and more people in the Middle and Near East, so that Eastern churches may well be entering a new era in their existence and becoming in a real way the "Church of the Arabs."[285]
- Many nations in Africa or Asia have Christian and Muslim populations in various proportions.

Through the media the whole world is being turned into a single society where ideas and values are shared and discussed, adopted and rejected by more and more individuals.

Encounters between men of various religions take place, not only on the religious level, but even more frequently on economic, social, and political levels. Christians perceive there is a way to manifest Christ at those levels "through disinterested service and identification with the needs of the Muslim world in crisis."[286]

All this may explain why the life of Jesus at Nazareth is seen by some as their own special personal vocation, and by the church as a whole, as an ideal to be translated into a more concrete presence to, and service of, the Muslim world.

THE MYSTERY OF CHRIST'S PREACHING: HENRI MARCHAL (1875-1957)

Born in France, Henri Marchal became a priest and missionary in North Africa. After several years in the Sahara (he was a personal friend of Charles de Foucauld), he was elected Assistant to the Superior General of his missionary society, the White Fathers, and continued in this post from 1912 to 1947.

Placed in a position of authority and responsibility, Marchal found himself obliged to translate into practical directives the main orientations given by the founder, Cardinal Lavigerie (1825-1892) about the African Apostolate in general and its applications to a Muslim milieu in particular.

A brief reminder of Lavigerie's views may be helpful here, especially with regard to Islam.[287] As an historian and church leader, Lavigerie saw the aim of the church's mission in a transformation of the whole world by the grace of Christ. Not only individuals but cultures, societies, and whole peoples would be transformed. Consequently he stressed the following points:

- The missionary must assume the culture of the people to whom he is sent: a theme of adaptation and inculturation.
- Evangelization of society as a whole is the work of centuries; it is a slow impregnation of a culture by Christ's life.
- There will be various stages in this evolution of the milieu, particularly in Muslim societies on account of past history:
  - Hostility must abate: priority must be given to a witness of disinterested love and service.[288] This may take generations of missionary lives.
  - Dialogue, meanwhile, must bear on common themes: God's majesty, our creatureliness, our need to repent and be forgiven.[289]
  - Christian teachings are for converts only.[290] The ancient discipline of the church had to be restored; only the catechumens could be initiated to the Christian doctrines because they had already given their faith to Christ. Thus, Christian dogmas were not to be preached to Muslims.

Marchal's Teachings

Marchal's teachings were naturally a sort of commentary on Lavigerie's ideas with more explanations and practical applications. Marchal wrote many books and booklets, for Christians and for Muslims, of which the following give some of the main ideas:

Only God converts people.

Only God can touch the heart of people deeply enough to move them freely. The missionary cannot change the ideas and the hearts of other men with arguments, influence, pressure; this would be proselytism. Real, true mission work means following the moves of the Spirit of God as he leads men from within. Each person has a vocation, a special destiny. The missionary is called to discern the way the Spirit calls each human and then to lend his person to the Spirit to make that call more explicit. Corresponding to this, each Muslim is continually solicited by the Spirit of God to answer his call, which does not necessarily include conversion to Christianity, here and now.

Man's resistance to God's grace.

As all the preachers of the past,[291] Marchal was sensitive to the ways in which humans can become deaf to God's call and resist his grace. Observing the behavior of ordinary people, both in Islam and in Christianity, he listed as more important:

> Pride, individual or collective, any feeling of superiority, complacency, even under the guise of a "sense of election, of being a chosen people," "the best Community."[292]

> Taking one's salvation for granted, i.e. believing that one is saved because one belongs to a certain group of people (Church, or Islamic Community) regardless of the way one responds to God and behaves in actual fact. With Muslim reformists, Marchal pointed out that many Muslims fell into that illusion and with it into moral laxism and serious sin.

> Social pressure, in so far as it inhibits a personal, free response to God's calls.

> Ritualism or Legalism, i.e. the belief that observing certain rules and rituals will, of necessity, ensure our salvation and make us God's creditors. This seemed to be frequent at the level of popular Islam or of popular Christianity.

All these prevent a man from humbly receiving the gift of God's forgiveness and love.

The Three Meanings of the Word "Conversion"

Marchal discerns three very different levels of conversion, each with its specific characteristics:

Conversion to God.

This means surrender (islam) of one's life and person to God as our Lord, Master, Creator, and Savior. It is an attitude of adoration, humble thankfulness, repentance, acceptance of God's will for our lives, prayer, and love. It is the basic conversion required for salvation[293] and the only attitude that makes further progress possible, since it allows man to be open to God's voice and action. From this starting point, a man can begin to discover God's plan for his life and respond in obedience.

This was the conversion preached by the Old Testament prophets, calling Israel away from ritualism to a deeper interior religion of the Poor of Yahweh, the *Anawim*. It was the conversion preached by Jesus himself in his public life.

Conversion to Jesus.

The New Testament shows us another sort of possible conversion, namely, the acceptance of Jesus as Lord and Savior. This conversion is presented as:

- a personal relationship: for you, who am I? (Mark 8:29)
- a progressive discovery: a friendship which develops from Galilee to Jerusalem at Pentecost through being with him (Mark 3:14).[294]
- an inner revelation given directly by the Father in heaven (Matthew 16:17). "No one can come to me unless the Father who sent me draw him" (John 6:44 NAB).
- an acceptance of Jesus' help: "Come to me, all you who labor" (Matthew 11:28 NAB); "if I do not wash your feet" (John 13:8).

Conversion to Christianity.

Often first to be mentioned in connection with mission work, conversion can be defined as changing one's loyalty from one religion to another, adopting new doctrines and rituals.

In the context of the Christian-Muslim confrontation described in preceding chapters, this means breaking with one human group to join another "enemy" community due to the traditional identification of religion with political entities. At this level, Islam has erected almost insurmountable barriers:

- controversies have vaccinated the minds against Christian dogmas
- laws punish with death the "apostate" and the missionary
- social pressure makes up for where the first two fail

Pastoral Applications

Marchal suggested that missionaries in Muslim societies follow the example of Jesus himself in his ministry to his own people. This meant in particular:

Gaining acceptance first.

In line with the idea of incarnation, Jesus was accepted by the Jews as one of them. The missionary had to become one of the group he was sent to, identifying with them in their language, way of life, and preoccupations. This meant a life of humble service until one was recognized for what one really was: a man of God and a friend.[295] Where suspicion and hostility were strong, this recognition might not come before several generations of missionaries had spent their lives in this gratuitous, selfless service. This was their mission and part in the church's apostolate.

Invite all to be converted to God.

All people including Christians and Muslims are susceptible to routine, negligence, tepidity, and nominal fidelity to their religion. All must be reminded through personal witness and informal sharing of the essential attitudes needed before God: worship, prayer (personal rather than ritual), humility, repentance, and the surrender of one's heart to God[296] leading away from a ritualistic conception of religion to a level of inner surrender[297] in total dependence on the Holy Spirit who alone knows what people need to hear at any given time.

Some may feel drawn to Jesus.

Here again the Spirit of God is the Master. To some who are attentive to God's will in this way, a certain inner call to discover Jesus becomes perceptible. If one feels that it is the effect of God's grace and not an idle curiosity, one may bear witness to one's own relationship with Jesus. One may also build on what is known in Islam about Jesus, sharing relevant facts, parables, and teachings of Jesus. Since Jesus did not merely preach to but also healed people, and called to himself those who labor and are heavily burdened (Matthew 11:28), Jesus must be presented as someone who helps and comforts his friends.[298] Dogmatic definitions of our Christology at this stage would only divert the attention from experiential and relational levels to that of past controversies. Instead, one should simply follow the work of grace which binds the person to Jesus in a loving, self-developing relationship.[299]

Conversions to Christianity.

In Marchal's experience, these were rare and had to be examined with care, under God's light, to discover whether the person involved was really responding to a call of the Spirit, and realized the social consequences of such a step in a Muslim milieu. Only then could one give teaching on Christian dogmas. Attempting to do so earlier would rebuild the defenses put up by Islam against Christian dogmas through centuries of controversies, as we have seen.

An Assessment

In many ways, Henri Marchal comes as a catalyst for ideas drawn from many periods and horizons: intuition from the Bible, directives from Lavigerie, ideas from Thomas Aquinas, Ignatius of Loyola, Charles de Foucauld, the trials and failures of missionaries in the field and the modern emphasis on sociology (which takes into account the influence of ideas in a group or milieu). All these are drawn together into a certain synthesis still relevant forty years after its formulation.

A comparison of Marchal's views and the teachings of Vatican II shows that much of what he said found confirmation in the Council's document *Ad Gentes* on the Missionary Activity of the Church (N° 11–18 for instance).

Many missionaries in various countries discovered in Marchal's ideas the answer to their need for prudent and practical guidance in their approach to Muslims.

Marchal wrote many booklets for a Muslim public. Faithful to his idea that one should always discern the work of the Spirit in a person before offering one's ideas, he never placed these books indiscriminately at the disposal of the general public, but distributed them to *confreres* and counted on them to see that they were only given to readers when they corresponded to their spiritual needs.[300]

Some books led to a conversion to God, while others stressed the moral attitudes needed in a believer, or again presented Jesus. None qualified as a work of apologetics or polemics. Their aim was not to convince, but to introduce a new experience of faith.

Of all the themes of Marchal's thought, those most followed in recent years seem to be:

- that the church has to speak to human groups, not just to individuals
- that the church has a ministry towards those who do not think of joining its ranks

- that foremost in that ministry is the proclamation of the kingdom of God, the help given to a whole milieu to enable it to become receptive to God's invitation and guidance.

THE MYSTERY OF CHRIST'S SACRIFICE: LOUIS MASSIGNON (1883-1962)

Louis Massignon was a French scholar who specialized in the study of Arabic and Islamic mysticism. After a few years of religious indifference he converted to Catholicism during a journey to Baghdad in 1908, thanks to the influence of a long-dead Muslim Mystic, al-Hallâj (d. 922). The circumstances of this overwhelming experience of God's love produced in him a twofold solidarity: solidarity with Christ and the church, and solidarity with Islam and the Arab World.

Massignon became a professor at the Collège de France and an authority in his specialty. The fact that he never divorced his studies from his prayer life gave his professional activities the dimensions of a spiritual ministry. In 1950, he was secretly ordained a priest in the Greek Melkite rite—the logical fulfillment of his whole life and work.

Massignon's Ideas

Massignon's thought is hard to follow and harder to sum up. He saw the history of the world as a kind of symphony with secret keys and harmonies between various events and lives, sometimes separated by centuries—a chorus where all voices blended as one, answering one another across a gap of several hundred years. Abraham, Isaac, Ishmael, Jesus, Mary, Muhammad, Muslims, Francis of Assisi, King St. Louis of France all corresponded to and completed one another in mysterious ways.

Without entering into this description of Massignon's unraveling of history, we could mention a few ideas which have sufficiently reverberated in the rest of the church to present them as possible calls addressed to us by God.

The work of grace in Muslim hearts.

Through his study of mysticism in Islam, Massignon discovered how God could use Islam to draw men to himself in marvelous ways. This was not due to Christian influence or elements of Christian doctrine, but to the invisible presence of Christ's Spirit using Islam to bring men to himself, beyond the limits set by dogmas and orthodoxies.[301] According to Massignon, Islam should be judged by these fruits of holiness, not only by the defects of its less faithful adepts.

Mutual hospitality.

Massignon never forgot the circumstances of his conversion and the way in which he as a foreigner had been received, protected, and cured by an Arab family in Baghdad. Translating his experience into spiritual terms, he stressed the fact that Christians and Muslims were strangers to one another.

Christians[302] were called to go to these "strangers" and become their guests. Psychologically, they had to begin by learning the language, categories, and doctrines of Islam from the Muslims themselves. This meant leaving one's home and critical point of view, and entering the Muslim's home to see his way of looking at himself and at his faith. Only then could the Christian, in turn, give hospitality to the Muslims. In practice this implied:

- finding a place for them in one's heart, mind, and prayer
- introducing suitable elements of Islamic prayer in one's own personal prayer (expressions, vocabulary, gestures), thereby giving them some Christian meaning — provided this was not in contradiction with their real sense
- this welcoming of Muslims in one's heart and prayer allows one to offer the Islamic Community to God in the Eucharist[303]

In this mutual hospitality, Massignon, with de Foucauld, saw the Pauline attitude of becoming all things to all men (1 Corinthians 9:19–22).

The Badaliyya or the Priesthood of Christ in us.

Here we are at the center of Massignon's thought: his contemplation of the Cross, with Christ offering himself to the Father in our place as priest and victim on behalf of mankind. Influenced by Catholic devotion of the nineteenth century, Massignon expressed this mystery in terms of "substitution" (the real meaning of Badaliyya), of "reparation"[304] for the sins of others. Nowadays, the same mystery is preferably expressed in terms of communion and solidarity with others.

The main points for our attention are as follows:

- The Priesthood of Christ continues in the church, as does his sacrificial death and resurrection.
- The church in the world carries on this ministry in both its dimensions of priestly function and of sacrificial suffering.
- The *Badaliyya* was a sort of "invisible community" of people who offered their lives to God for Muslims for their salvation, in union with Christ crucified for all men.

In practical terms, this vision encouraged Christians and missionaries living among Muslims to integrate their life, their joys and trials, their contact (friendly or otherwise) with Muslims into their daily Eucharist:

- with Christ, Priest, they could offer the whole Muslim community to the Father as bread to be changed into the Body of Christ.
- with Christ, Victim, they could accept all the sufferings and humiliations of this life so that Muslims might experience God's Fatherly love. This offering and acceptance were more especially relevant when the church had to suffer from Muslims themselves, as Christ suffered from us and for us.[305]

An Assessment

Massignon met with much opposition. His mystical and political options in favor of Arabs and Muslims were not always appreciated by his colleagues and many Christians. Nevertheless, it is true to say that his main intuitions (especially those presented here) have gained general acceptance among all Catholic "specialists" in Christian-Muslim dialogue. During Vatican II, passages concerning Muslims owed much to his ideas, well-known to the experts who prepared them.

Freed from certain personal dimensions — not necessarily shared by others — and from expressions linked with theological theories now discarded, his thought comes to us as a prophetic call to rediscover what love really means, lest we become no more than "resounding gong or a clashing cymbal" (1 Corinthians 13:1 NAB). And yet, accepted intellectually by all, this identification with Christ crucified — brought into the most practical details of our daily lives — has still little practical impact on many Christian communities confronted with the present Islamic revival.[306]

CONCLUSION

With these three servants of God, de Foucauld, Marchal, and Massignon, the church seems to have been reminded recently of three dimensions of her mission: the imitation of Christ in his thirty years of hidden life, his three years of public preaching, and his three days of passion and resurrection.

The striking common fact is that this reminder is connected with our present-day encounter with Islam. The attitudes called for were in striking harmony with those commended by pioneers in the field of Ecumenism (Couturier) or of dialogue with other religions (Le Saux, Monchanin) and milieu (Cardijn, de Chardin). It is this convergence and echo in many hearts which lead us to discern a divine call to missionary circles for new attitudes and approaches in their encounter with Muslims.

As we discover the many ways in which Christ, lifted up from the earth, draws everyone to himself (John 12:32), we are struck by the extraordinary variety of ways in which people, finding new faith in him, discover their new identity: they are changed and yet the same. We know that this diversity is only a small part of God's infinite skill in leading us to his house where Unity will combine with the fulfillment of each person's originality.

As one of the Trappist monks massacred in 1996 in Algeria wrote in his will: "Obviously, my death will justify the opinion of all those who dismissed me as naïve or idealistic: 'Let him tell us what he thinks now.' But such people should know my death will satisfy my most burning curiosity. At last, I will be able — if God pleases — to see the children of Islam as He sees them, illuminated in the glory of Christ, sharing in the gift of God's passion and of the Spirit, whose secret joy will always be to bring forth our common humanity amidst our differences."[307]

16

NESTORIANS, CONVERSION, AND MISSION ON THE EARLY SILK ROAD

JIHAN PAIK

The Nestorian Church is rarely acknowledged in mission history, even though it reached to Persia, India, the Arabian Peninsula, Central Asia, and Far East countries like Korea and Japan from the early days of the church through AD 1500. In fact, most Islamic countries were once considered Christian as a result of the work of Nestorians.

Their impact in the East was far broader than any other branch of Christianity in history as they made Christianity the dominant faith between the Caspian Sea and the borders of China. Twelve million people were associated with this church in 250 dioceses. By the thirteenth century, there were 72 metropolitans and 200 bishops in China and surrounding areas, representing 24 percent of all Christians in the world and over 6 percent of Asia's population.[308]

What was their secret and strength to carry out such scale of ministry over centuries? Why did they suddenly disappear? What was their legacy? In this article,[309] I will not focus on historical detail but look for lessons to guide mission work today. Two major qualities in the Nestorian Church equipped them for mission work in the East: a spiritual heritage rooted in the Jerusalem Church and their role as mediators between East and West on the Silk Road.

The Church of the East refers to Christian communities in Palestine, Syria, and Mesopotamia founded by those who had scattered northeast from Jerusalem after persecution. Developed in an environment and culture different from the West, it was rural based rather than urban, emphasized "a way of life" rather than dogma, and espoused monastic asceticism rather than ontological interpretation.[310] The people of this church were later known as the Nestorians.

Christianity in the West spread westward using Roman roads and sea routes along the Greek and Roman coastlines, whereas Christian faith in the East spread along the Silk Road trade route connecting the two worlds where the exchange of knowledge, cultures, and religions — the latter often coming into conflict — naturally occurred.

The Nestorians faced tremendous opposition and large-scale persecution over long periods (often more severe than the early days of the church in the West) as they encountered the powerful religions of Zoroastrianism, Hinduism, Islam, Confucianism, and shamanism. Nevertheless, they not only survived but made a tremendous impact on those religions. In spite of suffering, they grew to be key players on the Silk Road in trading, education, medicine, agriculture, and science. Significant evidence posits that Nestorianism was the inspirational source for Islam. Their success while under majority powers merits our understanding of implications for mission today.

Vasilli V. Barthold remarks,

> The chief factor in progress has always been the contact among peoples. The development and decadence of peoples can neither be explained by racial characteristics nor religious beliefs, nor even by natural environments. They are to be determined by the place that in the different periods of their history these peoples have occupied in such contacts. Whatever might be the racial superiority of the Indo-Europeans over other peoples, without these contacts they would have remained savages like the Lithuanians till the XIIIth century or the Kaffirs of the Hindu Kush. In the same way, whatever advantages might be adduced in favor of Christianity as compared to Islam, the culture of the Muslim world was higher than that of the Christians as long as the former held in their hands the chief trade routes of the world trade.[311]

For the sake of the work, we too need to take risks and suffer. We thank God for the wisdom and experiences of our brothers and sisters who walked ahead of us for a thousand years!

LESSONS FROM NESTORIAN MISSION

Throughout church history, theological rifts have, in the providence of God, fueled remarkable expansion of the church especially in new regions. Defending one's convictions can galvanize new movements of disciples into a high level of commitment in spreading their message. The Nestorians endured hardship and alienation for their beliefs and yet their perseverance was eventually rewarded.

Roots and Identity

The history of the Nestorians began with Nestorius' expulsion from the Byzantine Church. As Bishop of Constantinople, he was of the most respected school in the East, Nisibis, which functioned as a spiritual community rather than an academic seminary. Nestorius was a disciple of Theodore of Antioch, whose biblical exposition focused on what the Bible literally said, rather than interpretation of its meaning.

Fourth-century Christianity was sharply divided over the person of Jesus. Christ was in some sense both human and divine, but what was the relationship between these two elements? The monophysites' view was that Christ was the eternal *Divine Logos*, incarnate as a human being—God living under human conditions. Nestorius held the position of two distinct persons, one human and one divine, brought into coexistence in the person of Jesus; thus the Virgin Mary could not be "the Mother of God."

The monophysites' position was more acceptable in the Byzantine Empire. When the church council of the Roman Empire —chaired by Cyril as Bishop of Alexandria and representative of the monophysites—was held in AD 431 in Ephesus, where the worship of the fertility goddess Artemis had a strong influence, Nestorius was unfairly denounced as heretical.[312]

The Church of the East followed Nestorius' position (Christians were called Nestorians from then on). In AD 451, the Council of Chalcedon proposed a compromise between the monophysite and diophysite positions: Christ combined two natures, but not two persons. The Nestorians rejected this, insisting on two persons and referring to their statement "one divine nature only, in three perfect persons."[313] Later, when the Church of Byzantium held to the position of the monophysites, Nestorians moved their patriarch to Nisibis in the Persian Empire and declared independence from the Byzantine Church through a synod in AD 498. Nestorians moved their headquarters to Seleucia-Ctesiphon (a city near Baghdad), "the center of trade and travel between Europe and West Asia on one side, and India and China on the other."[314] Nestorians were now ready to go east.

Nestorians faithfully adhered to the creed of the Council of Nicaea.[315] Around AD 800, Patriarch Timothy listed their fundamental doctrines: the Trinity, the Incarnation, Baptism, Adoration of the Cross, the Holy Eucharist, the two Testaments; the resurrection of the dead, eternal life, the return of Christ in glory, and the last judgment.[316] According to the creed found among the rich Sogdian texts (eighth–thirteenth) in Turfan, there was nothing meriting a charge of heresy; their creed was very close to the Apostles' Creed.[317]

The Nestorian Church appeared to have preserved some orthodox positions of the Jewish Church. In fact, the Nestorians represented Eastern Christians along with Jacobites (Eastern monophysites) during that period, originating from Mesopotamia with a Syriac language related to the Aramaic of Jesus. This they consistently upheld as the liturgical language on the mission field, even though they used Persian, Sogdian, and Turkish in church life. Tracing their roots to the Day of Pentecost in Acts, Nestorians by the thirteenth century called themselves Nasraye — "Nazarenes" — referring to Acts 24:5, "We have found this man to be a troublemaker, stirring up riots among the Jews all over the world. He is a ringleader of the Nazarene sect." From this environment, Christianity spread east through the Nestorians.[318]

The Christian center of gravity has shifted over time first westward to Rome, Europe, North America, and now to the Global South of Asia, Latin America, and Africa. The conversion of Europe to Christianity was completed much later than often thought. Andrew F. Walls remarks, "It was not until comparatively recent times — around the year 1500 — that the ragged conversion of the last pagan peoples of Europe, the overthrow of Muslim power in Spain, and the final eclipse of Christianity in Central Asia and Nubia combined to produce a Europe that was essentially Christian and a Christianity that was essentially European."[319]

The Nestorian Church was deeply rooted to the Church of the East and its cultural background. Nestorians appeared to have kept the faith into the Mongol era.[320] The strength of the Nestorian Church — a key to its survival — was to spread the gospel eastwards.

Persecution

How did persecution affect the mission work of Nestorians? Persecution is interesting because it often produces diametrically opposite results than expected. The Nestorians underwent terrible persecution, beginning with Zoroastrianism in the Persian Empire until the period of Timurids, a Turkish-Mongol Empire in the fifteenth century.

Terrible persecution and torture in Persia spanned 130 years, beginning with the rule of Sapur II. The newly converted Emperor of Byzantine, Constantine, sent a letter to Sapur II to ask for good treatment of Christians there. This enraged the Persian Emperor, who ordered Christians to pay double tax for the cost of war, and that the Nestorian Patriarch should collect it. He refused, saying "they are poor and I am not a tax collector," was imprisoned and was martyred along with five bishops and a hundred minor clergy. His farewell blessing was: "May the cross of our Lord be protection of the people of Jesus. May the peace of God be with the servants of God and establish your hearts in the faith of Christ, in tribulation and in ease, in life and in death, now and for evermore."[321] This was the beginning of forty years' persecution during Sapur II's rule, continuing until the end of the fifth century, the worst being in AD 446 during the reign of Yez'gerd II at Kirkuk, 230 km north of Baghdad, where 153,000 Christians were martyred.[322]

Despite discrimination and persecution, the Nestorian Church continued to grow, nearly displacing Zoroastrianism in the Sassanid Persian period,[323] and was even popularly accepted under Islamic rule for subsequent centuries. Central Asian Muslim geographer and scientist Biruni in the eleventh century observed, "the majority of the inhabitants of Syria, Iraq, and Khurasan[324] are Nestorians."[325] In the restricted situation in Persia, it was a natural development to turn their eyes evangelistically to countries east along the Silk Road trade route.

The church's position in the West was completely different. When Christianity became an official state religion, the Kingdom of God took on a territorial concept advanced in particular by Augustine of Hippo. People dreamt of a Holy Roman Empire. As Samuel Moffett notes, Roman bishops regarded the war with Persia, for which Constantine prepared: "to battle with him and for him by their prayers to God from whom all victory proceeds."[326]

The Crusades were a truly tragic event in history which bequeathed an unforgettable image to Muslims. Surrounding nations and religions felt understandably threatened by the expansion of Christendom and became suspicious of Christians within their borders. Before, Nestorians had prospered under Islamic rule; this security contributed to their growth in Persia and Central Asia. But the situation now was different; Muslims changed their attitude towards Christianity to that of confrontation.

Moffett remarked: "History demonstrates that one of the reasons for the persecution of the church in Asia over the past 1700 years is the perceived alliance of church with Western territorial imperialism."[327] Islamic fundamentalism is a defensive movement against the imperialism of Christendom and/or a secularizing West.

Monasteries and Church

Nestorian monks played a crucial part in Christian life and mission in Persia, Central Asia, and further east, establishing monasteries wherever they went. Monks fulfilled various roles according to the requirements of the church.

First of all, monasteries were to raise committed, equipped manpower for mission work. Indeed, a number of church leaders came from monasteries. Patriarch Tomas Marga (AD 837-850) wrote of his home monastery, Bet Abe, that "at least 100 of its sons became bishops, metropolitans and governors of Nestorian dioceses in Mesopotamia, Arabia, Persia, Armenia, Kurdistan and China."[328] Monks were sent with envoys to other countries or asked to oversee major synods.

Monasteries were used as midway stations for mission network along the Silk Road. "The route from Persia to India was dotted with Nestorian monasteries which provided lines of communication and facilitated contact and support to congregations as far away as [Sri Lanka]."[329]

Monks were also sent as missionaries. Under persecution, conversion was forbidden both under non-Muslim and Muslim rulers. Converts faced the loss of property, expulsion, or suffering — even death. They found refuge and community support in monasteries. As the number of inhabitants grew excessive, monasteries turned their hearts evangelistically to other countries on the trade route to the east, across the Persian border. Monasteries thus played a crucial role in the preparation of workers, who always went as a team with medical skills and a commitment to education. Every monastery had a hospital and a school, teaching agriculture to nomads. All this made a great impact.[330]

Regarding monastic religious practice, according to the Turfan Texts, "it had emphasis on fasting, penance, mystic experience, and preparation for death and judgment and in community there was liturgy celebration, especially the Eucharist. Monks wore a tunic, belt, cloak, hood, and sandals, and carried a cross and stick. Their tonsure was distinctive, being cruciform. At first they met for common prayer seven times a day, but later this was reduced to four times. They were vegetarians, and ate only once a day, at noon. Celibacy, of course was rigidly enforced. Those who were more capable engaged in study and the copying of books, while others worked on the land. After three years a monk could, if the abbot agreed, retire to absolute solitude as a hermit."[331]

Monasteries worked closely with the bishoprics, which had jurisdiction over monastic property, thus strengthening church hierarchy and integration. The Patriarch[332] was the head of the church with authority to convene and lead synods, and consecrate and send bishops to remote regions. All metropolitans had to attend synods, but those in remote regions (further east over the Oxus River) were instead asked to send a reporting letter every six years. Church hierarchy was in place, but flexible according to the fields. Their decision to leave the historical religious city of Nisibis (presently Nusaybin in Turkey), and move their headquarters to Seleucia-Ctesiphon (a city beside Baghdad), strategically on the Silk Road in the East, for the sake of the gospel, evidenced their serious commitment to mission work.

Silk Road and Tent-Makers

Nestorians were key players on the Silk Road trade route between East and West. From ancient times, the Silk Road was used for trade (being the origin of the world's economic system), religious pilgrimage and cultural exchange. Even disease traversed this road, e.g. Black Death.

The Silk Road was the hub of Nestorian mission work. Yeshuyab II's (AD 628–646) vision was to set up monasteries and churches along all 5000 miles across Asia.[333]

Alopen, the first Nestorian missionary, arrived in Chang-An in AD 623, according to a famous Nestorian monument.[334]

Although many Nestorian monks went out as missionaries, lay people were also involved, especially merchants and traders. "One of the reasons for the spread of Nestorianism to Central Asia was certainly the fact that Nestorians engaging in missionary activity could live by the work of their hands and were thus not dependent upon monastic settlements along the way."[335] They were "a powerful army of devotees who strengthened the church and fearlessly penetrated the vast Asiatic continent in an attempt at large-scale evangelism."[336]

The Syriac and Sogdians were well known as merchants in West and Central Asia and played a crucial role in Nestorian mission. The Syriac language was the *lingua franca* of the West Asia trader and was also used in liturgy. Among early Christians, the Syriac word for merchant, *tgr*, was often used as a metaphor for those who spread the gospel. A fourth-century Syriac hymn includes the following stanza:

Travel well-girt like merchants,
That we may gain the world.
Convert men to me,
Fill creation with teaching.[337]

Sogdians were Iranian-speaking Central Asians gifted as traders who controlled the Silk Road network. When a Sogdian baby was born, glue was put on his hands and honey on his lips, so that money would not leave him and he would have ability to speak as a trader. They had a great influence upon the evangelization of Turks and Mongols and were good translators and teachers. They created Turkish and Uygur scripts, and translated a body of Christian literature from Syriac and Persian into nomadic peoples' languages.

The Nestorian mission team model is seen in the first historical record revealing Christians' presence in Central Asia. When the Patriarch sent a mission team to the Hephthalite (White Huns, Turks, in Bactria) in the sixth century, it was composed of two merchants (probably Sogdians), a bishop, and four priests. The Nestorian approach was holistic and pragmatic according to need. Nestorian historical records, Catholic missionaries, Islamic historians, and geographers record that many Turks and Mongols were converted by Nestorians. Merchants and traders were true pioneers on mission frontiers. One such record describes the conversion of the king of Keraits:

> (The king) was overcome by a violent snowstorm and, he saw a vision about a saint, who said he would lead his way, and wandered hopelessly out of the way. When he lost all hope of salvation, a saint appeared to him in vision and said to him, "If you believe in Christ, I will lead you to the right direction" ... and he reached his tents in

safety. He summoned the Christian merchants who were there, and discussed with them the question of faith, and they answered him that this could not be accomplished except through baptism. He took a Gospel from them, and he is worshipping it every day.[338]

As a result, 200,000 people, the majority of the Keraits, were moved into the church. Merchants were there when the king needed help. Merchants had a great advantage in accessing mission fields. Their trade and networking skills created open doors to extend mission work under different rulers and religions. Interestingly, the peak of Nestorian mission under the leadership of Patriarch Timothy I (AD 780–823) coincided with the golden age of Islam in the Abbasid period.

Contextualized Messages

The Nestorian Church was formed in a Mesopotamian cultural context and rooted to the early church in Jerusalem. Culturally, they were communal based rather than individualistic, experience oriented rather than logical or reasoning, and emotional in approach rather than intellectual. These are common Eastern values through which biblical messages are received.

Within this background, Nestorians communicated the message of the Bible well. A famous monument erected about AD 780 presented the message clearly yet through Buddhist and Taoist terminologies:

> The illustrious and honorable Messiah, veiling his true dignity, appeared in the world as a man ... he fixed the extent of the eight boundaries, thus completing the truth and freeing it from dross; he opened the gate of the three constant principles, introducing life and destroying death; he suspended the bright sun to invade the chambers of darkness, and the falsehoods of the devil were thereupon defeated; he set in motion the vessel of mercy by which to ascend to the bright mansions, whereupon rational beings were then released; having thus completed the manifestation of his power, in clear day he ascended to his true station.[339]

Patriarch Timothy (AD 780–823), had a religious conversation with the Caliph of Abbasid:

> We were all of us as in a dark house in the middle of the night. If night and a dark house, a precious pearl happens to fall in the midst of people, and all become aware of its existence, everyone would strive to pick up the pearl, which will not fall to the lot of one only,

while one will get hold of the pearl itself, another one of a piece of glass, a third one of a stone or of a bit of earth, but everyone will be happy and proud that he is the real possessor of the pearl. When, however, night and darkness disappear, and light and day arise, then every one of those people who had believed that they had the pearl, would extend and stretch their hand towards the light, which alone can show what everyone has in hand. The one who possesses the pearl will rejoice and be happy and pleased with it, while those who had in hand pieces of glass and bits of stone only will weep and be sad, and will sigh and shed tears.[340]

Both examples are beautifully presented according to their culture and way of communication: visual, using life stories, relationally based — very different from Paul's logical, Hellenistic approach in Athens (Acts 17:22–31).

Elijah, the metropolitan in Merv, performed a miracle for a Turkish king in AD 644.

When traveling ... he was met by a king who was going to fight another king. Elijah endeavored with a long speech to dissuade him from the fight, but the king said to him, "If thou showest to me a sign similar to those shown of my gods, I shall believe in thy God." And the king ordered the priests of the demons who were accompanying him, and they invoked the demons whom they were worshipping, and immediately the sky was covered with clouds, and a hurricane of wind, thunder, and lightning followed. Elijah was then moved by divine power, and he made the sign of the heavenly cross, and rebuked the unreal thing that the rebellion demons had set up, and it forthwith disappeared completely. When the king saw what Saint Elijah did, he fell down and worshipped him, and he was converted with all his army.[341]

Here we see how the miracle performed by Elijah affected the king's conversion. Calling for rain was popular in shamanism: "Yada Taşı," a sacred stone for Turkish people, was believed to have power to draw wind and rain. The shaman performed the miracle by lifting the stone to the sky. Among the Turfan texts, we find in a story of the birth of Jesus the stone element: Jesus gave a stone, taken from the stone manger, to the three wise men from the East as a gift.

Unfortunately, there were instances of shamanistic elements practiced in Nestorianism in the late period. In Central Asia, elements of shamanism whether in Islam or even Christianity are a potential syncretic danger. We should be watchful!

CONCLUSION

Although there is no cultural center for Christianity, the early church in the Greek and Roman (Western) world has been the default model for mission work. Yet another model, developed in an Eastern cultural background and spread along the Silk Road, could be far more relevant to mission work in the East.

Several points have been examined as lessons for today. As God prepared the Roman Empire as a conduit for the gospel, he also prepared the Silk Road as a trade route for cultural and religious exchange, using Nestorians as key players. Even in persecution, they kept their faith as a heritage from the Jerusalem Church and expanded their vision to the remote regions of the Far East. They worked as teams of bishops, priests, monks, traders, and other professionals. Churches and monasteries worked together for the same purpose, establishing mission stations along the Silk Road and developing needed manpower. Church hierarchy was arranged accordingly (a model of true missional church). Those from all walks of life were involved and made a great impact.

They continued to grow and expand their work even under Islamic rule. Islam was very much influenced by Nestorians in its formation and development. During the golden age of Islam under Abbasid Caliph Harun (AD 764–809), Christians and Jews made great contributions in science, philosophy, and medicine.[342] Although Muhammad did not favor monasticism, Nestorian monasticism contributed considerably to the formation of *madrassas* (Islamic schools) as well as to Sufism (Islamic mysticism).[343] Nestorians humbly approached authorities and religions in power which created open doors for their work. This was in stark contrast to the Church of the West with its vision of a Holy Roman Empire founded through brute force.

Concerning the decline of the Nestorians, hypotheses abound: the last blow from Timurids, the spread of Black Death, loss of influence on the Silk Road, compromise with other religions and authorities, their hierarchic structure and more. However, none explain their sudden disappearance in the fifteenth century (at least in Central Asia). Unfortunately, we do not have enough material to determine what precisely contributed to their final demise. We do not know how rooted they were in the Christian faith. Although their decline was mysterious, it is a good lesson. If they disappeared after 800 successful years in mission, what about us? Protestants have had only 500 years — we should continually examine ourselves.

17

THE ANOTOC STORY, CONTINUED: GROUP DYNAMICS WITHIN AN INSIDER MOVEMENT

JOHN KIM

In order to see a movement to Christ, we must understand group dynamics. Promoting movements on a wider scale demands resolution of issues such as socio-religious hierarchies, team dynamics between the community being reached and "inbetweeners,"[344] disharmony among expatriate workers, and discipling new believers. As a continuation of my previous work,[345] I return to the Anotoc case for lessons that apply to these issues, particularly in the context of a growing insider movement.

THE STORY OF ANOTOC AND NEARBY VILLAGES, CONTINUED

More than five years have passed since I described the group dynamics involved in a people movement to Christ that occurred in a Muslim village called Anotoc, where new believers in Jesus Christ have remained "insiders" within the social context and religious identity into which they were born.

Two group baptisms occurred in 2004 and 2005 following the first baptism in 2003, performed at the inbetweener's initiative. In 2004 the baptism was partly initiated by insiders; in 2005 it was fully initiated by them. Local leaders performed other baptisms in their own areas. The movement began to flow to lowland areas from the mountain village where it began.

In one lowland town some distance from Anotoc, Naya, an Islamic witchdoctor (and farmer) had been working with people in Anotoc village. He participated in the 2004 baptism and, simply from having seen what happened in Anotoc, he began to perform baptisms in and around his own village. At first his fellow villagers considered him a betrayer by becoming a Christian, persecuted him, and ordered him to leave. He insisted that he had never betrayed them and had not converted from Islam to Christianity, but merely accepted *Isa Al-Masih* (Jesus the Messiah) as his Lord and Savior. He boldly said that they should also believe in *Isa Al-Masih* as *Ruh Allah* (the Spirit of God). His testimony angered people who regarded it as proof that he had become a Christian. Yet despite this harsh situation, all his family members and other relatives came to the Lord.

Naya had been using a spell inherited from his father that included the name of *Isa Al-Masih*. One of his father's last words to him was that he should believe in that name as the strongest power giver. Even without any knowledge of *Isa Al-Masih*, Naya had used this name to heal many people. As a believer he seemed to be doing similar work, but now with faith and a clear knowledge of who *Isa* was. As time went on, people in his village accepted him as a strange Muslim, and gave him the name *Tukang Injil* (The Gospel Technician) since he was so skilled in using Bible passages to help people facing difficulties.

In 2005, Naya baptized eleven of his family members at one time and held other baptisms when there were new believers. Usually his wife baptized the women. An *ustad* (religious leader) named Zain was in one baptized group and began helping Naya. With Zain's help, there were 70 people in the next baptism. They insisted that people do as *Isa Al-Masih* commanded in the *Injil*, even though they were investigated by the police and the religion department, who were concerned that they were promoting Christianity.

A leadership training program was launched at an inbetweener's home at the initiative of some inbetweeners and expatriate workers. Many of Naya's neighbors came and listened to what was shared. The meeting began with the Islamic *sholat* prayer ritual, followed by the reading of Bible chapters. The insider leaders freely shared what they had learned with others.

Some neighbors who observed the meeting joined in a meal and asked many questions. A main question was about the meaning of *siratal mustaqim* (the Straight Way). Muslims perform a prayer ritual five times a day and memorize the "Show me the Straight Way"[346] verses from *Al-Fatiah* (the first chapter of the Qur'an). These verses have various interpretations but, in the training given, *Isa Al-Masih* was introduced as the only one among the 25 well-known prophets who introduced Himself as "The Way." Many were amazed to know this and committed themselves to The Way, including one woman who later married the inbetweener's nephew. The people met together and shared the gospel with great excitement. Very positive group dynamics were at work among families and neighbors.

We inbetweeners and expatriate workers were excited to see the movement develop. We also saw similar movements starting among the Bangunda people. To help, we prepared a video showing practices of worship and fellowship to offer suggestions to these and other "insider believers" (IBs) on how to have fellowship as followers of *Isa Al-Masih*. We hoped those groups would network to form a bigger community.

However, serious turmoil was about to hit one ministry area where we expected to see a movement similar to that in Anotoc. Some local leaders disagreed with the approach adopted by an inbetweener leader, an expatriate worker and local Christians who had been involved in an NGO-type ministry helping Bangunda refugees. Not long after the worship videos were made, the NGO-related workers approached their ministry place with an inbetweener leader and saw a crowd and TV reporters waiting for them, who asked about their religious identities. When it was the inbetweener's turn, they asked him to repeat the Islamic confession of faith, since he introduced himself as a Muslim. He recited the exact same phrases of the Islamic confession of faith, made a short pause, and then added, "*Isa Al Kalimatullah* (Isa the Word of God) and *Isa Ruh'lah* (Isa the Spirit of God)." Upon this confession the people mobbed him, screaming accusations of blasphemy. Even though some came close to attacking him with chairs and sickles, he was mysteriously protected as their arms were unable to move. As the situation worsened, policemen arrested the believers and took them to the station.

The expatriate worker was deported and the inbetweener was imprisoned for three years. Because he was a key leader influencing many IBs, he worked with expatriate workers in the area around Anotoc in providing training and, with the tense situation at hand, the expatriate workers decided to leave the area. Following this, I could not be directly involved in ministry around Anotoc for at least a year, but I heard periodically that Naya and Zain still ministered in their areas with great passion, despite the confrontation and arrest.

The year of hibernation ended when some inbetweeners and expatriate workers decided to restart leadership training in another town. Beginning in November 2006, three-month training sessions were held regularly and there was great joy among the twenty to thirty insider leaders gathered for the meeting. They were encouraged to take the initiative in Bible reading and free discussion. Even in the expatriate workers' absence, the gospel continued to penetrate Bangunda societies and many new believers met at the leaders' homes. There were even third-generation leaders as a result of the gospel's outflowing.

At the third leadership meeting, some participants proposed a special gathering of wives so that they could also grow spiritually and encourage one another as followers of *Isa*. In the Bangunda community, wives must not be seen at gatherings for men. Thus we saw this proposal as evidence of a behavioral change in the leaders; they were making decisions. Encouraged, we began to expect that an even bigger, community-transforming movement could become a reality very soon.

At this time, an inbetweener named Manggo was elected chief administrative leader in his village. Supporters of a rival candidate accused Manggo of trying to Christianize the Bangunda people. They produced several villagers who had participated in the leadership training meetings, including Naya's neighbor, a supporter of the rival candidate, who we later realized had been at the meeting as a spy. More than fifteen leaders were arrested and taken to the religious authorities and police station. Copies of the *Injil* they had were confiscated as proof that they were involved in Christianization efforts.

The candidates for village leader, including Manggo, along with Naya and other insider leaders, had their day in court. When interrogated, they continued to insist that they were not involved in any Christianization effort. After a long debate and interrogation, they all were released, and Manggo's new role as village leader was made official. In court, Naya and his relatives' strong social position in the community enabled them to calm the commotion caused by supporters of Manggo's rival.

At a recent meeting, Naya expressed his unchanging desire to see an even greater movement. He said that there were about a thousand IBs in areas near his village who wanted to gather as followers of *Isa*. He is now leading his own fellowship of about twenty people every Friday and Sunday at his home.

PRINCIPLES AND BASIC TOOLS

We established the incarnation of Jesus as the foundation for all our thinking and ministry approaches in the Bangunda context. Incarnational ministry is commonly related to missionaries' living standard in the field, but we applied it to every aspect of our lives, including how we communicate, build relationships, eat, dress, teach, learn, understand, and interact emotionally with others.

Training to mobilize "eleventh hour workers" was necessary,[347] but the traditional method of Christian evangelism often resulted in the extraction of new believers from their families and communities, which is ineffective and jeopardizes the stability of contextual ministry. We designed a training program to mobilize local long-term workers. These sessions ran intensively for one or three months. The latter session included field practice with help from experienced expatriate workers.

In most cases, those from other parts of the country with a strong affinity for mainline Christian structures did not fit in well for long-term work in an insider context. New believers from Muslim and other backgrounds adapted more successfully and were accepted by insiders as their kind of people. The inbetweeners who settled down successfully to live with local people play crucial roles in connecting insider followers of *Isa Al-Masih* with outsiders such as expatriate workers.

As described in my previous article,[348] family dynamics are very important. Even though male insiders were often responsible for pushing the movements forward, we encouraged inbetweeners and insider leaders to take advantage of family gatherings by interacting with other families to which the gospel might spread.

We held insider leadership training sessions on a regular basis. These sessions included a couple of expatriate workers, several inbetweeners, and IBs. We encouraged prospective leaders to take what they learned at the gatherings and apply it creatively. These sessions gave them role models of insider leaders and examples of fellowship among followers of *Isa Al-Masih*. We paid great attention to encouraging initiative. Insiders were encouraged to read Bible verses, meditate on what they read, talk about what they learned from the Holy Spirit, share how they would apply it, and ask questions of others at the meetings. There was no fixed format. Normally the leaders led *sholat* before they sat together to read and meditate on the Word of God. After eating together, they had an informal time of fellowship. We encouraged them to follow Paul's example recorded in Acts 28:31: "Boldly and without hindrance he preached the kingdom of God and taught about the Lord Jesus Christ."

Some IBs were sent to a training event for believers from Christian backgrounds, where the "Kingdom paradigm" was promoted rather than the "Christendom paradigm" (both described later in this chapter). Trainees' reactions depended on the speakers. When they spoke in traditional Christian terms, the insider trainees appeared unhappy, while I sensed that others reacted with joy. However, the insider trainees responded positively to trainers who used Muslim terminology. After one training session, an IB came to me quietly and whispered "Now I realize that *Isa* in whom I believe is exactly the same Lord Jesus in whom these Christians believe." We held this joint training session once as a test, using the "Kingdom perspective," thinking it could show our unity as members of the Body of Christ. We wanted to testify that the Kingdom of God is beyond the typical tradition of religions in conflict. However, the trainers decided not to do it again as it confused the IBs. Instead, we encouraged them to go through a self-theologizing process within their own context.

In fostering this insider movement, the expatriate workers' network was also crucial. We created a special training program — similar for those in the Anotoc movement — for expatriate workers to understand the remaining task and the ministry philosophies needed. After years of training expatriate workers, especially Koreans, through conferences and a cooperative partnership we are starting to see a similar vision to consider insider movements from a Kingdom perspective.

We encouraged inbetweeners to maintain a self-supporting lifestyle. Some settled down successfully within insider communities and became self-supporting, though from time to time outside help was necessary. Expatriate workers played an important role in helping inbetweeners settle in areas near IB villages so that the gospel could reach to these new communities.

THE PRESENT STATE OF KINGDOM DEVELOPMENT

A great insider movement was about to be kindled before the 2005 setback. Even though the movement seemed in hibernation after that, it was pushed forward by insider villagers such as Naya and Zain. When expatriate workers could not directly join in activities with the IBs, these men, on their own initiative and by their own efforts, kept the Kingdom advancing. Some inbetweeners continued successful ministries, but their role as a driving force seemed reduced due to security concerns regarding expatriate workers' involvement in the ministry teams.

The inbetweener who had been jailed was eventually released and continues to travel and share the gospel with the same passion as before. Manggo practices his leadership as an administrative authority in his village, and other inbetweeners continue to play roles as catalysts fostering insider movements.

Meanwhile, expatriate workers are moving cautiously to see even greater advances in the Kingdom, but without jeopardizing the insiders' initiative and the viability of their projects.

INHERENT GROUP DYNAMICS IN THE MOVEMENTS

I introduced the cluster model in my previous article. A family unit is the smallest feasible cluster that can cause reorientation in surrounding clusters which can be neighboring families, relatives or any group of people living in a similar context.

In the Anotoc case, almost all who joined the group baptisms in 2003–2005 were neighboring family units or extended families or clans, relatives living in different areas, and people working in similar professions. Naya, from a village some distance from Anotoc, shared the same job with some living in Anotoc. He was baptized in 2004 in Anotoc; in 2005, he baptized his own family members and relatives at the same spot. All baptisms were performed in contextually relevant ways—not as Christian events, but as a necessary step for insider followers of *Isa*—similar to the Bangunda tradition of bathing in a river when needing to repent of shameful deeds.

Every gathering resulted in further momentum. There was openness such that the gospel could flow freely throughout the group. Usually an inbetweener from the contextualized ministry team gave a message, starting with chanted quranic verses, then telling stories of key prophets, and ending with the unique story of *Isa Al-Masih*. At the end, they asked for repentance and called for baptism for those who accepted *Isa Al-Masih* as their Lord and Savior. In the group, those who had already been baptized encouraged those who were hesitant and confused. After the baptism, they usually performed the prayer ritual *sholat* as a group and shared the Word of God.

In doing so, they created a huge space for the gospel message to flow freely. This is the inherent character of groups: when the dynamics are good, the gospel can flow with fewer obstacles and people are much more open to hear the Good News. In the book of Acts, there are many cases of group dynamics at work. People often question whether all those who participate in group baptism are really saved. Who knows except the Holy Spirit? The matter of salvation is totally his work. However, when this kind of group dynamic is at work, the Holy Spirit seems to work so that each individual can respond in a spontaneous and cooperative way. This, in turn, gives many more opportunities to make disciples for *Isa Al-Masih*, a process that involves "baptizing" and "teaching all Jesus commanded" (Matthew 28:19–20).

Baptism and teaching all Jesus commanded are necessary in making disciples of Jesus. With good group dynamics, even though we do not know yet whether all in a group situation are really saved, the fact is that great opportunities become available for "making disciples" by encouraging new believers to obey the teaching and in baptism. This is what we attempted to do in Bangunda, including areas around Anotoc.

HINDRANCES AND AREAS OF CONCERN

There are several hindrances and areas of concern to be addressed in order to promote movements on a wider scale. Among them are the socio-religious hierarchy within the culture, team dynamics between insiders and inbetweeners, disharmony among expatriate workers, and discipling the believers.

Socio-religious Hierarchy

In the Bangunda context, different kinds of authorities influence clusters within a community. Clusters vary in nature, depending on the authority to which they give allegiance be it the *dukun* (witchdoctor), *kyai* (Islamic top leader), or regional governmental administrative authorities.

Villagers facing the struggles of daily living tend to visit the *dukun* to solve their problems. The *dukun* has many formulas based upon pre-Islamic beliefs. Even though the *kyai* usually deals with Islamic teachings, in the folk Islam context the *dukun's* role is often encroached upon by the *kyai*. Tensions can arise between leaders who may try to test the other's power. This power encounter happens even among *kyais* in the same village or between them and *kyais* in a neighboring region; when that happens, even local governmental leaders are powerless to intervene.

This socio-religious hierarchy needs to be determined when attempting to focus on a specific cluster.

In the case of the NGO team setback, there was competition between different *kyais* during the planned governmental leader election in the district. While one *kyai* showed great hospitality to the team and allowed the team to do their NGO work publicly, a competing *kyai* was opposed, directed the conspiracy against the movement, and succeeded in halting it.

In Manggo's case, *kyais* in his village actually came to suggest that he be a candidate in the village leader election. He was greatly supported by local religious leaders. However, there was another cluster around a *hajji* who was also a candidate and in competition with the *kyais* who supported Manggo. When Manggo was elected, the cluster following the *hajji* accused him of being a Christianizer.

Socio-religious hierarchies exist in any human society. However, when hierarchically formed clusters collide, the movement can be halted—a major concern when a chain reaction is about to happen throughout local clusters. This is particularly true when political leadership is intermingled with religious leadership, as happens in Muslim communities.

Team Dynamics between Insiders and Inbetweeners

Inbetweeners are usually trained team members cooperating with expatriate workers; together they have occasional team meetings to sharpen their vision, discuss new issues, struggles, and other concerns. For long-term work, they agree to cooperate by sharing not only vision but also resources including manpower, finances, and ministry methodologies and tools.

Problems often arise as new IBs appear and, it is assumed, the inbetweeners' role should be transferred to insiders. Inbetweeners are not contract workers cooperating with expatriate workers. Rather, both are servants of God called at the eleventh hour into God's vineyard (Matthew 20:1–16). There are many IBs who have never had a relationship with Christian workers or believers within their societies until they meet inbetweeners. Inbetweeners also model what new life is like in *Isa*. In the initial stage of the movement, teamwork with inbetweeners and potential IB leaders is essential and requires regular gatherings for training and getting to know and trust one another.

I have worked with two teams, each with a couple of inbetweeners and several IB leaders. In Anotoc, where the movement collapsed along with the NGO team in 2005, most of the leaders lost momentum in spreading the gospel. As coworkers, the Anotoc leaders should have had the same authority as the inbetweeners, but they tended to wait for inbetweeners to make decisions. Whether this reflected dependency or ill-advised directive leadership, the team wasn't working. However, Naya and Zain enjoyed working with an inbetweener couple who wanted to be learners as well as team members. They were not directive, but patient and practiced the kind of teamwork found in an extended family. Consequently, they have high expectations of an even bigger movement.

Disharmony among Expatriate Workers

Disharmony among expatriate workers has been a huge issue in the post-modern mission era and often arises from debate over mission paradigms, namely the *Christendom* perspective and the new *Kingdom* perspective. The former maintains a definite Christian identity, employing terms and traditions well known and understood in worldwide Christianity. The latter finds equivalent terms and forms to convey the same meanings while being readily understood within non-Christian societies.

Contradictory paradigms naturally result in different mission practices on the field[349] and, when present in a team, can engender serious disharmony. For example, a radio broadcasting project in the Bangunda language involved three different groups: staff members at the radio studio, national field workers, and expatriate workers. They agreed to contextualize the program by using Muslim-friendly terms such as *Isa Al-Masih* instead of *Yesus Kristus*, the term commonly used in Christian circles. One day the radio station's chief of staff decided to change the name *Isa Al-Masih* to *Yesus Kristus* without consulting others. He thought the name *Isa Al-Masih* had been used long enough for Muslims to finally know *Yesus Kristus*, who gives salvation when they become Christians.

A typical conflict caused by the two paradigms involves priority in mission practice. Should unity and fellowship among workers from different backgrounds be a manifestation of the body of Jesus, or should agreement as team members on the same goal take precedence? In the NGO case, team members had different identities: national Christians, an inbetweener of Muslim identity, and a Western expatriate. The inbetweener recognized himself as an insider and that the others were not. When asked to confess the *shahada*, he did so without hesitation but, because of the special intervention of the Spirit, he also confessed who *Isa* was. When he went to court, Christians were willing to help him. However, he wanted to make clear his position as an insider who believed in *Isa* and, since the question of Christianization had surfaced, he refused any assistance from Christians. Unfortunately, many insiders he knew well did not want to become involved in the court process out of fear of being connected to any Christianization effort.

On the other hand, if a similar case happened in the area of Anotoc — where there were no apparent Christians on the team and the inbetweeners were of Muslim identity — the IBs may have shown the initiative to defend themselves. The NGO team practiced networking and cooperation, even though some had an apparent Christian identity while the latter team consisted of all Muslim-identity followers of *Isa*. There was harmony among the NGO team members from different spectrums of

Christianity, yet they seemed uncertain about their goal; members merely decided to join a good Christian work. However, the Anotoc team did well in encouraging strong initiative among insider members.

When a team consists of members from different macro-paradigms, attention must be given to the threat of disharmony. It would be good for field practitioners and mission leaders to discuss this and achieve agreement on principles to apply to the remaining missions task.

THE ISSUE OF TRAINING

Jesus commissioned us to the great task of making disciples of him (not ourselves) among all the nations. In discipleship training, leadership issues seem to take a central position. Fostering insider movements requires us to uphold the importance of insiders taking the initiative in training rather than deferring to inbetweeners or expatriates.

Normally we tend to practice a prescribed way of leading training. What expatriate or inbetweener leaders often contribute is formulated content from their own cultural backgrounds which, in this case, cannot be used because it is foreign to the insiders' contexts. Leaders trained with such material cannot successfully use it in trainings they lead, and so the movement can come to a halt.

There are many well-prepared packages often used to mobilize national workers which may be sufficient to mobilize and encourage national workers to become inbetweeners. Problems usually arise when new IBs need discipleship or leadership training. When inbetweeners are trained using a well-formulated program but have never experienced unforeseen situations, their ability as coordinators declines remarkably.

In running training sessions to recruit national workers, I have found that some nationals could become inbetweeners and long-term team members. Then, when insider believers appear, training activities could be arranged. This underscores the importance of good group dynamics within our own expatriate and national teams, which allowed us to invite a prospective leader group for a group-to-group meeting so that insider leaders could observe and learn different leadership roles.

At the first meeting, each inbetweener or expatriate worker took different roles in turn, each leading the group through *sholat*, chanting, reading, praying, and sharing. At the second meeting, we encouraged insider leaders to set up their own roles, which they did, and they continued from there. We did not encourage any leader to be dominant and we practiced the inductive way of interacting: leading, thinking, talking, and studying the Bible. In order to keep a movement going, we need as many insider leaders as possible to learn good group dynamics.

CONCLUSION

For several years, I worked with an international organization whose members were mostly Westerners. I enjoyed the fellowship among people of various nationalities which was a confirmation of our union in the body of Jesus. The activities I was involved in were a continuation of sorts of my Christian experience in my home country. Still, a foggy skepticism arose in my mind about whether this was the best way to approach the Bangunda people. In time I realized that I could do nothing for the Bangunda people as long as I remained a Christian worker within the Christendom paradigm.

This people group ministry focus drove me through a paradigm shift in understanding what must be done among unreached peoples. I began to understand the ideas of people movements to Christ within a Muslim context and insider movements. As I observed group dynamics among the Bangunda, I was convinced that God was at work in nontraditional ways, even as many field workers focused on people groups struggled with mission paradigm issues.

The case of the Bangunda people may provide understanding into the group dynamics resulting in the free flow of the gospel through clusters. The greatest advantage of the insider approach is the huge space that can be created to make disciples for Jesus. In our home countries, churches invite non-believers into existing structures to have the opportunity to hear the Good News. Similarly, movements such as in Anotoc create even more opportunities so that even more people can hear the Good News.

18

THE "DISCONNECT" IN THE DISCIPLESHIP OF SOUTH ASIAN WOMEN: SOCIO-CULTURAL AND RELIGIOUS BARRIERS AMONG MUSLIM BACKGROUND BELIEVERS

KAREN SCOTT

"Sister, can we do this again? We want to meet together like this more often."

"You mean it is alright for you to travel two hours away from your village to meet together like this on a regular basis? What will your Muslim neighbors think?"

"Oh, yes, of course it is okay; we can tell our neighbors that we are going to visit relatives."

These Muslim background believer (MBB) women's words challenged several of my assumptions that day! The scene was the rented site of a local non-governmental organization (NGO) where several rural Bangladeshi MBBs and I were meeting for purposes of my research. For thirty years I assumed that rural women of Bangladesh were relegated to stay, for the most part, within the confines of their villages — unreachable for evangelistic or discipleship purposes — yet that day I learned differently from the women themselves. Therefore, I am honored and privileged to stand with them as they tell their heart's cry.

In this chapter[350] I intend to draw attention to the alarming fact that women followers of *Isa* (Jesus) in Bangladesh are not typically receiving training through intentional discipleship programs. Given the importance of the woman's role in the family and society, including leading her children and women relatives and friends to Christ, why might this be the case? How can women be more adequately honored, discipled, and given opportunity to fulfill their important role as followers of Jesus? Failing to address this may lead to a disastrous future for the Muslim background church. This dilemma is illustrated through an MBB woman's personal testimony:

> I am from Bangladesh and am a librarian with a Bachelor of Theology degree. I have worked in a well-known NGO and currently work as a development worker. I am the wife of a pastor; we have three children. My family has been Muslim from generation to generation.
>
> My husband heard the gospel of Jesus Christ and received him as Savior, but I did not. Although my husband tried to discuss this with me and encouraged me to listen to Jesus' word, I could not stand to listen to him because my family members were conservative followers of Islam. I read the Qur'an and prayed to God according to the law of Islam. After one year of trying to make me a follower of Jesus, my husband tried something new: every night, he put the Holy Scripture under my pillow. Even though I saw the scripture, I did not touch it. Early one morning, I heard a sound in my heart, "Take the scripture from under the pillow and read it." That very moment, I took the scripture and began to read these verses, "Come to me all of you who are tired from carrying heavy loads and I will give you rest. Take my yoke and put it on you, and learn from me, because I am gentle and humble in spirit and you will find rest. For the yoke I put on you is easy and the load I will put on you is light" (Matthew 11:28–30). I compared this with what Hazrat Mohammed said in his holy Qur'an: if we do lots of right works we would get into heaven; otherwise not. I completed the New Testament in one month and then compared the teaching of Jesus and Mohammad.
>
> As a Muslim woman, I have seen the negative attitude that Bangladeshi men have toward women, considering them to be of low status and illiterate. In this culture, wives have to depend on their husbands for everything. Normally, women do not express their opinion in the family and have no opportunity to help make decisions. The veil is

only for women, not for men — this is the way it was in my family. Slowly things became better. Many believing families retain one or two of these points because they do not forget their background or culture easily; change happens slowly.

After beginning to follow Christ, it has been my experience that many believing men do not encourage women to come to the weekly meetings nor do they explain salvation to them. They do not know how important they are or how necessary women are to the life of the *jamaat* (congregation). We know this is true, since women have to obey their husbands; if husbands said they must go to the weekly meetings, they would go. Their absence means that their male guardians are not telling them to go, because the men do not understand the importance of women being taught spiritual truth: without them, their children will also not know how to follow Jesus.

All this results from their habits from Islam. When I first asked my husband if I could go to the *jamaat* with him, he said no. After some time, the mission organization called a meeting for families and he took me along. Because of the teaching he received, from that time I was able to go to the meetings.

The weekly *jamaats* that women do attend are mostly for worship and brief teaching. There is no opportunity to learn the deeper truths of scripture. Once they have this training and if they can read, women can continue on in their homes.

I have been a follower of Jesus since 1986. I graduated with a BTh in 1992. Although I have been able to teach at several women's meetings, December 16, 2008 was the first time I was asked to speak in front of both men and women in a meeting. It is like this because they say there are no women pastors in the Bible and therefore I cannot preach. They also look back at the Islamic experience where only men can preach. I believe this attitude toward women must change.[351]

BARRIERS TO WOMEN'S SPIRITUAL GROWTH IDENTIFIED

Several factors resulting in barriers to women's spiritual growth become evident through this woman's story:

1. A culturally and socially ascribed negative attitude toward women
2. Certain religious beliefs and practices of Islam
3. The lack of special meetings for women and children
4. The lack of appropriate discipleship materials stressing the importance of each family member's spiritual growth and the importance of women's roles in the *jamaat*
5. Our evangelical assumptions regarding cultural and religious customs

BACKGROUND TO CHURCH PLANTING IN BANGLADESH

The pluralistic history of Bangladesh has resulted in an expression of Islam that is unique. The national Christian church, founded by William Carey in the late 1700s from a Hindu population, used cultural forms and terms from Hindu language and culture for its religious expression. Thus, to Muslims, many Christian terms were an abomination. During the mid-1970s, a group of missionaries began experimenting with contextualized church planting strategies as they witnessed to Muslims.

In the 1980s the *Injil Sharif* (the New Testament translation incorporating Muslim terms) was printed by the Bangladesh Bible Society. The *Kitabul Mokaddos* (the complete Bible) was printed by the Society in 2000. Thousands of Muslims are now reading God's Word in their own heart language.

The result is astounding. To those familiar with the monsoon season, that is what this movement of the Holy Spirit resembles — a "monsoon downpour" of the Spirit of God. There are now thousands of Muslim background believers in Bangladesh. One can only stand in awe of what God is doing.

As exciting as this is, all is not well. Among the many challenges facing the new *jamaat* (MBB church) is the troubling fact that women and children are not normally the focus of discipleship programs nor are they attending local *jamaat* (congregational) meetings in numbers that come close to those of adult male *Isa-i* (follower of Jesus). An expatriate worker reports that there is a *jamaat* that has met in a university town for more than twenty years. It has survived persecution and its members have retained their respect in the community, even though recognized as followers of *Isa*. On Friday mornings, eight to twelve men gather at one of the *jamaat* member's homes to study the Word and pray together. Except for one woman, there is no indication that any of the other wives have come to faith.

The expatriate woman's husband had an opportunity to teach English to the young boys of this *jamaat* and did so to find out how much they knew of the Bible and their Christian faith. He was surprised to discover a relative lack of knowledge about spiritual matters. Sometime later, this expatriate woman was asked to meet with the daughters and daughters-in-law of *jamaat* members. She was appalled that the young girls and women knew almost nothing of the Scriptures. One young woman interviewed did not seem to know that her father was a follower of Jesus — she thought he was a member of a Muslim cult. What hinders the women from full participation in these *jamaat* meetings? Why do the children know so little about their faith?

FIELD RESEARCH

This lack of opportunity for the spiritual formation of women and children was confirmed by my doctoral research. Field research through qualitative and quantitative methods in two geographic locations indicated that the above was the rule rather than the exception.[352]

Other than in one instance, none of the mission agencies, *jamaat* leaders, or members reported special meetings for women or children in the work they were involved in or knew about. In some cases, women were invited to infrequent leadership training meetings with their husbands; however, few attend. It was expected and hoped that men would pass on teaching to their families. A key *Isa-i* leader reported that there are a few women *jamaat* leaders but, when leaders are called together for training, these women are not invited. Where there was some concern evidenced during the interviews, there was a lack of ideas on how this problem could be surmounted.

It is important at this point to highlight a few findings from the quantitative questionnaire used in my research. In summary, 82 percent of children from age two to five learn about religion primarily from their mothers. From age six to ten that statistic changed and the local *imam* (religious leader) became the primary teacher. Of the eighty-two persons surveyed, 60 percent had attended a *madrassa* (an Islamic school) when they were young, including twenty-five out of thirty-eight women. In these rural *jamaats* women attended weekly meetings in fairly equal proportion to men, but children did not usually attend. This reveals a clear lack of special meetings for women and children.

A few questions come to mind:

- How is a mother going to be able to teach her small children if she does not receive teaching?

- Who within the believing church is replacing the local Muslim *imam* that taught religion to the boys and girls in their homes or villages?
- After coming to faith, what is replacing the *madrassa* education that so many of the young girls (and young boys) received as Muslims?
- Why do women avoid attending meetings with their husbands even when they have been invited and why are there no meetings — or so few — specifically for women?

A look at the status and role of Muslim women in Bangladesh will shed light on these questions.

SOCIO-CULTURAL STATUS AND ROLE OF MUSLIM WOMEN

While rural Muslim women of Bangladesh have rich and varied life experiences, their cultural and religious status and roles are socially ascribed from birth. Popular Islamic practices often dictate their response to life situations. Within this patriarchal society, male superiority and female inferiority is a generally accepted norm. A woman must rely on a male guardian from birth to death for food, shelter, and clothing as well as for social security. Women work long hours in jobs that are not measured in economic terms. They have inferior status in education, religion, and other social institutions, including marriage. Traditionally, they are not supposed to take part in activities outside the homestead.

STATUS AND ROLE WITHIN ISLAM AND CHRISTIANITY

As the social status and role of rural women in Bangladesh are discussed, we must keep in mind that lines between religious and social status and role are blurred. It is not always possible to determine if an action is culturally or religiously ascribed. However, for the most part, women are not allowed to participate fully in the Muslim *ummah* (brotherhood, community) in public festivals or prayer in the mosque.

Faith is interpreted by men from the local *madrassa* and nearby mosque to which women have no access. This does not mean they regard their spiritual lives as unimportant. On the contrary, one study suggests that around half of all women in Bangladesh claim to pray five times a day.[353]

Both religious and cultural norms apply in the area of purity/pollution as it applies to the identity of womanhood. A negative identity stems from the religious or social norms applied to her purity or pollution, which are nothing more than natural, life-giving, biological functions as females. Women about to give birth and menstruating women — considered to be in a state of pollution — may not take part in religious activities.[354]

Because of their exclusion from public expression of religious faith, women are forced to look elsewhere to express their spirituality; the ready availability of ancient traditions is close at hand. The nature of married women's contacts with the supernatural varies from that of men; the array of powers wives invoke in the supernatural realm is much wider than that of men.[355] Although not recognized officially, it would appear that within Bangladeshi culture it is the purview of women to have responsibility in dealing with the supernatural world — within the homestead. However, there is also a precedent in Islam for women's participation in more public religious activities. Historical sources have preserved a large number of names of ascetic and *Sufi* women who are witnesses of Islamic mysticism and have been given titles such as *shaykha* (authority in religion), *mudarrisa* (teacher in the religious colleges), and *faqihiyya* (doctor in Islamic law).[356]

Santi Theresa Rozario's research offers reasons why men still do not usually seek a woman's opinion on important matters:

- Men claim that women are less intelligent, believing their brain is only one-half or one-quarter the size of a man's.
- Men say that women do not go out and therefore do not understand or know anything.
- Women do not earn or have money, implying that they are of less importance.
- Men are concerned that women will become too free, bossy, and clever if their opinion is sought.
- Men are concerned about losing their honor or losing face if they seek a woman's opinion.
- Sometimes, if women go to meetings, people in the *samaj* (society) do not like it and the women will get a bad reputation.[357]

I would argue that male guardians — also products of their historical, cultural, social, and religious upbringing — do not normally realize the potential of the women in their families. Deeply embedded in their worldview is the traditional ascribed status and role of women. Since men and women move in different social circles, a new faith will not normally be passed on to women in the "trickle-down" effect assumed effective by current discipleship methods. A radical change of heart and mind is necessary. Until men affirm women's value, the women themselves will not realize the importance of their contribution to their families and communities. Unless current beliefs change, women will have little motivation to attend meetings that they imagine are "above their heads" or for people with more intelligence. However, God in Christ makes this paradigm shift possible.

THE BIBLICAL STORY OF THE STATUS AND ROLE OF WOMEN

There are many similarities between the status and role of rural Bangladeshi women and that of women in the Bible. Contrary to the Greek and Roman gods and goddesses, the Creator God of the Hebrew Bible formed men and women to share in origin, destiny, tragedy, and hope.[358] Denise Carmody, chair of the religion faculty at the University of Tulsa, says that the Bible has so strongly influenced Western religious and cultural imagination that anyone seeking a perspective on central matters such as the status of women has to confront the biblical materials. When doing so, to the student's surprise, the confrontation turns out to be liberating, as John Carlisle's poem, "Proving the Pertinence," so well describes.

> *Statistically men*
> *(predictably too)*
> *predominate the text*
> *and concordance*
> *of scripture*
> *but the women*
> *manage to infiltrate*
> *at crucial times*
> *and prove their pertinence*
> *to all the sacred story.*[359]

JESUS AND HIS "UPSIDE DOWN KINGDOM" APPROACH TO WOMEN

Says Paul Jewett, "It was not so much in what he said as in how he related to women that Jesus was a revolutionary ... He treated women as fully human, equal to men in every respect; no word of deprecation about women, as such, is ever found on his lips."[360] Jesus enhanced the status of women and broadened their role by going so far as to allow them to follow him as his disciples. This dramatically expanded their sphere of influence outside the domestic role ascribed to them by society. "Here was a man with the wisdom of a prophet who readily violated social custom when it oppressed people."[361] Mary Evans, lecturer at London Bible College, writes:

Jesus healed women, he allowed them to touch him and to follow him; he spoke without restraint of women, to women and with women. He related to women primarily as human beings rather than as sexual beings; that is, he was interested in them as persons, seeing their sex as an integral part but by no means the totality of their personality.[362]

Most importantly, in the stories from Jesus' experience with women, we see the attitudes and values of Jesus himself. He knowingly overthrew customs of the day when he allowed women to follow him and he brought them before God on an equal footing with men.[363] In the same manner, Jesus is stepping outside the norms of current Bangladeshi culture as he calls women to be leaders of *jamaats*, including *jamaats* of mixed men and women believers.

Remarkably, Jesus used the everyday world of women's cares to enrich his parables. In the story of the woman searching for the lost coin, the woman represents God (Luke 15:8). Jewett responds, "the woman stands for God himself, a matter which bears directly upon the time-honored (but hardly honorable) argument that since God is masculine, only men may represent him in the office of the Christian ministry."[364]

The gospels offer several other examples of Jesus' actions with women. Speaking about the Samaritan woman, Donald Kraybill, sociologist and lay theologian, says that in an "upside down kingdom" kind of a way, Jesus reveals who he is, not to the members of the Sanhedrin, nor to the scribes, but to a Samaritan woman — "I who speak to you am he."[365]

Mary and Martha: A Spiritual Response to Jesus

Mary and Martha were friends of Jesus. Luke tells of Mary sitting at Jesus' feet — the traditional position of a disciple or rabbinical student — listening to him as he taught. Jesus approved of and allowed Mary to learn of him. He affirms women's need and desire for intellectual and spiritual growth.

On the occasion of Lazarus' illness and death, John records Jesus' conversation with Martha on the road near their home. He says to her, "I am the resurrection and the life; he who believes in me shall live even if he dies, and everyone who lives and believes in me shall never die." Jesus then asks Martha, "Do you believe this?" With astounding spiritual perceptiveness, she responds, "Yes, Lord; I have believed that you are the Christ, the Son of God, even he who comes into the world" (John 11:25–27 NASB).

Likewise, Bangladeshi women participate in spiritual events and show remarkable persistence as the following story reveals. One man related this to me in 2004:

I was out on a boat for an eight-day trip where we were handing out the Book of Luke in Muslim Bangla. One day, an old woman was on the river bank yelling to us. We came over to where she was standing and she asked, "Are you the men? God came to me last night and told me to come here today because some strangers would be coming by with His word for me. Do you have a copy of God's word for me?" We did have a few complete Bibles with us and we gave her one. Upon receiving it she held it up and said, "Thank you Allah for giving me your Word, now let me go and read it to my children and grandchildren so they know your truth, so I may die in peace."

Woman with a Hemorrhage—Jesus' Response to Ritual Pollution

After healing the paralytic, and on his way to the home of a synagogue official, Jesus felt power flowing out from him. When he asked who had touched him, a woman came and fell at his feet. She had been hemorrhaging for twelve years and had used all her resources to find a cure. Because she was ritually unclean, she could not participate in religious observances. Jesus did not recoil from her touch in concern over his own ritual purity; rather, he praised her faith, "Daughter, your faith has made you well; go in peace, and be healed of your disease" (Mark 5:34).

Jesus deliberately called attention to the fact that the woman had touched him and yet he apparently felt no necessity to undergo ritual purification after her doing so. According to the biblical record, Jesus traveled on to the home of Jairus in what would have been considered a ritually impure state. Nevertheless, God heard his prayer and raised Jairus' daughter from the dead. Consider the absolute gratitude of MBB women in Bangladesh as they hear stories that free them from the bondage of spiritual pollution and that allow them free access into the presence of God.

Joseph Grassi, author and professor, portrays fascinating female counterparts of Jesus. He claims that each woman is not merely an example, "instead, *she is a necessary part without which the Gospel could not have been written*" (italics his). He reminds us that Mary Magdalene was the only one to see the risen Lord. Bringing that message to the disciples entitles her to be called "apostle to the apostles." He contends that without women's participation there would have been no witnesses to Jesus' death, burial, empty tomb, and resurrection. "Hence, Jesus would have died alone, and the story would have ended there."[366] As this gospel is preached and taught in worship services and through intentional discipleship programs in Bangladesh, women will be bold heralds of this good news to their children, families, and neighbors.

SUMMARY

Bangladeshi society and Islam have failed to recognize the worth and value of rural women whereas biblical examples abound that raise their position in society and widen their areas of responsibility. The lives of Muslim background believing women are much the same as when they were Muslims. These long-held beliefs will not be changed merely by receiving Christ as Savior. On the other hand, as men and women consider an interpretation of scripture that offers women a higher status and expanded roles, they will recognize the numerous ways women are of inestimable value to their family and community. If children are not learning of their faith, this movement of the Spirit of God in Bangladesh may very well not make it to the next generation.[367] If for no other reason than this, women must be esteemed as coworkers in the activities of the *jamaat*.

Without despising the customs of his time, Jesus subordinated them to the needs of the people he encountered, treating women as fully human and equal to men in every respect. He enhanced their status and broadened their role outside what society had prescribed by allowing them to follow him as his disciples. How can we offer them less? As men and women reason together about the seriousness of women being absent from *jamaat* activities, every hindrance will be broken down in order to ensure their presence and active participation in the *jamaat*.

Out of my thirty years' experience in the field and my PhD research, I recommend the following in order to nurture women toward a fulfilled life within the local *jamaat*.

It is imperative that we count the cost of women not being discipled. We must train women to teach and assume leadership responsibilities in the *jamaat*. The gap left by the local *imam* must be filled through materials that offer biblical stories and examples that raise the status of women. It is vital that we surmount any and all barriers to the early conversion and discipleship of women, identifying and equipping godly women whom God has already placed in the *jamaats*. We must teach all believers, especially women, in the area of power encounter/spiritual warfare. It is important that church planting teams be well-trained in the principles of discovering cultural values and worldview change. In order to offer teaching to those who hunger for it, it is critical that we pray the Lord of the harvest to send out laborers into his harvest field. We must mobilize the global church to pray for protection from the Evil One over the new Muslim background *jamaat* and all who work within Muslim church planting.

It is appropriate to conclude this paper with words of the Bangladeshi woman whose testimony is found at the beginning of this paper. She offers three ways that attitudes could be changed. I suggest that, if these were followed, women would eagerly participate fully in the life of the *jamaat*. Thus, their families and communities would benefit and the *jamaat* would glorify the Lord through carrying on a strong witness to the future.

1. They can be changed as men and women receive teaching about the importance of women — positive stories of women in the Bible must be stressed so they can recognize women's value from Jesus' teaching and example.
2. They will be changed if men leaders give the opportunity for women to take an important role in the *jamaat*. Without this, the women's fathers, husbands, and sons will not release women to learn deep spiritual truths.
3. They will be changed as women are taught that they are created in the image of God and that they have an important role in the kingdom of God. They need to know they are necessary to the life of the *jamaat*. When they are aware of their identity in Christ, men will refrain from oppressing them and women will be able to share their opinions in appropriate ways.

19

WOMEN'S GATHERINGS AND LEADERSHIP

MARY DAVIDSON

Muslim women gather together and exercise leadership during family gatherings for rites of passage, in women's religious gatherings in the extended family or neighborhood, in taking up "sacred" space in mosques and textual hermeneutics, and in more extended Muslim women's movements. How may these existing roles and needs be taken up in a Christian community for more effective discipling?

This chapter draws on my research on a women's program in a Middle Eastern mosque and two decades of living in the Middle East, together with insights from scholars on other geographical and ethnic Muslim contexts around the world.

RITES OF PASSAGE

In the Qur'an men and women are equal before God (33:35).[368] Women are required to carry out the same basic duties of Islam as men, within the limits of ritual purity and domestic duties. Performing the five duties of Islam brings merits towards the "great reward" in the next life.

Women also seek God's blessing and power for this life, to fulfill their practical duties of care for their families. In the official space of Islam, men have preference in the mosque, giving the Friday sermon to the (male) community gathered to pray, and issuing *fatwas* and rulings. However, women take central place at many rites of passage—times of transition when divine blessing is needed to help family members negotiate perilous crossings from one life stage to another. A woman in Cairo described her work of rearing and marrying off her children—caring for the family—as her *risalah* (mission).[369] The vocation of Muslim women is to ensure the *salam* (peace) of their family—their health, well-being, and success in study and life. Men's place may be in the marketplace or the mosque, earning the family income, studying texts or debating dogma. But a woman's first place of responsibility, where she is primarily judged, is family and home. Here, women are often the conservers of family tradition and faith practices. Mullin comments: "Religious power and authority resides both with the Muslim *imams* and with women. While the power and authority of the Muslim *imam* is community-based and exercised through established authority in the mosque, women will engage in rituals and superstitious practices quietly within the family context."[370]

TYPES OF RITES

The shape of rites of passage and responsibilities varies across cultures and over time. Following are a few examples from the Middle East.

At birth, women are in attendance. I went with my neighbor in a small Egyptian town to visit our neighbor's niece who had begun labor. When we arrived, the baby was just born and midwives were cleaning up. We congratulated the exhausted mother and viewed the baby while the new father was still anxiously waiting outside the house. This space and time belonged to women, not men.[371]

While men must sign the contract of marriage, women are usually closely involved in negotiations. In Damascus, women would ask if I had a daughter of marriageable age for their nephew or son. Women in the family will often visit a prospective bride to get an idea of her beauty and physical build before the potential groom meets her (dressed in more concealing clothes). Young women were once assessed and marriages planned at communal bath houses. Now it occurs at wedding celebrations, when the young women dance, and the older women watch them and talk together. At the consummation of marriage, it is the mother of the bride who visits the couple the next morning.

Women are responsible to care for sick family members. They may read the Qur'an over sick or possessed people for their healing.[372] In Cairo, a woman's role helping prepare dead bodies for burial validated her as someone who "knew her religion" and could teach others.[373]

Gatherings for life-cycle transitions are often shaped by pre-Islamic animistic customs and reveal a deeper culturally-based worldview underlying official formulations of belief and piety.

WOMEN'S PLACE

Muslim women are involved in the day-to-day messy realities and responsibilities of family and home, around which more formal faith practices must find their place. Men cannot change nappies because they would become unclean and have to purify themselves again for ritual prayers. Women have to fit in prayer around domestic duties. When women have their monthly period, they cannot participate in ritual prayer, fasting, or reading the Qur'an.[374]

The instructor in the women's program in a Damascus mosque listed the occasions when the word of one woman is sufficient for a verdict (against al-Baqarah 2:282, where the word of two women equals one man as evidence); nearly all relate to rites of life passage.

- One woman is sufficient to testify to a birth.
- If a woman breastfeeds a child, she stands in a mother relationship to it which will guide future marriage decisions (the child of the wet nurse has a sibling relation to the breastfed child, and is not eligible as marriage partner). The witness of one woman that she has seen the other breastfeeding the child is enough.[375]
- In examining a girl's virginity, the witness of one woman is enough.
- The witness of four people, whether men or women, is necessary to prove adultery.[376]
- In sighting the new moon for the beginning and end of Ramadan (times of community transition in the religious year), the word of one man or one woman is sufficient.

Instead of viewing women as on the margins, we should see their place as on the boundaries, the places of transition and movement from one stage to another. They preside, Janus-like, over border crossings from the old to the new. Muslim custom reinforces women's place amid physical realities of everyday life. Women have authority in times of ensuring life's continuity in all its messy physicality.

NEIGHBORHOOD RELIGIOUS GATHERINGS

Throughout the Muslim world, women meet together in gatherings with neighbors or extended female family members. These may be around times of birth, marriage or other life-cycle rituals, or for more overtly religious purposes such as reciting the

Qur'an or *dhikrs* (remembrance). The two categories often overlap, with religious activity bringing blessing into a life-cycle transition or difficult family situation.

In one Middle Eastern city, I would sometimes sit with my neighbors as they read through the Qur'an. Using the popular division of the Qur'an into thirty sections, each woman would quietly recite one or two sections, all murmuring concurrently until the whole Qur'an had been recited.[377] In the middle a few bottles of water stood with lids off; the water gained efficacy as the Qur'an was read over it. The house where we gathered received blessing, which compensated the hostess for her work in preparing a meal for everyone. Others outside the group would ask that the Qur'an be read with intent for someone sick in hospital or a business starting; the one making the request might contribute towards the meal. The hostess was responsible for organizing the day, but the woman leading the time of supplication at the end was chosen on the basis of having memorized the Qur'an, or having a more affective voice in eliciting the tearful response in supplication considered beneficial. Another variation was reciting the *B'ism Allah* (In the Name of God the Compassionate the Merciful) 1000 x 1000 plus 100 times. The women sat with a pile of broad beans in front of them, moving one bean to mark each repetition.[378]

In the same city, other groups of women linked by extended family or through membership in a Sufi *tariqa* will gather in a house to do *dhikr* together, and then enjoy catching up with each other over a glass of tea. During the month of Muhammad's birth (*Rabi'a al-awwal*) a woman may invite family members or friends to gather to sing songs of praise of Muhammad, read the Qur'an and enjoy food together.[379]

Other women's gatherings include ritual vows at shrines and tombs, Shi'ite mourning ceremonies, Ismaili ritual meal trays, regional pilgrimages in India, *zar* ceremonies in Egypt, Sudan and North Africa, and Bori cult rituals in Hausaland.[380]

Increasingly in the past decade, in the women's carriage on the Cairo metro, I saw young women initiating a sermon or leading in quranic recitation. Other passengers might quietly join in, murmuring the recitation under their breath. This publicly defined women's space became a place for the exercise of women's *da'wa* (to call or invite).[381]

Neighborhood gatherings may be economic-based. Jansen describes Uighur women in Kazakhstan meeting together for a meal provided by the hostess. Each participant puts in a pre-agreed amount of money for the hostess, who then pays it back in turn at other hosted feasts. Similar gatherings have occurred among Syrian women.[382] These groups may continue for years,[383] fulfilling some of the needs of women for community and life resources.

MOVING INTO MOSQUES

The movement of women into mosques and textual hermeneutics has been a notable trend in the last couple of decades. This derives partly from growth in women's literacy and education which, together with the widespread availability of material on theological issues and faith duties in various media, give women more access to religious discussion and resources. Popular media feeds and is fed by growth in conservative Islamic movements across the Muslim world which prioritize religious education, particularly for *da'wa*. Mahmood describes the place of the *da'iyya* (preacher/missionary): "In many ways the figure of the da'iya [sic] exemplifies the ethos of the contemporary Islamic Revival, and people now often ascribe to this figure the same degree of authority previously reserved for religious scholars."[384]

The leader of a women's program in a Middle Eastern mosque described the *da'iyya* as *khalifa* (successor) to the Prophet (Muhammad)—a radical shift from women seeing their *risalah* (divine vocation) only in terms of domestic space and responsibility. In that mosque, the extensive upper section was dedicated to the women's program, including a large hall, office, smaller rooms, and a library and computer area specifically for women. Only on Fridays men filled the mosque, including the women's space, for the Friday address and prayers; on that day, women did their prayers at home.

The women's program included two weekly lectures, times of *dhikr*, and smaller classes teaching quranic memorization and recitation (*tajwid*), Islamic practices, and history. When in the mosque at prayer times, women would make their *salat* (prayer) there. During Ramadan, evening *tarawih* prayers were always attended by many women as well as men, even those who never attended the mosque during the rest of the year. At the main religious feasts, times of celebration together included chorus-led religious songs of devotion accompanied by a drum—a time for women to testify how they had benefited from the program, followed sometimes by light refreshments. Women's mosques in China also offer space to do their full ablutions there.[385]

WOMEN'S MOVEMENTS

Women join in wider regional and even international networks. The following examples traverse theological and geographic spectra: Sufi women's movements, the Qubaysi movement from Syria, and women in the Tablighi Jama'at on the Indian subcontinent.

Sufism

Historically, Sufism has been a home for women's movements. Rabi'ah, a slave-girl-turned-mystic, is a famous early exemplar from Islamic history. As Sufism became more institutionalized, women's orders developed, including convents led by women.[386] Strong describes Somali Sufi women belonging to their own order and tracing their "spiritual lineage and *barakah* (blessing) back to Muhammad's daughter, Fatima."[387]

Qubaysi Movement

The Qubaysi[388] Sunni women's movement includes thousands of adherents in Syria and has spread beyond neighboring countries into Europe and the United States. Originating from the al-Nur mosque in Damascus, they met in homes for years, but their growing influence through numbers, influential family connections and the further spread of their teaching through elementary schools they run, encouraged the government to license them to meet in mosques. Some observers suggest that the movement deliberately recruits women from wealthy influential families. In the Sufi Naqshabandi order (with influential connections in the al-Nur mosque), disciples have to give unconditional allegiance to their *sheikh*.[389] A Qubaysi tenet teaches: "No knowledge can be attained and there is no way to reach God without a mentor."[390] This movement appears to combine features of the women's pious mosque movement with Sufi elements of absolute obedience to the teacher.

Tablighi Jama'at

This Islamicist movement on the Indian subcontinent is now focusing more on Muslim women as "bastions of 'Hinduistic' customs and traditions."[391] They encourage women to take time off from domestic responsibilities to form a group preaching reformist Islam to other women in the areas they visit. Beginning with three days every two months, with experience they are encouraged to go for up to forty days visiting other countries. They are accompanied by male-permitted (*mehram*) relatives, who make all decisions about the working of the whole group and the women's daily program. As well as spending time praying, reading, and listening to lectures (usually from a man) about Islamic faith and practice, women have this opportunity to share each other's lives, joys, and sorrows.

ROLE OF GATHERINGS

What role do these gatherings have? Why are they so widespread throughout the Muslim world? I suggest they fulfill five principal functions for women.

Community.

Where faith defines a woman's primary place as the home, and bonds with husband and affinal family (mother-, sisters-in-law) may be weak,[392] an opportunity to gather with other women offers important social interaction, a connection with wider community events, information and news, and often access to social and material resources. Doumato comments, "Women's meetings for ritual prayer and sacrifice, I suggest, are more than social occasions for which ritual provides a pretext. The ritual and the sacrifice (whether offered as a meal, as in the shrine picnic, or as simply the serving of coffee or food) create bonds of obligation among those who participate, and those bonds are forged into networks of women's communities."[393]

Chance to Get Out.

In the Middle East, people still quote a woman's three movements: from her mother's womb to her parent's house, from her parents' house to her husband's house, from her husband's house to the grave. Other groups are starker: Hegland cites the Pukhtun saying, from the North-West Frontier Province of Pakistan, "Women: either the house or the grave."[394] Religious gatherings give women an acceptable reason to leave their homes and meet with other women, perhaps even to travel beyond their immediate home or village environs.[395]

Roles of Leadership.

Religious gatherings offer women the chance to take on new roles outside the domestic domain. Hegland describes women competing to be "the best and most dedicated singers, preachers, Qur'an readers, hostesses, and donors." Similarly Ghadially mentions women cantors, and Tadjbakhsh has women "leading others in prayers or in problem-solving ceremonies."[396] I saw a younger sister-in-law, both quieter and more impoverished than other family women, given the role of leading supplication because she had memorized the Qur'an.

Some of these women gained their position as leaders through ability; some by being taught at home, usually by a father; or by membership in the aristocratic class, such as relatives of the king.[397] The leader of the women's mosque program which I attended was from a leading family in the city, and her brother was an internationally known *imam*.[398]

Blessing: Access to God's Power.

These rituals enable the participant to gain access to God's power, especially when she occupies a more marginal place in official religious space. Women are involved in the daily life dramas of family relationships and caring for children, responsible for family welfare in crises of sickness, poverty, or political unrest. How can they get God's *barakah*, the power needed to meet the challenges of life and its uncertainties?

Daily life is often lived without the security of financial resources, good health-care, a well-resourced education system or even political stability. Add to this the risk of the evil eye (envy) affecting a new car, a young pregnant bride or a healthy child and women face daily challenges in meeting responsibility with meager re-sources: restricted access to the official sacred spaces, unable even to do the *salat* prayer or read the Qur'an when menstruating (about a quarter of their life between the age of thirteen and fifty). So they look for ways to access God's power or *barakah* for daily life and needs through rituals.

Gathering to completely recite the Qur'an brings blessing on the house, partici-pants, and sponsors.[399] Doumato comments, "In vowing rituals women can try to bargain with God or a saint and to come away with hope."[400] Ghadially describes Shia women's ritual meal trays, "each with a set form, structure and menu," that "celebrate and invoke the presence and help of a particular historical Islamic fig-ure," such as Fatima or Ali. She mentions pregnancy, and vows related to family finances, problems, or illness as frequent causes for ritual meal trays. Tajik women are among the many women who visit shrines seeking fertility or healing.[401] Hausa women are involved in rituals for fertility, and also work "in conjunction with rural priests to open and close the hunting and planting seasons."[402]

As well as seeking *barakah*, women's gatherings also offer a way for those seek-ing to grow in religious knowledge or experience.

Maintaining or Challenging Community Norms.

Much of the writing about women's rituals views them in terms of contesting or reinterpreting women's freedom, agency or autonomy.[403] In becoming preachers or leaders in women's gatherings, they are implicitly contesting the *hadith* which teaches that "Women are lacking in intelligence and religion."

We need to see their role in social maintenance and continuing faith traditions as conservers and purveyors of the faith to the next generation. Ghadially comments that Bohra Ismaili rituals in India "facilitate both the maintenance and reproduction of the community as a social and religious unit over time. Due to their domestic role, women are the socializers of the next generation of Bohras. Children and young girls often accompany women at religious gatherings and this instills in them an awareness of the traditions and practices of the community. By bringing them together, Hajari and other women's ceremonies reinforce a distinct Bohra identity and make community cohesion possible."[404] Women seek *barakah* to preserve family and social structures.

Rituals offering women alternate or normally-disallowed roles give space to vent, which can enable women to continue in a restrictive environment. Doumato suggests that women involved in *zar* rituals were often those most restricted by physical segregation: "Women could find relief and enhanced self-esteem in the

Zar ritual, because there they could express themselves in ways otherwise not open to them or acceptable in the larger society."[405]

Life-cycle rituals reinforce cultural values and traditions, especially in times of pressure or persecution. Mother will whisper secrets of group identity to daughter, and continue proscribed religious practices in the home away from state supervision. Under seventy years of Soviet rule, Tajik women continued practices of prayer and fasting, and in women's group rituals in village communities "a female learned in religious matters would lead others in prayers or in problem-solving ceremonies."[406]

Women may be a conservative force in the face of religious change.[407] Cooper's work in Hausaland provides an interesting study of patterns of change and continuity in female leadership under pressure to move from folk Islam to more Wahhabi-influenced practices. While "jihadists" (Cooper's word to describe the conservative, Wahhabi-influenced Muslims) opposed the more animistic Bori cult and women's role within it,[408] they offered women training in Islamic scholarship. "Jihadist" women who were well-educated scholars, poets, and historians used poetry to teach women and children their specific understanding of faith and women's roles. Tomb visits were used for women to study religion together. "The leadership of this movement mimicked and drew upon the authority implicit in the titled positions for women in the pre-jihad kingdoms, even as the jihadists worked to eliminate women's access to such positions within the conquered territories."[409]

CHRISTIAN LIFE AND FAITH

In the Muslim world, women commonly gather in family and neighborhood groupings and in networks across regions and sometimes countries. In these gatherings they have opportunity to exercise leadership in a variety of roles. The gatherings offer religiously/socially sanctioned reasons for women to leave their homes for a little while, and situations where they can access community and blessing/power from God for everyday needs. In these contexts, women may either challenge or reinforce religious and social values, passing on traditions and practices across generations.

What then are the implications in evangelizing and discipling Muslim background women? Some questions may help our thinking:

Rites of Passage

- How can we help women draw on God's protection and power during times of life-cycle transitions or crisis?
- What rituals were used in biblical times?

- What are biblical symbols of God's protection and power? (e.g. laying on of hands, oil, water, bread, and wine.)
- What are the powers that threaten the women we relate to? (e.g. the mischievousness of *jinn*, the evil eye.)
- What are times of crisis or dangerous boundary crossings in their lives?
- What are ways to enable women we meet to appropriate God's protection in the power of Christ against hazardous powers or at times of risk?
- What are the everyday contexts of women's lives? How can they remember God and draw on his blessing at such times? (e.g. cooking, changing baby/feeding, cleaning, washing clothes, cleaning rice, healing, funerals.)

Neighborhood Groups

- What are the neighborhood or extended family groups in which women in our locality meet?
- How might these be a model for groups for women to learn the Bible, worship, and be discipled?

Earlier I mentioned the Uighur women's tea groups. In Kazakhstan, Christian women from different churches and of different ages started a tea group. They initially included a money exchange but dropped it when it caused relational problems. Jansen describes the groups: "When there was a decision to be made, everyone had her say. The final decision rested with the more mature (not necessarily the oldest). These teas were six-hour parties where we ate, sang, danced, told stories and testimonies, read from the Bible, prayed and ate some more."[410]

- What other models for such groups exist?
- Do we need to look at incorporating women into community groups before we look for conversion?
- How can we integrate stories of faith and life into such gatherings, so that women can see how their own stories can be linked to the great narrative of God's redeeming work in Christ?
- How can we use practices of prayer and relating to sacred text that both honor God and his complete revelation to us in Christ, and honor the lives and culture of the women with whom we meet?

Church Life

- As a church, are we ensuring that women are in programs where they are being taught and trained to share their faith?
- How do we recognize their role as conservers of the faith, and disciple them accordingly?
- What local patterns of leadership exist? What should be carried over into church life?
- At key feasts or fasts, are we giving women the opportunity to meet and participate or celebrate together?

Women's Movements

- How much do women have the chance to see themselves as part of a wider network?
- Do they have opportunity to travel with each other (or in a group with male relatives) for learning, study and teaching?
- In evangelism and discipling, how can we meet in women's groups that allow them to become part of the community in ways that meet their need for fellowship as well as a chance to get out?
- How can we offer different roles in leadership and give them access to God's blessing/power in ways that reinforce godly traditions and values within their culture, even as they become part of challenging and reforming others?

CONCLUSION

Popular images of the silent, enclosed Muslim woman overlook the extent to which women gather together and exercise leadership in family and neighborhood through to international contexts. This chapter has explored some of the common patterns of women's gathering and leadership around the Muslim world, and asks how these patterns might appropriately be taken up in forming Christian communities.

20

LITURGY TO FOCUS MIND AND HEART: FOSTERING SPIRITUAL GROWTH AMONG MUSLIM SEEKERS

RUTH NICHOLLS

In an Asian country where Muslims form a strong majority of the population, I was part of a team that used Bible correspondence courses and radio programs to reach Muslim seekers. One issue constantly raised was how to foster these seekers' spiritual growth.[411] Upon my return to Australia, exploring that question became the basis for my doctoral thesis[412] for several reasons. Firstly, I wanted to clarify my own understanding of spiritual growth, development and maturity. Secondly, I wanted to provide non-English speaking colleagues with a practical resource incorporating scholarship they would otherwise be unable to access. My prayer is that my work will provide a theoretical foundation on which others can develop fruitful practices.

My search took me down many paths and became an interesting personal journey with an unexpected result: that Muslim seekers' Christian spiritual growth is fostered by using culturally relevant, purposefully created liturgies that function like spiritual disciplines within the context of corporate worship.

THE CLAIM

The primary foundation underpinning this paper is a concern for the maturing of Muslim seekers. Within the New Testament, there is an embryonic understanding of spiritual birth (John 3:3) which is assumed to lead to maturity (1 Corinthians 3:1–3, Hebrews 6:1–3). The Apostle Paul desired this while realizing it was a goal yet to be fully attained (Philippians 3:5–15). Undoubtedly, the purpose of every epistle was to lead a particular group of Christians into a fuller relationship with and experience of Jesus Christ, their lives reflecting their understanding of spiritual truth within their cultural setting. The letters to the churches in Revelation also hint at issues of growth and maturity. The New Testament, however, reflects a church in its spiritual infancy, grappling with growth pains. Not surprisingly, issues of spiritual growth and maturity lack definitive prominence.

However, in asking questions relating to the actual nature and process of spiritual growth and maturity, finding answers proves more difficult, though some have attempted it. The mystics suggested various stages,[413] Jim Engel proposed a scale,[414] and James Fowler[415] endeavored to formulate stages of growth based on Erik Erikson's physical development scale. One complication in assessing spiritual growth is the sovereignty of God: He chooses the path people will tread that will draw them and cause them to grow. Nevertheless, Robert Clinton[416] and Janet Hagberg, together with Robert Guelich,[417] have identified broad areas of commonality and postulated stages of development. Within the confines of this paper, it is not possible to explore all the issues associated with spiritual growth and development leading to spiritual maturity. By way of analogy, if pianists are to excel in mastery and performance they must practice basic routines. Historically-based observation also points to the spiritual disciplines as a foundation and path for growth. The Fruitful Practice Descriptive List[418] recognizes the importance of applying the reading of the Word and prayer, which are fundamental to spiritual development. Yet the spiritual life requires other disciplines to be adopted as well, many of which are exercised in the context of worship.

A particularly helpful metaphor for spiritual growth in a Muslim context is that of a journey. For many Muslim seekers it is difficult to pinpoint the "birth" moment, though for some it occurs when a "power encounter," such as a dream or a healing, propels them forward. The journey concept also recognizes that salvation is not an end point but rather a position on a continuum. Further, the concept of a journey parallels and complements that of growing into maturity.

Following my exploration into spiritual maturity, I became aware that there is much more yet to know about the nature of spiritual development in terms of growth that leads to maturity. Understanding how God works in creating maturity would equip us to be more fruitful in our practice.

Given our limited understanding of this process and goal, is there a way forward? I believe it is through using the spiritual disciplines, especially since most of them are exercised together in the context of worship whether practiced as a group or individually.

THE CASE FOR CULTURALLY RELEVANT AND PURPOSE-FOCUSED LITURGIES

What I propose is the creation of culturally relevant and purpose-focused liturgies for particular contexts, i.e., with a particular Muslim-seeker audience in mind and specific to a particular situation. In terms of contextualization, this reflects an anthropological model where people endeavor to faithfully respond to God's revelation from within their own cultural perspective. Such liturgies need to be created from within the culture, in response to particular situations and in forms which both reflect and are being critiqued by God's revelation, as expressed through the Bible in that culture.

In addition, such liturgies foster a positive response to the spiritual needs of these seekers. Moreover, choosing liturgies is to adopt a form used in Islam, which has a number of liturgical forms — the *shahada* and the *salat* are primary examples. Much of the *hajj* ritual is liturgical in form. Each of these forms plays an important spiritual role within the Islamic community and affects an individual's spirituality.[419] Historically, some would claim that the *salat* was modeled on the monastic practice of the Daily Office. Indeed, while recognizing that Islam has its roots in Judaism and Christianity, others would claim Islam is a Christian heresy.

CULTIC RITUALS

From an anthropological perspective, liturgies — whether belonging to Christianity or Islam — are considered cultic ritual. Because cultic ritual serves the community/society in various ways, liturgies have those same benefits and functions. Rituals organize and structure the whole of society and culture, forming a complex web of interrelated behaviors, attitudes, and emotions while governing interaction. Rituals are determined by but also influence the worldview of a society/culture, and provide its distinctive character. Many rituals are informal, unrecognized and unspoken, while others are formal and observable, and at times incorporate pageantry and symbolism. Some have also been legalized. Many rituals lie in between these two extremes.

While rituals are the web underlying the functioning of a culture, it is cultic rituals which give visibility to a society's (culture's) cosmic (cultic) beliefs. "Cosmic" is used here in the widest sense of the word to include not only a society's interpretation of Earth and the universe but also as encompassing that society's beliefs about gods and spirits, thus underlying the society's moral and ethical decisions. Cultic rituals are forms invested with meaning which reflect a culture's spiritual worldview, much of which is embodied in the *mythology* or sacred stories.[420] Paul Hiebert, R. Daniel Shaw, and Tite Tiénou claim that the study of ritual is a necessity for "winning converts and planting vital churches."[421] They are not alone in this claim. Darrell Whiteman, introducing Matthias Zahniser's *Symbol and Ceremony*, notes that religious structures "enable new Christians to move beyond conversion to a deeper engagement of their culture with their faith."[422] Zahniser himself maintains that "symbols and ceremonies represent indispensable means for connecting Christian meaning with life's daily routines."[423] In essence, both Whiteman and Zahniser are referring to rituals in general and specifically to cultic rituals.

William G. Doty details how society is served by rituals. Below is a summary of the twelve functions that he lists:

1. convey or establish personal identity
2. provide cohesiveness
3. convey the society's ideal
4. create a sense of continuity
5. involve symbolic condensation
6. relax social tensions
7. convey or reinforce systems of meaning (cf. religious values)
8. allow dramatic enactment of feelings
9. provide for transitions
10. mobilize the community for action
11. regularize behaviors
12. for enjoyment [424]

Rituals thus serve a wide variety of functions. However, while most rituals have benefits, some are more particular in their function and in the aspect of society that they serve. Understandably, it is not possible here to detail the nature and roles of ritual within society.

What is striking to note is that each of the functions that Doty has identified parallels the needs of Muslim seekers as they journey towards giving allegiance to Jesus Christ. By way of example:

- Muslim seekers need to reestablish their (spiritual) identity (1)
- they need to learn the ideals of the Kingdom of God (3)
- having been separated from their past identity and allegiance, they need to develop new continuities (4)

- because many face significant opposition, they need to be able to relax tensions (6)
- the new worldview that they are developing needs to be extended and re-enforced (7)
- they also need to understand the nature of this new worldview and be able to express it (10, 11).

While the above list elaborates the needs of seekers primarily at a surface level, they also have significant needs at the deep core, highly emotive level of their own personal worldview where, usually, only a dramatic personal experience facilitates change.[425]

WORSHIP MORE THAN RITUAL

From a Christian perspective, worship is more than cultic ritual; it is also a spiritual discipline with both individual and corporate forms. Historically, the spiritual disciplines have been associated with fostering spiritual growth. That is, just as physical exercise develops physical prowess, so liturgies function as spiritual exercises whereby spiritual growth can be fostered. For the purposes of this paper, spiritual growth is the process leading to spiritual maturity or attaining the "full measure of the stature of Christ" (Ephesians 4:11–16). 2 Peter 1:4 expresses it as "partaking of the divine nature" or "Christ-likeness." Worship incorporates training models from many spiritual disciplines such as praise, confession, Word-related disciplines and prayer. Merely becoming proficient in training exercises does not automatically result in profitable performance; personal application of the exercises is necessary. The worshipper not only needs instruction on using those disciplines personally but also opportunity to practice them. In such a situation, a mentor plays a significant role. While it is possible for the disciplines to become mere habit, their effectiveness in fostering spiritual growth depends upon the individual's attitude and responsiveness to the Holy Spirit in allowing spiritual growth to occur. Growth is not automatic; it requires purposeful and diligent attention.[426]

Liturgy gives a worshipping community its own identity and character, allowing Muslim seekers to establish a new identity within the cultural expression of their society. Liturgy fosters cohesiveness, in contrast to the insecurity and sense of loss incurred as they move towards allegiance to Christ. It also provides a safe environment in which seekers can learn to exercise leadership roles and develop gifts (cf. 1 Corinthians 12, 14).[427] Here the word "liturgy" is used in two ways, referring both to a formalized order of worship as well as to various spoken/sung liturgical practices such as readings, prayers, litanies, and confessions of faith within that formalized order.

In addition, liturgy facilitates engagement in worship.[428] Consequently, the effectiveness of a liturgy is directly related to the degree of an individual's involvement, determined by the extent of one's emotional, spiritual, and intellectual identification with the liturgy, the relationship of the content to particular life circumstances past and present, and also the individual's personality.

Central to the Christian concept of worship is the notion that God meets with his people (through the Word) and that the people meet with God (through prayer) while expressing their love to him through service. As Hiebert, Shaw, and Tiénou note, cultic ritual "enable[s] people to experience and relate directly to the gods and supernatural forces within the context of sacred time and space."[429] While the expression "experiencing God" is difficult to define, many Muslim seekers are indeed confirmed in their journey towards Christ through an "experience of God." This "power encounter" can take various forms, though frequently it is a vision of a "man in white" who is understood to be Jesus. The testimonies of those declaring their allegiance to Christ reveal how God's sovereign intervention is intertwined with each individual's personality, past history and experiences, and current situation. Nevertheless, since the purpose of worship is to "encounter God" — whatever form that may take — and since an "encounter with God" appears to play such an important role in the spiritual development of Muslim seekers, can that be enhanced through liturgical worship?

POSSIBLE LITURGICAL FORMS

When Muslim seekers continue on their journey towards Jesus Christ, their worldview — with its philosophical/theological conceptualization, its moral and ethical stance with accompanying attitudes and behaviors, including allegiance to Muhammad — undergoes considerable transformation to a new way of living, attitudes, and aspirations. The Bible describes this as *metamorphosis*. Theological terms take on new meaning while still tinged by their Islamic and/or Islamized context. (I use the word *Islamized* because Islam overlays previous cultures which give Islam in that particular area a distinct quality and character not shared by another *Islamized* country.) For inward Christian spiritual change to occur, teaching relevant to their situation and particular needs is necessary. In both education and communication, meeting the needs of listeners is fundamental. As seekers undergo incredible mental, emotional, and in many cases social change, they need support. Taking something from the past into the future facilitates that change. Their circle of allegiance is being redirected away from their previous community and their former worldview. Thus it is important to develop an appropriate community that re-enforces their

AFFIRMATION *of* FAITH

GOD IS LIGHT

I believe that in the beginning the earth was without form and void
and that God said, "Let there be light," and there was light.

I believe that the Creator God separated the light from the darkness.

I believe that God Himself is Light and that in Him there is
no darkness.

I believe that Jesus Christ said, "I am the light of the world."

Whoever follows Him will never walk in darkness but will have the
light of life.

I believe that Jesus Christ is the true Light for anyone who sits in
darkness, and for those who sit in the shadow of death He is the Light.

I believe that God sends forth His light and His truth and with them
leads, guides, and directs those who accept His Light.

I believe that His Word is a lamp to my feet and a light to my path.

Yes, I believe Jesus Christ is the Living Word, the Light for
my world.

I also believe that He has called me out of the darkness of sin
to walk in His Holy Light. I believe that He has made me a
Child of Light.

I believe that when I walk in the light, as He is in the light, I will have
fellowship with others, and that the blood of Jesus, His Son,
purifies me from all sin.

Amen.

Figure 20.1: An Affirmation of Faith

CATECHETICAL LITURGY

LIGHT IN DARKNESS

———————

To be used responsively either by the leader with the group or
divided between the group.

———————

**Who said, "Let there be light," and separated the light and
darkness?**

When the earth was without form and void, God said, "Let
there be light," and there was light. It was the Creator God
who separated the light from the darkness (Genesis 1:3-4).
God Himself is light and in Him is no darkness (1 John 1:5).

What claim did Jesus make?

Jesus Christ said, "I am the light of the world. Whoever follows
me will never walk in darkness but will have the light of life"
(John 8:12; 9:5).

**Who brings people out from the depths of darkness into light
and teaches them to remember their God?**

All praise to Jesus Christ, the Lord. For the people who sat in
darkness have seen a great light, and for those who sat in the
region and shadow of death light has dawned (Matthew 3:16).

What does sending forth this light and this truth accomplish?

Praise the Lord! He sends forth His light and His truth and with
them leads, guides, and directs us (Ps 43:3).

How can His light and truth guide me?

Praise the Lord! His Word is a lamp to my feet and a light to my path (Ps 119:105). Praise the Lord! Jesus Christ is the Living Word, the Light for my world.

Who are the Children of Light?

Praise the Lord! He has called us out of the darkness of sin to walk in His Holy Light (1 Pet 2:9). It is He who has made us the Children of Light (John 12:36; Eph 5:8).

What is the blessing of walking in the Light?

Praise the Lord! When we walk in the light, as He is in the light, we have fellowship with one another, and the blood of Jesus, His Son, purifies us from all sin (I John 1:7).

Praise the Lord for the gift of Light! Praise the Lord for His Salvation!

O Lord God, Light of the World, help us to walk each day in Your light, Jesus Christ, reflecting it brightly to those around us, knowing that one day we will walk forever in Your eternal light.

Figure 20.2: A Catechetical Liturgy

new worldview, provides social and emotional support, and facilitates this transition, without which people can feel lost and isolated.

Purposefully created liturgies which function as models reflecting an ancient and tried educational form are able to fill this very significant role. For centuries, the Psalms have been models for prayers and hymns. The Lord's Prayer is another well-known model. Sadly, the "liturgical model" as an educational form can degenerate into mere rote learning and recitation. While rote learning plays a significant role in the educational process, it does have the following limitations, which can be compensated for, including:

- content being irrelevant to the learner at the time of introduction
- lack of personal interaction with content
- being educationally inappropriate at the time.

On the other hand, rote learning or repetitive use of training exercises can result in the mastery of techniques leading to greater facility in a person's ability, greater creativity, and more effective use of the skill. However, does greater facility in the spiritual disciplines foster spiritual growth leading to continuing spiritual maturation? While there may be a practical correlation, the degree of personal willingness to apply the skill is also a factor.

In considering Muslim seekers, the ministry of the Word is primary. Through it they are taught truths about the Kingdom of God and living as Kingdom people. Liturgical forms such as catechetical liturgies and creedal statements or affirmations of faith play a significant role. These forms, however, require engagement if such teaching is to be effective. Using catechetical liturgies (such as in Figure 20.1)[430] relevant to teaching provide those involved an opportunity to review the teaching and to engage with it as they personally rehearse it. The advantages of a catechetical liturgy are its use of question and answer, its enunciation of truths, and its ease of use. However, it also has limitations. It may not have immediate relevance to the learner; it does not allow for questioning or challenging, and it assumes a single form of learning. While historically creedal statements have tended to emerge as a response to a current situation, creedal-type statements or affirmations of truth, such as in Figure 20.2,[431] can highlight biblical teaching on a specific truth under consideration. In the world of Islam, the *shahada* creed is a fundamental statement of identity and theology. As a Muslim moves towards Christ, their previous worldview is challenged and changed. Having creedal-type statements (affirmations of faith) to ponder gives them the opportunity to "meditate" on the truths of the divine revelation that come from the God and Father of the Lord Jesus Christ. Its weaknesses are similar to those of a catechetical liturgy, but it is possible to compensate for these. Compensating for irrelevance is achieved by creating liturgies appropriate to seekers and their situation. Involving them in the creation of such liturgies strengthens their relevance. If the Word segment of a service is to have practical consequences for spiritual development, then it is important that seekers be given the opportunity to personally engage with the Word through discussion and application, thereby discerning how to obey it. Only then will personal spiritual growth be possible.

Within sections of Islam, repetitive recitation (*dhikr*) plays a very important role, often facilitated by using beads. Within Orthodox Christianity, the use of beads in association with the recitation of the "Jesus Prayer" is considered productive in facilitating spiritual growth. There are many who choose to meditate on the Names of Christ as part of their spiritual journey. But what place is there in Christianity for repetitive recitation? Some dismiss it as an example of "the vain repetition of the heathen." Yet the memorization of Scripture and its recitation is enjoined within the Scriptures; the call to "bring to mind" and "remember"[432] is a constant theme. For people from an oral social background, remembering through recitation, sometimes using song, is important.

If the Word segment focuses on God's desire to meet with his people, then prayer is the means by which people respond to God. For Christ-followers, prayer is the personal expression of their relationship with their God. Prayer for the Christian has many modes of expression. The mnemonic ACTS—Adoration, Confession, Thanksgiving, and Supplication—identifies some of the major forms of Christian prayer. Muslim seekers are well-acquainted with set ritual prayers, but their experience with extempore prayer can be limited. While prepared prayers are focused and purposeful, extempore prayer best reflects the personal response of the heart. Many of the Psalms that serve as models of prayer were first the prayers of individuals before becoming prayers of the community. Although it is assumed that people "automatically" pray, the reality is that most need to learn how to pray. Along with providing prepared prayers as models, assisting people to personally pray is an important part of spiritual growth.

In formulating worship that incorporates liturgical forms, the principles of cultic ritual are not only instructive but also provide a model. Formal cultic ritual begins with delineation or separation, such as entering a sacred space and any preparation needed to enter that space. Having entered the space, the next phase is that of *limitas*—of "not yet being but becoming." In Christian worship, this closely relates to the Word section. What follows is that of *communitas*—of fellowship and being part of the community. This is especially reflected in participation in the Eucharist, though it is also expressed in the life of prayer and service of the worshipping community. Since it is believed that the *salat* is modeled on the structure of the Daily Office, I have used it to construct several models that reflect some of the principles outlined above. Available in my dissertation, referenced earlier, these are suggestive only of possible practices.

CONCLUSION

The purpose of this paper was to present a case for using culturally relevant dedicated liturgies such as creedal statements, catechetical liturgies, chants, and prayers to foster Muslim seekers' spiritual growth. As cultic ritual forms, they service the needs of Muslim seekers on their journey towards Christ. When worship is considered a composite spiritual discipline, modeling features of other spiritual disciplines, the possibility of achieving spiritual growth is enhanced. While liturgical forms have their own benefit, including that of being a customary cultural form, spiritual growth only occurs when an individual personally engages with the content of the forms, allowing the Holy Spirit to bring transformation which leads to growth. Most importantly, if spiritual growth is to be fostered, then Muslim seekers must be encouraged to personally engage with those liturgical forms and put them into practice.

21

AGAINST WINDS AND WAVES: THE COUNTERCULTURAL MOVEMENT OF A TURK AND THE TURKISH PROTESTANT CHURCH

JAMES BULTEMA

A few years ago, a friend sent me a paper he had written entitled "From Sailing the Seas to Seeking the Strays," subtitled "A Brief Sketch of the Life of Hasan Unutmuş." Only later did I recall that Hasan Unutmuş was the first Turkish believer I met after moving to Istanbul in 1990. I realized that Hasan's steadfast course of faith not only paralleled but also typified the emergence of the Turkish Protestant Church.

The Turkish Protestant Church today has approximately 4,000 members, gathered into about 115 local church fellowships throughout the country, particularly in its western half. Two-thirds of its members are Muslim-background believers, while one-third come from various ancient Christian traditions whose numbers have greatly diminished due to persecution, discrimination, and emigration. The Turkish Protestant Church, however, has gone against the wind and waves of local religious culture and has, on average, grown at a noteworthy annual rate of 14–15% between 1960 and 2009 — more than ten times the current population growth rate of the country.[433]

When Hasan Unutmuş came to faith in 1970, in all of Turkey the number of evangelical Turkish believers from a Muslim background was only about ten; there was no distinctly Turkish congregation. There were, in Istanbul at least, a small number of Christian-background evangelical congregations, such as Bible House and Gedikpaşa, and foreign-language congregations such as the Union Church.[434] But there was no group of believers that Hasan could join and sense that he was among like-cultured people. Although he had accepted the teachings of the Bible as true, for him the Christian faith must have seemed highly unpatriotic; the earlier condemnation of the captain of a ship on which he had served must have haunted him.

THE WORD

While working for that captain, Hasan received a life-changing portion of the Word. Their ship moored in New York harbor, Hasan disembarked and headed for the nearest bar. He was actually hatching a plan to get drunk, start a fight, get fired, and be sent home to Turkey. Once there, in Erzincan, he would kill a man who had recently wronged a close Unutmuş family member. But suddenly the voice of a complete stranger interrupted his thoughts, asking, "What nationality are you?"

"Turk," replied the surprised Hasan.

The stranger then placed in Hasan's hand the gift of a booklet: the Gospel of John in Turkish. After reading some lines while standing there, Hasan forgot his plan, and returned to the ship where he read the Gospel from beginning to end. John 15:13 particularly convicted him: "Greater love has no one than this, that he lay down his life for his friends." He thought about how very different such love was from his own current attitude of vengeance and violence.

While this is just the beginning of Hasan's story of coming to faith, I have analyzed the full telling of his story along with more than thirty other conversion stories of Turkish believers. Three main reasons emerge as to why these Turks made the unconventional decision to go against the assertive secularism of the Turkish Republic and the defensive Islam of Turkish society, summed up as Word, witness, and worship: the Word of God encountered in various ways, but most often in printed, intelligible form; the witness of believers experienced in myriad ways; and the worship of God's people observed or engaged in with a local church.[435]

Hasan's story fell neatly into a Word-witness combination of reasons (the most common accounting for conversions of Turks to Christ). The influence of Christian witness upon him will be discussed later, but here we have God's Word making an initial impact upon his life. After reading the Gospel of John, Hasan abandoned his vengeful plan, chose to remain true to his duties on the ship, and wrote a response letter requesting that a complete New Testament be sent to him at a future port of call.

One could hardly overemphasize the importance of the written Word of God in the emergence of the Turkish Protestant Church. Christian workers, mostly from countries where the printed Word is abundantly available, often fail to fully appreciate the esteem and desire that predisposed Turks have for the Holy Books of God. Workers who have conscientiously gifted Turks, particularly through formed friendships, with the Bible or portions of it have seen the most fruit from their labors.[436]

In the history of the Turkish Protestant Church, there have been two periods of peak numerical growth. The first period was 1988–1994, right after the New Testament was published in modern Turkish; the second was from 2000–2002, right after the whole Bible was published in modern Turkish. It behooves the researcher to explain what happened in a subsequent period, 2002–2005, when the growth rate dropped to an apparent all-time low; nevertheless, the point remains that hot-off-the-press availability and distribution of the Spirit-illuminating Word of God in contemporary Turkish has fueled church growth to an utmost degree.[437]

OPPOSITION

Upon reaching the port of Mombasa, Kenya, Hasan was eagerly hoping to receive a complete New Testament in Turkish. As usual, the ship's mail was collected by the captain, who took the liberty to open the intriguing package addressed to the ship's cook, Hasan Unutmuş. The captain's subsequent scolding of Hasan revealed that he sensed treachery brewing in the heart of his chef. The captain summoned him.

"Aren't you a Turk?" he shouted. "Aren't you a Muslim?"

"Yes!" Hasan replied, without hesitation.

"Then what are these?" He displayed not just the New Testament, but other Christian books that had been included in the package. "Since you are a Muslim, we will throw these into the sea." Hasan could not bring himself to do it, so the captain himself hurled the yearned-for books into the water below, warning as he did: "Mark my word, there will be consequences for this."

And there were. Upon later arriving in the port of Haifa, Hasan was officially fired, due to a bad report from the captain and was then sent home, jobless.

To properly understand the mindset behind such opposition, one must first understand the assertive secular nature of the Turkish Republic established in 1923. While the founders and shapers of the republic largely sidelined Islam from the public sphere, it remained an essential identity marker for the modern Turk. Individualized and idealized though it became for secularly minded citizens, Islam has continued to be a controlling force in society. "To be a Turk is to be a Muslim" a popular saying goes, and to even consider turning backwards and downwards to Christianity is to toy with betraying the widely held notion of Turkishness.[438]

Thus, we can understand the captain's condemnation of Hasan who, in seeking a better way, was judged with betrayal. Convert after convert, both before and after conversion, has experienced such opposition from family members, friends, foes, employers, and colleagues.[439] Harsh consequences often follow, not always material in nature; the most painful is often psychological.

> Since only Turks are full members of the nation and considered loyal citizens, this perception is key to joining the mainstream society of the country. On the other hand, not being regarded as a Turk leads to the stigma of being an imperfect citizen. ...

> Non-Muslims, especially Christians, are not viewed as Turks. ... An example of this was the recent controversy involving Turkish Protestant churches. News appeared in the press ... that small grassroot churches had sprung up in the major cities. There was an immediate backlash against this ... Christianity was seen as unfit for Muslim Turks (and) alien by the larger Turkish society. ... (It is) a painful situation for the country's small Christian communities.[440]

TIME

After relating the firing of Hasan as the ship's cook and his return to Turkey, Thomas Cosmades writes, "Quite some time passed. We didn't hear anything from Hasan."

Who is to say exactly what happens during these quiet, presumably reflective periods on the road to conversion? They seem to be in virtually every conversion story, although their duration varies greatly. Perhaps, in some cases, they are simply made up of distractions, and all intentional searching for truth and journeying toward commitment are temporarily set aside. In other cases, they serve the purpose of active reorientation as one's mind, heart, and will are trying to find each other so that, hand-in-hand, they can enter the kingdom of light.

Perhaps the average Muslim's journey to the bosom of Christ is simply longer and harder than the average Christian-background believer's journey. There is danger in generalization, but I cannot help but think that believers like me have made that journey on a kind of "public transport system," with comforts and companions on the way, while Muslims, especially the earliest converts in Turkey, have made that journey largely alone, on foot, so to speak, and with an array of hazards and hardships on the way.

WITNESS AND WORSHIP

Eventually Hasan did write another letter to Cosmades, who put him in touch with two Christian workers in Istanbul. Hasan was overjoyed to meet these men. At his invitation, the two men began teaching Hasan the Scriptures, and their wives met with Fatma, Hasan's wife, on a regular basis for the same purpose.[441] Both Hasan and Fatma soon made professions of faith, as did his mother.

The family apparently worshiped at Gedikpaşa Armenian Bible Church where the pastor, Misak Günay, baptized Hasan in the summer of 1974, roughly five years after he received the Gospel of John in the port of New York. Soon thereafter, the ex-seaman Hasan embarked upon a tea-house venture as a new livelihood which consumed his time and energy to the point that Sunday worship services in far-off Gedikpaşa became impractical to attend.

The two Christian worker families began to hold regular worship services in the home of Hasan and Fatma — among the first of what infamously came to be known as "apartment churches" in Turkey. The Lord no doubt used these worship meetings to grow the young converts in the faith. But the seeds of persecution were growing.

An extensive study conducted by J. Dudley Woodberry discovered that the "lifestyle of Christians" ranked as the number one reason for Muslims around the world becoming followers of Christ.[442] From my albeit less extensive but more focused research in Turkey, it seems clear that the influence of the Word, both in Scripture and less often in supernatural dreams and visions, surpasses other reasons for Turks choosing to follow Christ.[443] Nevertheless, the witness of believers was depicted as essentially a synergistic reason in the majority of narratives. One can be confident of the enduring importance of Christlike cross-cultural workers settling among and socializing with indigenous peoples — especially in countries such as Turkey, where relatively few nationals have committed their lives to Christ, and even fewer have matured in him.

Sincere, Spirit-filled worship with believers also presents a powerful pull toward faith in Christ.[444] I think of Zinnur Turan: as a young man in his twenties, he was strongly grounded in his family's Islamic faith. He lived in Istanbul and worked in the computer industry. One day, a colleague invited him to a Turkish Christian worship service. Hardly able to believe that such a thing existed, Zinnur joined the meeting with his colleague, and the modern, lively, spiritual worship experience drew him in as no other religious ceremony had ever done. After regularly attending those worship services for many months or years, Zinnur chose to trust Christ as his Savior and Lord and be baptized.[445]

While the experience of Christian worship emerged as the key factor for conversion in Zinnur's testimony, in actuality God's Word, Christian witness, and corporate worship probably all played roles in leading Zinnur, Hasan, and the vast majority of other Turkish believers through the process of confession, repentance, and the forging of faith in Jesus Christ. However, for them all, the post-conversion Christian experience has had its dangers.

EXTRACTION AND EMPLOYMENT

The tea house that Hasan owned and operated was a financially profitable but all-consuming undertaking. When a visiting pastor came to Turkey and met Hasan, he offered to provide support for the Unutmuş family if Hasan would abandon the tea house venture. This was a difficult sacrifice for Hasan to make, but he finally agreed.

It was then decided, apparently as much for Hasan as by him, that he would open a shop and sell religious literature there as well as typical groceries. Customers became few when word spread regarding what he was selling. Anonymous threats began to come his way. Then the first drive-by shooting occurred, the bullet closely missing his head. When the second drive-by shooting occurred Hasan, husband and father of two, was nearly killed. After this shooting Cosmades writes, "The decision was made to terminate this ministry ... Hasan closed the shop."

Let us reflect upon what happened. Hasan owned his own modest business that evidently enabled him to make ends meet. Not only that, it was a tea house which afforded him frequent interaction with scores of different men. One wonders what some subtly but strategically placed Christian literature might have accomplished there. One wonders what redemptive opportunities might have arisen if Christian workers had chosen to mingle with the men there. And what if they alternately volunteered their service to free up Hasan on Sundays so that he could attend church with his family?

Instead they, or the visiting pastor, arranged for support-with-a-string: give up your business, and we will give you money. That kind of offer is difficult to resist, especially when the money comes from overseas: tax-free, even work-free, or so it may have seemed at first.

One also wonders whose idea the Christian-literature-selling shop was. Currently my family and I live in Antalya, probably the most open-minded city in all of Turkey, but I doubt how well a Christian-literature-selling shop would fare here. After the threats and the first shooting, why was the vulnerable shopkeeper allowed to carry on? After the second bullet came, and "the decision was made to terminate the ministry," who made that decision? Who, at this time, was in charge of Hasan?

He and his family were then moved to Izmir, to be near Fatma's parents. Hasan was given the assignment of visiting short-wave radio respondents in various parts of Turkey. This seemed like a pleasant enough job but, for Hasan, the worst of persecution was still to come.

In critiquing the decisions, actions, or inaction of the workers who had assumed some degree of responsibility for the Unutmuş family, I also indirectly critique myself. I too have made my share of mistakes while working, well-intentioned, with Turkish believers. Nonetheless, extracting Turkish believers from their social contexts and employing them with money from abroad has often led to ill-fated, and sometimes even ruinous, results. Great humility, exceptional wisdom, and strong love are vitally needed to serve them as we should.

PERSECUTION AND SUFFERING

After Hasan visited contacts in Nazilli, alone, and consequently suffered severe near-fatal torture, why was he allowed to travel alone to Bingöl in the east, a city almost certainly more closed-minded and perilous than any city near the western coast? Only after one safe, encouraging visit there did Christian workers accompany Hasan on his second visit to Bingöl. When police order the two foreigners to leave the city and Hasan to stay, why did they abandon their brother to the sure torture to follow?

I relate these events only to illustrate the hard realities for the Turkish Protestant Church and the missionary effort that brought it into existence. Turkish believers suffer various forms of harassment and persecution far more often than foreign workers realize. I recall many heartrending accounts I heard during my interviews with national brothers and sisters. Their suffering is real, even when not physical, and often intense, even as they praise the Lord. We as foreign workers could do more than we have to empathize with our fellow believers in their suffering and to be by their sides when they need us the most.

On March 6, 2008, I interviewed Fatma Unutmuş. Hasan had died a year and a half before; their son Ercan had been murdered some time before that. Encouragingly, a close friend and Christian worker sat by her side to give aid and support.

I asked her one question not once, but twice, because Fatma was reticent to respond: "Fatma, you've had interactions with many Christian workers over the years; sometimes we manage to do good, sometimes we make mistakes, and we can even do harm. From your perspective, what kind of mistakes have you seen us make?" The friend by her side encouraged her to be open and honest.

Finally, Fatma was ready to answer. As you read excerpts from her words, listen to her pain:

> I have two things then, if I can be honest. I mean, this is very difficult for me, because I don't want to say anything unkind ... we were asked to go to a small city, and help lead a fellowship ... they actually, I shouldn't say lured us away from another job, but it was true. Hasan was in a full-time job, and these people promised that they would make sure that all our needs were met if we would just go to this one city every week ... and then we went to this place, and then in their country they had an economic problem, and so some of the money ran out, but instead of just saying, "Look, we don't have as much money anymore, we're going to have to shut down this

project," they came to us, and acted like we were the problem ... we didn't have enough money to take the bus there, and yet somehow it was our fault, because we couldn't go there every week.

The second thing would be ... after Ercan died ... and now as a widow it's very hard for me, because we, my husband toiled for the Lord, and then, I know it's difficult, and there's reasons why they stopped supporting, but ... I just feel like there's no communication now, even though I'm still left here. I'm still alive; it would be helpful if they maybe thought of me, or maybe tried to find out how I was doing ... you would think that they would think about the family that's left.

FRUIT OF FAITHFULNESS

Despite the seemingly inordinate amount of persecution and suffering that Hasan and Fatma have undergone, their steadfastness and service yielded much fruit over the years. One noteworthy example is the establishment, under the leadership of Pastor Mesut Cevik, of the Buca Baptist Church in an historic Anglican Church building in Izmir. Hasan greatly assisted Pastor Cevik in bringing about this unlikely development and in serving the needs of the congregation. Fatma still serves faithfully, Sunday after Sunday, in the church kitchen.

During our interview, I listened intently to Fatma's version of her and Hasan's history, and found it complementary to Thomas Cosmades' version. Reflecting upon listening to her and so many others like her, it strikes me that perhaps by giving our time to really listen to the stories, opinions, insights, and even criticisms of Turkish believers, we may serve them best.

"What keeps you going in the faith, Fatma?" I asked, sensing how much she had endured.

"I fear God and not anything else," she said. "His Word is true. He's done miracles in our lives. Who else do I have besides him?"

That is right, Fatma. That is right, Turkish believers. Keep voyaging against the winds and waves of this fallen world, because you have him. And when you have him, you have everything.

22

CONCLUDING REFLECTIONS

DAVID SMITH

It has been humbling to meet the authors of these papers when they presented them at the second "Coming to Faith Consultation" early in 2010 and to then reflect on the finished product at a later stage. While the basic principles on which they have been working have once again been spelt out in a straightforward and convincing way, there is so much here that is new which pushes the boat out into the deep. It is encouraging to see so much attention given to issues relating to women, to read a fresh and deeply challenging Roman Catholic perspective, and to find many contributors creatively building on and moving us beyond the "C Spectrum." I am struck by the wide variety of contexts represented, rural and urban, in countries very different from each other. And I am impressed by the academic rigor in using sociological and anthropological disciplines to understand new data and to listen to many moving stories.

My contribution will simply be to offer two short biblical reflections and to raise questions concerning further work that may be needed.

BIBLICAL REFLECTIONS

Barnabas and the church in Antioch (Acts 11:19–26)

This short account may tell us something about our attitudes toward new developments in Christian mission. Up until Acts 7, the action is confined to Jerusalem.

When the believers are scattered following the stoning of Stephen, Philip proclaims Christ to the traditional enemies of the Jews in Samaria. This is followed by the conversion of the Ethiopian eunuch, no doubt a black God-seeker or proselyte who had come to worship in Jerusalem. The conversion of Saul in Acts 9 is followed by the next significant breakthrough when the Roman Cornelius responds to the good news proclaimed by Peter. The leaders of the Christian movement were probably surprised — and even shocked — to hear that "*the Gentiles also* had received the word of God" (11:1). Peter had some explaining to do before they could rejoice with him and conclude, "So then, God has granted *even Gentiles* repentance unto life" (11:18).

Until now, however, there is no suggestion that a church fellowship has come into being which includes both Jews and Gentiles, and this is what makes the account of events in Antioch so significant. Luke begins by relating this development once again to the persecution following Stephen's death. Some believers went to Phoenicia (modern Lebanon), Cyprus, and Antioch (near to the coast and to the southern border of Turkey), "*telling the message only to Jews.*" But then some Jewish believers from Cyprus and Cyrene (the present Libya) "went to Antioch *and began to speak to Greeks also*, telling them the good news about the Lord Jesus." Breaking out of the Jewish community in this way was revolutionary! Could it be that it needed believers who had *not* been nurtured in the Jerusalem Church to pioneer this incredibly significant development — people more open-minded, flexible, and adaptable than those brought up in "the mother church" and familiar with the thinking of "the headquarters of the church"?

What happened in Antioch was that "The Lord's hand was with them, and a great number of people believed and turned to the Lord." What did church leaders in Jerusalem think when they heard what had happened? Would they not be worried at the thought of *Gentiles* flooding into the community of *Jews* who were following the way of Jesus, the Jewish Messiah? Gentiles might not have the same moral standards as Jews, and they would not have any idea of the right way to worship Yahweh!

We can be so thankful that their response was to send Barnabas to Antioch. He has earlier been introduced in Luke's account as "Joseph, a Levite from Cyprus, whom the Apostles called Barnabas (which means Son of Encouragement)" (4:36). Note that he was not from Palestine but from the island of Cyprus. And what did he do when he reached Antioch? "When he arrived and saw the evidence of the grace of God, he was glad and encouraged them all to remain true to the Lord with all their hearts. He was a good man, full of the Holy Spirit and faith, and a great number of people were brought to the Lord" (11:23–24).

Barnabas realized that he was not omnicompetent and, being a talent spotter and the one who had introduced Paul to the Church in Jerusalem, he went to Tarsus to recruit Saul to work with him in Antioch. "So for a whole year Barnabas and

Saul met with the church and taught great numbers of people. The disciples were called Christians first at Antioch" (11:26).

Barnabas must have had a genuinely open mind as the official representative of the Jerusalem Church sent to investigate this new development. He did not come with the rulebook or liturgy of the Jerusalem Church in his pocket, intent on making sure that these people forming a mixed Jewish and Gentile church would do things exactly as they were done in Jerusalem. He was willing to be convinced that this new development was a genuine work of God. And when he "saw the evidence of the grace of God," he was glad — perhaps even excited and thrilled — to see this new thing coming into being: the very first multicultural and multiethnic church. So he simply "encouraged them all."

I hope that readers of this book will have read every chapter with the open-mindedness of Barnabas. We hear many questions and doubts — even harsh criticisms — being raised in mission circles about the insider movement and contextualization. These need to be expressed and some may be justified. But in these chapters there is so much "evidence of the grace of God" at work in a variety of ways that most readers will, I believe, simply want to encourage the writers and those with whom they live and work to "remain true to the Lord with all their hearts" and to press on in their work.

The gradual development of the disciples' understanding of Jesus

One problem for Western Christians in general and Western missionaries in particular is the considerable mental baggage we bring with us in learning how Muslims in different contexts are becoming disciples of Jesus. We know the Creeds and have some understanding of their development throughout the Christological controversies of the first centuries. We are aware of the way Protestant Reformers of the sixteenth century defined their understanding of salvation — as distinct from that of the Roman Catholic Church — and set about reshaping churches in their own countries. We are also aware of how evangelical Christians articulated their understanding of scripture and basic Christian doctrines in response to nineteenth and twentieth century liberalism. We therefore bring to the study of new movements among Muslims pre-conceived ideas about what is "correct" or "orthodox" Christian belief. Inevitably, we become anxious when new believers seem rather vague in the ways they speak about Jesus and even sometimes have reservations about using terms like "Son of God."

If we can admit that this is a genuine problem *on our part*, it may help to read the New Testament with this question in mind: how did the first disciples of Jesus come to believe that he was "more than a prophet"? Although this expression is used by Jesus to refer to John the Baptist, it may be helpful to apply it also to Jesus for two reasons. Firstly, some of the disciples at one stage described him simply as "a prophet, powerful in word and deed before God and all the people" (Luke 24:19). Secondly, it gives us a starting point with Muslims. Of course the expression does not describe adequately who Jesus is for Christians, but it does provide common ground in our conversation with Muslims who have no difficulty in recognizing Jesus as a prophet.

How then did the disciples' ideas about Jesus develop during their three years with him? As orthodox Jews who believed in the oneness of God, they followed Jesus at the beginning simply as a rabbi, an itinerant Jewish teacher. They heard him telling parables about the coming of the kingdom of God and suggesting that it was through him that God was going to establish his kingly rule. They also heard him claiming to be able to do things that only God can do, like forgive sins. They saw him perform miracles—calming the storm, healing the sick and raising the dead—things that only God can do. They were therefore forced to ask themselves: how can this man Jesus be related to Yahweh, the one true God?

Jesus never made the claim "I am God" or "I am divine" but he used several titles to describe himself which were all taken from the Old Testament. His favorite way of speaking about himself was the title "Son of Man," which certainly emphasizes his humanity, but is also associated with the heavenly Son of Man in Daniel 7:13–28 who comes into the presence of God to receive "authority, glory and sovereign power." He identified himself with the Suffering Servant of Isaiah chapters 43–53, the mysterious figure who "bore the sins of many." When he spoke of himself as "the Son" who enjoys a special relationship with "the Father," these terms would have been understood initially in their Old Testament context, where "the Son" refers to the Children of Israel as a whole (e.g. Exodus 4:22–23; Hosea 11:1) and sometimes is used as a title for the king (e.g. Psalm 2:7). Jesus claimed in effect that he was the "Son of Man" described in Daniel's vision, he was Isaiah's Suffering Servant and he was the descendant of David, the Messianic king through whom God was going to establish his kingly rule in the world—all incredibly bold claims suggesting that he enjoyed an especially close relationship to God.

When Jesus was raised from the dead, the disciples understood that he had been vindicated by God and shown to be who he had claimed to be. Then came the experience of Pentecost, when the disciples were filled with the Holy Spirit and given the confidence and the courage to communicate to others what they believed God had done through Jesus. The early chapters of Acts describe how these very Jewish disciples explained the identity of Jesus to fellow Jews. The Epistles (written between around AD 49 and 63) and the Gospel of John (probably written in the 90s) express many years of reflection about the identity and work of Jesus. Jewish believers still believed passionately in the oneness of God, but gradually came to understand this oneness as a more complex kind of unity, and used many different expressions to sum up their belief that he was both fully human and fully divine. The precise formulations of the Creeds and the introduction of words like "trinity" and "person" came more than two hundred years later.

If the faith and understanding of the disciples developed *gradually* during the three years they were with Jesus and then continued to develop *gradually* over several decades, should we be surprised that Muslims who are attracted to the person of Jesus do not always articulate their understanding of who he is and what he has achieved in the words of the Creeds or of later evangelical statements of faith? As Muslims, they have started their journey with an understanding of the oneness of God very close to the understanding of the Jewish disciples of Jesus. They had to go through an incredible "Copernican Revolution" in order to believe that the man Jesus could be so closely identified with God. There are therefore real and significant parallels between the experience of the first Jewish disciples and the experience of Muslims drawn to the person of Jesus. Thus, trying to get inside the minds of the disciples should help us walk with our Muslim brothers and sisters.

If the worldview of many Muslims has more in common with the Semitic worldview of the Bible than with the worlds of Greek philosophy, Roman law, the Enlightenment, the Reformation or nineteenth century skepticism, should we not be willing to walk with new believers and share, slowly and patiently, in their pilgrimage of faith? Muslims are not being asked to abandon their belief in the oneness of God. It will inevitably take time for them to understand how the man Jesus could be "more than a prophet," how he reveals God to us and how, in his own person and not just in his words, he communicates the love and forgiveness of God to us. At the risk of being misunderstood, I dare say that perhaps we *can and should* be prepared to put the Creeds and later theological formulations to one side, at least temporarily. New believers will not go far wrong as long as they and we are reading the scriptures together in the light of the real struggles that they have to go through.

SOME QUESTIONS

Have we found ways of communicating with "honor and shame" cultures?

We may assume that, in mission circles today, the difference between cultures based on honor and shame and those based on guilt is understood. How are we to explain the death of Jesus to people who only think in terms of honor and shame? Some Christians have suggested that we simply point to Jesus as the one who bore our shame (rather than our guilt) on the cross. L. R. Burke, however, suggests that it is vital that we help Muslims to understand the root of the problem: our guilt in the presence of God. And Colin Edwards explains how Bangladeshi Muslims use ideas like "connectedness to a savior" and being "joined with Jesus" as the person who has "the highest honor." Can we therefore say that we have resolved how to explain the death of Jesus to Muslims who think in terms of honor and shame? Can we be satisfied that we have found a way of explaining how the death of Jesus on the cross relates to the honor of God and deals with our shame before him?

Have we listened seriously enough to the critics of the Insider movement?

In the last few years, I have read more than one serious critique of widely accepted approaches to contextualization. Some draw attention to the excesses and extremes which most practitioners are acutely aware of and strenuously seek to avoid. Other criticisms sound to the practitioners as if they come from "armchair" spectators observing what is happening in far off countries from the safety of seminaries or mission headquarters. Yet some concerns may be very genuine and need to be taken seriously. If the contributors to this book have been too busy analyzing the significance of what they have been witnessing and lack time to answer the critics, perhaps it is up to others to engage seriously with what they are saying, and thus discern which concerns can be laid to rest and which might sound a necessary note of genuine caution.

Is there any reason why we are so slow to ask ecclesiological questions?

In all the research presented in this and similar volumes, I see little evidence of questions related directly to our understanding of the church. When new groups of believers are formed, they clearly have some kind of structure and understanding of how to worship, organize themselves, and relate to other believers. Are these structures and practices, including patterns of worship and approaches to pastoral oversight, determined by what seems appropriate in a particular cultural context or by the denominational preferences of the evangelists? Am I alone in wondering why there has not been much research as to what is understood by "the church" and how this relates to the realities of how these new "churches" (if we are allowed to use the term) actually function?

How can we encourage those who have followed these principles but have still not seen any fruit?

In one group discussion at the conference, I was struck by the contribution of a missionary who had been working in an African country for many years. "We've heard all these stories from other situations," she said, "and we've tried all these new approaches, but we still haven't seen any Muslims coming to faith." It is easy for us to play the role of Job's comforters and think what we might say to colleagues in such situations. We might need, first of all, to sit on the ground with them for seven days and nights as Job's comforters did. But would we then have anything more reassuring and encouraging to say than the unhelpful kind of half-truths that probably immediately come to mind?

Have we done enough research on those who have gone back to Islam?

I picked up hints in at least one chapter of some who have come to faith in Jesus but then gone back to their previous faith. I suspect that this happens more often than we are prepared to admit, and wonder whether this deserves further study. Some reasons are only too easy and painful to mention: hostility from family and economic hardship; cool reception from other believers and the inability to find a genuine family and community to which to belong. One fruit of contextualized approaches is that there is far less extraction of new believers who are able to remain within their community to a greater extent. But we are still confronted with the challenge of how to stir Christians who are comfortable with their warm, homogenous fellowships. How can we motivate them to embrace people seen as "outsiders" so that these new believers feel that they really do belong to the people of God, the body of Christ, and to this local expression of that worldwide family?

Can we see our worship as part of our witness?

In reflecting on the papers in *From the Straight Path to the Narrow Way*,[446] based on a similar conference five years earlier, I mentioned that I have always taught that there are three major factors in the stories of Muslims who have come to faith in Jesus: the reading of scripture, the lives of Christians and their sacrificial action, and some experience of the power of Christ (through visions, dreams, or healing). Having read James Bultema's chapter, however, perhaps I should add a fourth: observing Christian worship. Ruth Nicholls has asked about the possibility of developing simple liturgies which new Muslim believers would be happy to use.

And for the communities of Roman Catholic missionaries which Jean-Marie Gaudeul has described, regular patterns of worship have been an integral part of their witness. So I cannot help relating this issue to my earlier concern about ecclesiology, admitting that I myself come from (and continue to appreciate) a liturgical tradition. Does it not make sense to recognize that observing and taking part in vibrant and thoughtful Christian worship can encourage others to draw closer to God in worship? Should we not put as much time, energy, and thought into our worship as we do into our research?

How much do we share their suffering?

I was deeply moved by this simple sentence in Sufyan Baig's chapter in which he tells of the painful experiences of several new believers in an Indian context: "The church must also be prepared to suffer and sacrifice, following the example of Christ, if it is to become effective in reaching Muslims." We know about the suffering that new believers so often experience, but how much do *we* suffer — we the missionaries, the supporting churches, those who teach and write about these issues?

What am I actually doing?

I end by repeating this simple story narrated in J. Dudley Woodberry's chapter, to remind us that, at the end of the day, what we *do* counts far more than what we *say*. Did the idea come to these Christians from something in scripture, the example of Jesus at the Last Supper?

> A Christian organization imported thousands of sandals for children in a very primitive Afghan refugee camp in Peshawar. However, they decided not just to hand out the sandals, but first to wash the feet and dress the wounds of the children. Months later, a local grade school teacher asked her class, "Who are the best Muslims?" A girl raised her hand and said, "the Kafirs." When the shocked teacher asked why, the girl responded "The mujahidin killed my father, but the Kafirs washed my feet."

(ENDNOTES)

1. Paul G. Hiebert, *Transforming Worldviews: An Anthropological Understanding of How People Change* (Grand Rapids: Baker, 2008), 308.

2. David H. Greenlee, ed., *From the Straight Path to the Narrow Way: Journeys of Faith* (Waynesboro, GA: Authentic and Secunderabad, India: OM Books, 2005).

3. See, among others, Samuel Jayakumar, *Dalit Consciousness and Christian Conversion: Historical Resources for a Contemporary Debate* (Delhi: ISPCK and Oxford: Regnum, 1999); Sebastian C. H. Kim, *In Search of Identity: Debates on Religious Conversion in India* (New Delhi: Oxford University Press, 2003); and Chad M. Bauman, *Christian Identity and Dalit Religion in Hindu India, 1868-1947*, Studies in the History of Christian Missions series (Grand Rapids: Eerdmans, 2008).

4. This despite the prescient focus of Seppo Syrjänen's landmark *In Search of Meaning and Identity: Conversion to Christianity in Pakistani Muslim Culture* (Vammala: Annals of the Finnish Society for Missiology and Ecumenics, 1984), 45.

5. See Brian M. Howell and Edwin Zehner, eds., *Power and Identity in the Global Church: Six Contemporary Cases* (Pasadena: William Carey Library, 2009). The chapters of Jens Barnett and Tim Green provide many further references on this topic.

6. John Travis, "The C1 to C6 Spectrum: A Practical Tool for Defining Six Types of 'Christ Centered Communities' ('C') Found in the Muslim Context," *Evangelical Missions Quarterly*, 34,4 (October 1998): 407–408.

7. John Kim, "Muslim Villagers Coming to Faith in Christ: A Case Study and Model of Group Dynamics," in Greenlee, *Straight Path*, 239–253.

8. See his "Conclusion: Looking Ahead," in Greenlee, *Straight Path*, 285–303.

9. Daniel Bell, "The Return of the Sacred?" *The British Journal of Sociology* 28 (1977): 419–449; Rodney Stark, "Secularization, R.I.P. — Rest in Peace," *Sociology of Religion*, (fall 1999): 23; Philip S. Gorski and Ates Altinordu, "After Secularization?" *The Annual Review of Sociology* 34 (August 2008): 55–85.

10. Gary D. Bouma, "The Challenge of Religious Revitalisation and Religious Diversity to Social Cohesion in Secular Societies," in *Religious Diversity and Civil Society: A Comparative Analysis*, ed. Bryan S. Turner (Oxford: The Bardswell Press, 2008); John D'Arcy May, "Political Religion: Secularity and the Study of Religion in Global Civil Society," and Adam Possamai, "Australia's 'Shy' De-Secularisation Process," in

Religion, Spirituality and the Social Sciences, ed. Balia Spalek and Alia Imtoual (Bristol: The Policy Press); and Rodney Stark and Roger Finke, *Acts of Faith – Explaining the Human Side of Religion* (Berkeley: University of California Press, 2000).

11.   Stark and Finke, *Acts of Faith*.

12.   David Smilde, *Reason to Believe* (Berkeley: University of California Press, 2007).

13.   There is good reason for adopting the term "Protestant" as it locates a movement of a collection of Christian groups (Baptist, Pentecostal, etc.) that are not the Russian Orthodox Church, nor groups that are considered "sects" such as the Jehovah's Witnesses. It also reflects the term "Baptist," which was used during the Soviet era when referring to non-Russian Orthodox and non-Catholic Christians.

14.   The data for this chapter comes from interviews that were conducted by the author as part of PhD research that took place in Kyrgyzstan between 2004 and 2008.

15.   Mehrdad Haghayeghi, *Islam and Politics in Central Asia* (New York: St. Martin's Press, 1996); Beatrice Manz, ed., *Central Asia in Historical Perspective* (Boulder, CO: Westview Press, 1998).

16.   John Anderson, *Kyrgyzstan: Central Asia's Island of Democracy* (Amsterdam: Overseas Publishers Association, 1999); Anara Tabyshalieva, "The Kyrgyz and Spiritual Dimensions of Daily Life," in *Islam and Central Asia*, ed. Roald Sagdeev and Susan Eisenhower (Washington D.C.: Center for Political and Strategic Studies, 2000).

17.   Haghayeghi, *Islam and Politics*; John Glenn, *The Soviet Legacy in Central Asia* (New York: St. Martin's Press, 1999); T. Jeremy Gunn, "Shaping an Islamic Identity: Religion, Islamism, and the State in Central Asia," *Sociology of Religion* 64,3 (2003): 389–410; Sebastian Peyrouse, "Christianity and Nationality in Soviet and Post-Soviet Central Asia: Mutual Intrusions and Instrumentalizations," *Nationalities Papers* 32,3 (2004): 651–674.

18.   These included groups as varied as the Baptists, Pentecostals, Seventh Day Adventists, Jehovah's Witnesses, the Baha'is, the Unification Church, and the Hare Krishnas. See John Anderson, "Religion, State, and Society in the New Kyrgyzstan," *Journal of Church and State* (Winter 1999); and Gunn, "Shaping an Islamic Identity."

19.   From personal observation and interaction with local Christian leaders (including in-depth interviews undertaken as a part of this research) estimates close to 20,000 seem to be reasonable, about 1 percent of the titular Kyrgyz. See Mathijs Pelkmans, "'Culture' as a Tool and an Obstacle: Missionary Encounters in Post-Soviet Kyrgyzstan," *Journal of the Royal Anthropological Institute* 13,4 (December 2007); Julie McBrien and Mathijs Pelkmans, "Turning Marx on His Head: Missionaries, 'Extremists' and Archaic Secularists in Post-Soviet Kyrgyzstan," *Critique of Anthropology* 28,1 (March 2008); Mathijs Pelkmans, "The 'Transparency' Of Christian Proselytizing in Kyrgyzstan," *Anthropological Quarterly* 82,2 (spring 2009); Damir Ahmad, "Proselytization Eats Away at Muslim Majority in Kyrgyzstan," June 26, 2004, <www.islamonline.net/English/News/2004-06/26/article04.shtml>.

20.   Stark and Finke, *Acts of Faith*, 37.

21.   Smilde, *Reason to Believe*.

22.   Ibid., 52.

23.   Ibid., 77.

24.   The names of the respondents have been changed to maintain confidentiality and anonymity.

25.   The author engaged in both qualitative (participant observation and in-depth semi-structured interviews) and quantitative research methods (questionnaire: 427 respondents). I interviewed 49 Kyrgyz Christians (28 women and 21 men) from various age groups (all 18 years or older) and different locations around Kyrgyzstan. There are clearly more female believers than men and the data from the questionnaires indicate that there is a 2:1 ratio between female and male Kyrgyz Christians overall.

26.   *Kozuachyks* often use a combination or synthesis of Muslim religious rituals with spiritist practices.

27.   Kyrgyz generally associate Christianity with Russian ethnicity. To be Kyrgyz is to be Muslim and to be Russian is to be Christian. For a Kyrgyz to be called 'Russian' is a tremendous shame as it is understood that one has become Russian and now accepts Russian religion and the Russian God thus betraying their family, community, and faith.

28.   Conversion in sociological writings refers to any turning, changing, or redirecting of faith or of thinking. One very stringent definition is "a definite break with one's former identity such that the past and the present are antithetical in some important respects." Irwin R. Barker and Raymond F. Currie, "Do Converts Always Make the Most Committed Christians?" *Journal for the Scientific Study of Religion* 24 (1985): 305; see also Richard V. Travisano, "Alternation and Conversion as Qualitatively Different Transformations," in *Social Psychology through Symbolic Interaction*, ed. G. P. Stone and H. A. Faberman (Waltham, MA: Ginn-Blaisdell, 1970). Other theorists emphasize that it is difficult to define an individual as a convert, as anyone who has undergone any change may be defined as such David A. Snow and Richard Machalek, "The Sociology of Conversion," *Annual Review of Sociology* 10 (1984): 167–190; Clifford L. Staples and Armand L. Mauss, "Conversion or Commitment? A Reassessment of the Snow and Machalek Approach to the Study of Conversion," *Journal for the Scientific Study of Religion* 26 (1987): 133–147; Robert M. Carrothers, "Identity Consequences of Religious Conversion: Applying Identity Theory to Religious Changing" (PhD dissertation, Department of Sociology, Kent State University, Kent, Ohio, 2004), 109. Based on this understanding, while I am aware of the sensitivities in many circles of the term "conversion," I use it throughout this paper, in recognition of its academic meaning, to refer to people who have broken with or weakened their loyalty to former beliefs and developed an allegiance to Christ.

29.   The use of both terms, "Christ" and "Christianity," here reflects what could be considered a fourth conversion process, but which will not be investigated further in this paper. That process follows external social vs. internal psychological factors motivating conversion. Some converts may be attracted to the new faith or religion due to the appeal of the religious community, either material/financial or social,

while others begin considering a change due to more emotional/spiritual driving factors. As with the other processes, it can be argued that most, if not all converts, experience and in fact pursue a degree of change in both of these realms.

30.   This chapter is based on interviews of thirty-three individuals I conducted in Egypt and Lebanon as reported in my 2008 PhD dissertation, "Community and Identity among Arabs of Muslim Background who Choose to Follow a Christian Faith," Department of Sociology, University of Bristol, Bristol, England.

31.   Emile Durkheim, *Suicide: A Study in Sociology* (London: Routledge and Kegan Paul, 1952); Richard Sennett, *The Corrosion of Character* (London: W. W. Norton and Company, 1998); David Downes and Paul Rock, *Understanding Deviance* (Oxford: Oxford University Press, 2003), 111.

32.   Janet Jacobs Liebman, *Divine Disenchantment* (Indianapolis: Indiana University Press, 1998), 6.

33.   Peter Berger, "The Pluralistic Situation and the Coming Dialogue between the World Religions," *Buddhist-Christian Studies* 1(1981): 35.

34.   Sennett, *Corrosion of Character*, 118.

35.   Ali Kose, *Conversion to Islam* (London: Kegan Paul International, 1996); Nicole Bourque, "How Deborah Became Aisha: The Conversion Process and the Creation of Female Muslim Identity," in *Women Embracing Islam*, ed. Karin van Nieuwkerk (Austin: University of Texas Press, 2006), 233–249.

36.   Laurence R. Iannaccone, "Risk, Rationality, and Religious Portfolios," *Economic Inquiry* XXXIII (1995): 291.

37.   The narratives in this chapter are extracted from my master's thesis, "Conversion's Consequences: Identity, Belonging, and Hybridity amongst Muslim Followers of Christ" (Redcliffe College, Gloucester, England, 2008), in which I used grounded theory principles to study multiple belonging and hybridization among several of my friends in a Middle Eastern country. I use the term 'friends' since they *are* my friends, and also due to the clumsiness, inadequacy, or inappropriateness of other commonly used expressions or acronyms to describe this group. Pseudonyms are used and some non-relevant details are changed to protect the privacy of these individuals.

38.   The evangelical churches in Thani's homeland tend to be ethnically homogenous; that is, almost all members have "Christian" written on their birth certificates. Since this label is inherited, it primarily denotes a baby's tribal or ethnic heritage. Many local 'Christians' bolster this sense of ethnic identity by claiming to be pure descendants of the land's indigenous inhabitants prior to Islamic colonization from the Arabian Peninsula.

39.   Wolfgang Simson, *Houses that Change the World: The Return of the House Churches* (Waynesboro, GA: Authentic Media, 2003), xv.

40.   I assume that readers will have a basic familiarity with Travis' "C Spectrum" and the discussion surrounding it. See John Travis, "The C1 to C6 Spectrum: A Practical Tool for Defining Six Types of 'Christ Centered Communities' ('C') Found in the Muslim Context," *Evangelical Missions Quarterly*, 34,4 (October 1998): 407–408.

41. The term "Third Culture Kids" was coined by Ruth Hill Useem to describe cultural multiple belonging and hybridity in expatriate children. It has several parallels to the phenomena highlighted in these chapters. See John Useem, Ruth Hill Useem, and John Donoghue, "Men in the Middle of the Third Culture: The Roles of American and Non-Western People in Cross-Cultural Administration," *Human Organization* 22,3 (1963): 169-179 and David C. Pollock and Ruth E. Van Reken, *Third Culture Kids: Growing Up Among Worlds* (Boston: Nicholas Brealey, 2001).

42. Robert J. Schreiter, "Christian Identity and Interreligious Dialogue: The Parliament of the World's Religions at Chicago, 1993," *Studies in Interreligious Dialogue*, 4,1 (1994): 72. I comment briefly on multiple religious belonging and *syncretism* in the following chapter. See also Schreiter's chapter on religious identity, hybridity, and syncretism in *The New Catholicity: Theology between the Global and the Local* (Maryknoll: Orbis, 1997).

43. John Ridgway, "Insider Movements in the Gospels and Acts," *International Journal of Frontier Missiology*, 24,2 (April 2007): 78.

44. Rebecca Lewis, "Insider Movements: Honoring God-Given Identity and Community," *International Journal of Frontier Missiology*, 26,1 (January 2009): 16-17.

45. A basic familiarity with the "Kingdom Circles" paradigm is assumed here, Rebecca Lewis, "Kingdom Circles," *International Journal of Frontier Missiology*, 26,1 (January 2009): 18.

46. For example, the debate over whether MBB (Muslim background believer) or BMB (believer of Muslim background) is the more appropriate acronym illustrates this sort of hierarchical thinking. See also Peter Gottschalk, *Beyond Hindu and Muslim: Multiple Identity in Narratives from Village India* (Oxford: Oxford University Press, 2000), 35-38, a study of religious group-identities in India, in which he critiques four common Cartesian models scholars have used to 'map' Muslim and Hindu identities in the subcontinent.

47. Mikhail M. Bakhtin, "The Problem of Speech Genres," in *Speech Genres and Other Late Essays*, ed. Caryl Emerson and Michael Holquist, trans. Vern W. McGee, (Austin: University of Texas Press, 1986), 91.

48. T. R. Sarbin, "The Narrative as a Root Metaphor for Psychology," in *Narrative Psychology: the Storied Nature of Human Conduct*, ed. T. R. Sarbin (Westport, CT: Praeger, 1986), 3-21.

49. Hubert J. M. Hermans, "The Dialogical Self: Toward a Theory of Personal and Cultural Positioning," *Culture and Psychology*, 7,3 (2001): 243-281.

50. Hubert J. M. Hermans and Giancarlo Dimaggio, "Self, Identity, and Globalization in Times of Uncertainty: A Dialogical Analysis," *Review of General Psychology*, 11,1 (March 2007): 31-61.

51. Hermans, "The Dialogical Self," 248.

52. Presumably his use of this acronym was inspired by the term "TCKs."

53. Schreiter, "Christian Identity," 72-73.

54. Salman Rushdie, "The Courter," in *East, West* (New York: Pantheon, 1994), 211.

55. William James, *The Principles of Psychology*, vol. 1, (New York: Dover Publications, 1950), 294.

56. Peter L. Berger, *The Sacred Canopy: Elements of a Sociological Theory of Religion* (New York: Doubleday, 1967), 14.

57. George A. Lindbeck, *The Nature of Doctrine: Religions and Theology in a Postliberal Age*, (Philadelphia: Westminster Press, 1984), 34.

58. Lausanne Committee for World Evangelization, *The Willowbank Report: Report of a Consultation on Gospel and Culture*, Lausanne Occasional Papers, No. 2 (Wheaton, IL: Lausanne Committee for World Evangelization, 1978).

59. Inspired by a diagram in Hermans, "The Dialogical Self," 253, an earlier attempt of my own, Barnett, "Conversion's Consequences," 65, and the insights of Tim Green, "Beyond the C-Spectrum: Testing a Model of Multiple Identity amongst Christ-Followers in Pakistan," Second Coming to Faith Consultation, (England, February 2010).

60. Hubert J. M. Hermans, "The Construction of a Personal Position Repertoire: Method and Practice," *Culture & Psychology*, 7,3 (2001): 329; Hermans, "The Dialogical Self"; and Yoshihisa Kashima, Margaret Foddy, and Michael Platow, eds., *Self and Identity Personal, Social, and Symbolic* (Mahwah, N.J.: Lawrence Erlbaum Associates, 2002), 85.

61. Benedict R. O'G Anderson, *Imagined Communities: Reflections on the Origin and Spread of Nationalism*, 2nd ed., (London: Verso, 1991), 12–13.

62. Berger, *The Sacred Canopy*, 3–28.

63. Ibid., 19; Bradd Shore, *Culture in Mind: Cognition, Culture, and the Problem of Meaning* (New York: Oxford University Press, 1996), 42.

64. Ingrid E. Josephs, "'The Hopi in Me': The Construction of a Voice in the Dialogical Self from a Cultural Psychological Perspective," *Theory & Psychology*, 12,2 (2002): 161–163.

65. Hubert J. M. Hermans, "Construction of a Personal Position Repertoire," 360.

66. Indeed, in the following chapter I argue that suppression of a voice is potentially harmful.

67. Schreiter, "Christian Identity," 73.

68. See for example Catherine Cornille, ed., *Many Mansions? Multiple Religious Belonging and Christian Identity* (Maryknoll: Orbis, 2002); Gideon Goosen, "An Empirical Study of Dual Religious Belonging," *Journal of Empirical Theology* 20,2 (2007): 159–178; Jyri Komulainen, "Is a MultiReligious Identity Theologically Plausible? Some Post-Liberal Reflections," from the Conference of the International Association of Mission Studies (Port Dickson, Malaysia, July 31–August 7, 2004).

69. Some notable exceptions are Jonas Adelin Jørgensen, *Jesus Imandars and Christ Bhaktas: Two Case Studies of Interreligious Hermeneutics and Identity in Global Christianity*, Studien zur interkulturellen Geschichte des Christentums, Vol. 146 (Frankfurt: Peter Lang, 2004) and Pim Valkenberg, *Sharing Lights on the Way to God: Muslim-Christian Dialogue and Theology in the Context of Abrahamic Partnership* (Amsterdam: Rodopi, 2006), 113–150.

70. The narratives in this chapter are extracted from my 2008 master's thesis, "Conversion's Consequences: Identity, Belonging, and Hybridity amongst Muslim Followers

of Christ" (Redcliffe College, Gloucester, England). Pseudonyms are used and some non-relevant details omitted to protect the privacy of those whose stories are told here.

71.   An explanation of the terms "friend" and "ethnic Christian" is given in the preceding chapter.

72.   Derek Attridge, *Peculiar Language: Literature as Difference from the Renaissance to James Joyce* (London: Routledge, 2004), 190.

73.   Homi Bhabha, *The Location of Culture* (London: Routledge, 2004), 313.

74.   Homi Bhabha, "The Third Space: Interview with Homi Bhabha," in *Identity: Community, Culture, Difference*, ed. Jonathan Rutherford (London: Lawrence and Wishart, 1990), 211.

75.   David C. Pollock, and Ruth E. Van Reken, *Third Culture Kids: Growing Up Among Worlds* (Boston: Nicholas Brealey, 2001).

76.   Bhabha, *Location of Culture*, 121.

77.   Ibid., 122–123.

78.   Bart Moore-Gilbert, "Homi Bhabha," in *Key Contemporary Social Theorists*, ed. Anthony Elliott and Larry J. Ray (Malden, MA: Blackwell Publishers, 2003), 73.

79.   See, for example, Frantz Fanon, *Black Skins, White Masks*, trans. Charles Markman (New York: Grove Press, 1967).

80.   Paul-Gordon Chandler, *Pilgrims of Christ on the Muslim Road: Exploring a New Path between Two Faiths* (Lanham, MD: Cowley Publications, 2007), 29.

81.   Paul Henry Lysaker and John Timothy Lysaker, "Narrative Structure in Psychosis: Schizophrenia and Disruptions in the Dialogical Self," *Theory & Psychology*, 12:2 (April 2002): 211–212.

82.   Bhabha, *Location of Culture*, 172–173.

83.   Jan Nederveen Pieterse, *Globalization and Culture: Global Mélange*, 2nd ed., (Lanham, MD: Rowman and Littlefield, 2009), 119.

84.   Arnold van Gennep, *The Rites of Passage*, trans. Monika Vizedom and Gabrielle Caffee (London: Routledge, 2004), 11.

85.   Ibid., 21.

86.   Victor Turner, *The Ritual Process: Structure and AntiStructure* (New York: Aldine de Gruyter, 1995), 95.

87.   Victor Turner, "Variations on a Theme of Liminality," in *Secular Ritual*, ed. Sally Falk Moore and Barbara G. Myerhoff (Assen, the Netherlands: Van Gorcum, 1977), 40. There are also strong parallels here to Mikhail Bakhtin's analysis of *carnival*, Mikhail M. Bakhtin, *Problems of Dostoevsky's Poetics* (Minneapolis: University of Minnesota Press, 1984), 126.

88.   Hubert J. M. Hermans, "The Dialogical Self: One Person, Different Stories," in *Self and Identity Personal, Social, and Symbolic*, ed. Yoshihisa Kashima, Margaret Foddy, and Michael Platow (Mahwah, NJ: Lawrence Erlbaum Associates, 2002),78, 95.

89.   Turner, *Ritual Process*, 128. See also John 10:9.

90. John McLeod, *Beginning Postcolonialism* (Manchester: Manchester University Press, 2000), 218–219.

91. Mikhail M. Bakhtin, "Discourse in the Novel," in *The Dialogic Imagination: Four Essays,* ed. Michael Holquist, trans. Caryl Emerson and Michael Holquist (Austin: University of Texas Press, 1981), 293–294.

92. The Qur'an contrasts *islam* (submission) and *iman* (faith) declaring: "The desert Arabs say, 'We believe.' Say to them, 'You do not believe'; you should rather say, 'We have become Muslims [lit. we submitted],' for faith has not yet entered your hearts'" (Surah 49:14, my translation). Ibn Kathir, in his commentary on this verse and its related *ahadith* states, "the Prophet made a distinction between the grade of believer [*mu'min*] and the grade of Muslim, indicating that Iman [faith] is a more exclusive grade than Islam." Isma'il ibn 'Umar ibn Kathir, *Tafsir ibn Kathir,* abridged ed., ed. and trans. Ṣafi al-Raḥman Mubarakfuri (Riyadh: Darussalam, 2003).

93. Chandler, *Pilgrims of Christ*, 187.

94. Bhabha, *Location of Culture*, 322.

95. Dale Eickelman and James Piscatori, "Social Theory in the Study of Muslim Societies," in *Muslim Travellers: Pilgrimage, Migration, and the Religious Imagination*, ed. Dale Eickelman and James Piscatori (Los Angeles: University of California Press), 17.

96. Chandler, *Pilgrims of Christ*, 196.

97. Ying-yi Hong, Michael W. Morris, Chi-yue Chiu, and Verónica Benet-Martínez, "Multicultural Minds: A Dynamic Constructivist Approach to Culture and Cognition," *American Psychologist*, 55:7 (July 2000): 710.

98. Maykel Verkuyten, and Katerina Pouliasi, "Biculturalism among Older Children: Cultural Frame Switching, Attributions, Self-Identification, and Attitudes," *Journal of Cross-Cultural Psychology*, 33:6 (November 2002): 596–609.

99. Ingrid E. Josephs, "'The Hopi in Me': The Construction of a Voice in the Dialogical Self from a Cultural Psychological Perspective," *Theory & Psychology*, 12:2 (2002): 162.

100. cf. 1 Corinthians 14; 2 Peter 1:21.

101. Chandler, *Pilgrims of Christ*, 107.

102. Clifford Geertz, "'Internal Conversion' in Contemporary Bali," in Clifford Geertz, *The Interpretation of Cultures: Selected Essays* (New York: Basic Books, 1973), 170–189.

103. Lewis R. Rambo, *Understanding Religious Conversion* (New Haven: Yale University Press, 1993), 13.

104. Anthony Wallace, *Revitalizations and Mazeways: Essays on Culture Change,* vol. 1, ed. Robert Steven Grumet, (Lincoln: University of Nebraska Press, 2004).

105. See Awal's comments in the preceding chapter.

106. A. Scott Moreau, s.V. "Syncretism," in *Evangelical Dictionary of World Missions*, ed. A. Scott Moreau, Harold A. Netland, Charles van Engen, and David Burnett (Grand Rapids: Baker, 2000), 924.

107. Jonathan J. Bonk, "The Defender of the Good News: Questioning Lamin Sanneh," *Christianity Today*, October 2003, <www.christianitytoday.com/ct/2003/october/35.112.html>.

108.   This quotation was given to me in 2010 by a personal contact. For the remainder of this chapter I will not reference personal conversations.

109.   Seppo Syrjänen, *In Search of Meaning and Identity: Conversion to Christianity in Pakistani Muslim Culture* (Vammala: Annals of the Finnish Society for Missiology and Ecumenics, 45, 1984).

110.   Paul-Gordon Chandler, *Pilgrims of Christ on the Muslim Road* (Lanham, MD: Cowley Publications, 2007), 105.

111.   Ibid., 106–107.

112.   Ibid., 104.

113.   Kathryn Kraft, "Community and Identity among Arabs of a Muslim Background who Choose to Follow a Christian Faith" (PhD dissertation, Bristol: University of Bristol, 2008). See also Kathryn Kraft, *Searching for Heaven in the Real World: A Sociological Discussion of Conversion in the Arab World*, Oxford 2012 Regnum, Regnum Studies in Mission series.

114.   Psychologists writing on identity include William James, Erik Erikson, and Galen Strawson; sociologists include Kurt Lewin and Evaitur Zerubavel; social psychologists include Henri Tafjel, George Herbert Mead, and Sheldon Stryker; sociologists of religion include Peter Berger and Thomas Luckmann; but the list is almost endless.

115.   Anthony Giddens 1990, cited in Stuart Hall, "The Question of Cultural Identity," in *Modernity and its Future*, ed. Stuart Hall, David Held, and Tony McGrew (Cambridge: Polity Press, 1992), 275–316.

116.   Jean-Marie Gaudeul, *Called from Islam to Christ: Why Muslims become Christians* (Crowborough, England: Monarch, 1999), 225–26.

117.   Stuart Hall, "The Question of Cultural Identity," in Hall, *Modernity and its Future*, 275–31. Michel Foucault has strongly influenced postmodern notions of identity.

118.   Benjamin Beit-Hallahmi, *Prolegomena to the Psychological Study of Religion* (London: Associated University Press, 1989), 96–97. Emphasis added.

119.   I slightly adapted his descriptions of each level and have added the "individual-corporate" axis. Kathryn Kraft and I, in jointly presenting our model of identity at the "Bridging the Divide" consultation in 2012, decided that "core identity" is more readily understood than the technical term "ego identity" derived from psychology.

120.   Rudolf C. Heredia, *Changing Gods: Rethinking Conversion in India* (London: Penguin, 2007), 3.

121.   Kraft, "Community and Identity," 156.

122.   Kenneth Cragg, *The Dome and the Rock* (London: SPCK, 1964), 148.

123.   Peter Berger, *The Sacred Canopy: Elements of a Sociological Theory of Religion* (New York: Doubleday, 1967).

124.   Erik Erikson, "Identity and the Life Cycle," *Psychological Issues*, 1:1, (New York: International Universities Press, 1959), 102, cited in V. B. Gillespie, *The Dynamics of Religious Conversion* (Birmingham, AL: Religious Education Press, 1991), 136.

125.   James Fowler, *Stages of Faith: The Psychology of Human Development and the Quest for Meaning* (San Francisco: Harper & Row, 1981). I notice strong links here with theories

of transformative learning in the field of adult education in the writings of Paulo Freire, Jack Mezirow, and Stephen Brookfield.

126.   Benjamin Beit-Hallahmi, *Prolegomena*, 100.

127.   Chandler, *Pilgrims*, 102.

128.   Dilwar Hussain, "British Muslim Identity," in Muhammad Seddon, Dilwar Hussain and Nadeem Malik, *British Muslims Between Assimilation and Segregation: Historical, Legal and Social Realities* (Leicester, England: Islamic Foundation, 2004), 83. Note how crises have proved a catalyst for Muslim communities in the West to reflect on, intensify, and declare their personal commitment to Islam. This happened in Britain with the Salman Rushdie affair in 1989, and in the USA with the 9/11 attacks in 2001 and their aftermath.

129.   See, for example, the postings at <www.ex-muslims.org.uk>.

130.   Lewis R. Rambo, *Understanding Religious Conversion* (New Haven: Yale University Press, 1993).

131.   Peter Berger and Thomas Luckmann, *The Social Construction of Reality: A Treatise in the Sociology of Knowledge* (New York: Doubleday, 1966).

132.   Heredia, *Changing Gods*, 127.

133.   See also Rom. 6:6 and Gal. 2:20.

134.   Note that in Islamic thought *jihad* includes the spiritual struggle, not just the military.

135.   Berger and Luckmann, *Construction of Reality*, 145.

136.   Ibid., 131, 144.

137.   Berger, *Sacred Canopy*, 22.

138.   Ziya Meral, "Conversion and Apostasy: A Sociological Perspective," *Evangelical Missions Quarterly*, 42:4 (October 2006): 508–513.

139.   Thomas Walsh, "Voices from Christians in Britain with a Muslim Background: Stories for the British Church on Evangelism, Conversion, Integration and Discipleship," MA thesis, Birmingham: University of Birmingham, 2005. Don Little, "Effective Insider Discipling: Helping Arab World Believers from Muslim Backgrounds Persevere and Thrive in Community," DMin dissertation, South Hamilton, MA, Gordon-Conwell Theological Seminary, 2009.

140.   Chandler, *Pilgrims*, 102.

141.   Mariam al Hakeem, "Saudi Man Kills Daughter for Converting to Christianity," *Gulf News*, <http://archive.gulfnews.com/articles/08/08/12/10236558.html>, August 12, 2008. The poem is available on many websites including <www.strateias.org/fatima.pdf>.The blog was posted originally at <http://muslmah.blogspot.com/2008/08/blog-post.html>.

142.   "Nazir" is a pseudonym. The interview was recorded February 14, 2009. Throughout this chapter references are not given in cases where I received the information personally.

143.   The traditional long shirt and baggy trousers worn in Pakistan.

144. Ron Geaves believes that recent years have seen "a shift from notions of a fragmented self torn between culture and religion and ethnicity" and "Britishness" to that of a "multi-layered self" with a genuine "hybrid British Muslim identity" now emerging; Ron Geaves, "Negotiating British Citizenship and Muslim Identity," in *Muslim Britain*, ed. Tahir Abbas (London: Zed Books, 2005), 76-77. Humayun Ansari and Philip Lewis agree.

145. This adjective is derived from "Isa" (Jesus), in the same way as "Christian" is derived from "Christ."

146. Jens Barnett and I developed this diagram based on Abu Taher Chowdhury's categories.

147. Paul G. Hiebert, "The Category 'Christian' in the Mission Task," *International Review of Mission* 72 (July 1983): 421-27. Hiebert helpfully draws distinctions between "bounded," "centred," and "fuzzy" sets.

148. I am told that this is exactly what happened to a previous movement to Christ from Islam in Bangladesh several decades ago.

149. John Travis, "The C1 to C6 Spectrum: A Practical Tool for Defining Six Types of 'Christ Centered Communities' ('C') Found in the Muslim Context," *Evangelical Missions Quarterly*, 34,4 (October 1998): 407–408.

150. This is different from the many believers who manage to sustain a semi-secret identity for years quite successfully; they reveal to some people their allegiance to Christ, but not to all.

151. Roland Müller, *The Messenger, The Message, The Community*, (n.p.: Canbooks, 2006), 108–109.

152. Kenneth Cragg, *The Call of the Minaret* (Dublin: Collins, 2001), 318. (First published in 1956.)

153. David Greenlee, *One Cross, One Way, Many Journeys: Thinking Again about Conversion* (Atlanta: Authentic, 2007), 68.

154. Kevin Higgins, "Speaking the Truth about Insider Movements," *St. Francis Magazine*, 5:6 (December 2009) <www.stfrancismagazine.info/ja/7%20KevinHiggins-SpeakingTruth.pdf>.

155. The debate continues especially in the journals *International Journal of Frontier Missions* <www.ijfm.org> and *St. Francis Magazine* <www.stfrancismagazine.info>.

156. Peter Mandaville, *Transnational Muslim Politics: Reimagining the Umma* (London: Routledge, 2001), 115.

157. Ghulam Haider Aasi, *Muslim Understanding of Other Religions: A Study of Ibn Hazm's Kitab al-Fasl fi al-Milal wa al-Ahwa' wa al-Nihal* (Islamabad, Pakistan: Islamic Research Institute Press, 1999), 9.

158. M. Houtsma, A. Wensinck, H. Gibb, W. Heffening, and E. Levi-Provencal, *The Encyclopaedia of Islam*, vol. 4 (Leyden: Late E. J. Brill Ltd., 1934), 1015.

159. Robert Nisbet, *The Sociological Tradition* (New York: Basic Books, 1996), 47–48.

160. L. Broom and P. Selznick, *Sociology: A Text with Adapted Readings* (New York: Harper and Rowe, 1968), 31.

161.   Hammudah Abd-al Ati, *Islam in Focus* (Indianapolis: American Trust Publications, 1975), 38.

162.   Tariq Ramadan, *To Be a European Muslim* (Leicester: The Islamic Foundation, 1999), 158.

163.   Allama Abdullah Yusuf Ali, *The Meaning of the Illustrious Quran* (New Delhi: Kitab Bhavan, 1982), 34.

164.   Phil Parshall, *Beyond the Mosque* (Grand Rapids: Baker, 1985), 30.

165.   Dale Eickelman and James Piscatori, "Social Theory in the study of Muslim Societies," in *Muslim Travellers: Pilgrimage, Migration, and the Religious Imagination*, ed. Dale Eickelman and James Piscatori (London: Routledge, 1997), 4.

166.   Henri Tajfel, *Differentiation between Social Groups: Studies in the Social Psychology of Intergroup Relations* (London: Academic Press, 1978), 63.

167.   Arun Shourie, *Missionaries in India* (New Delhi: ASA Publications, 1994), 11.

168.   Unless otherwise noted, the stories in this chapter are drawn from my interviews with individuals — names changed to protect their privacy — that took place in various locations of central and northern India in May and September 2002.

169.   Gordon Nickel, *Peaceable Witness Among Muslims* (Windsor, Ontario: Herald Press, 1999), 57.

170.   "Fruitful Practices: A Descriptive List," in *Where there was No Church: Postcards from Followers of Jesus in the Muslim World*, ed. E. J. Martin (n.p.: Fruitful Practice Research and Learning Together Press, 2010), 195–196.

171.   Bevan Jones, *The People of the Mosque: An Introduction to the Study of Islam with Special Reference to India* (Calcutta: Association Press, YMCA, 1932), 327–328.

172.   I was involved in discipling Abdul during his search for Christ and, after his death, interviewed members of the church Abdul attended.

173.   I was an eyewitness to the incident related.

174.   H. B. Dehqani-Tafti, *Design of My World: Pilgrimage to Christianity* (New York: Seabury, 1982), 79–80.

175.   See "Fruitful Practices, A Descriptive List" in Martin, ed., *Where there was No Church*, 165.

176.   Jones, *People of the Mosque*, 330.

177.   Howard A. Snyder, "The Church as Community: Subculture or Counterculture?" *Christianity Today*, April 8, 1983: 32.

178.   Nickel, *Peaceable Witness*, 47.

179.   Mdimi G. Mhogolo, "A Vision of Full Humanity: An African Perspective," *Transformation* (January 1998): 6–10.

180.   For a good introduction to these issues see Jerome H. Neyrey and Bruce Malina, eds. *The Social World of Luke-Acts* (Peabody, MA: Hendrickson 1991), 25–96. For a fuller, more nuanced approach and the descriptions of horizontal and vertical collectivism see Harry C. Triandis, *Individualism and Collectivism* (Boulder, CO: Westview Press, 1995).

181. Triandis, *Individualism and Collectivism.*

182. Louis Dumont, *Homo Hierarchicus: The Caste System and its Implications*, rev. English ed. (New Delhi: Oxford University Press, 1980).

183. David Abecassis, *Identity, Islam and Human Development in Rural Bangladesh* (Dhaka: University Press, 1990), 38.

184. Most leaders are indeed male in this patriarchal setting.

185. S. N. Eisenstadt and Louis Roniger "Patron-Client Relationships as a Model of Structuring Social Exchange," *Comparative Studies in Society and History* 22,1 (1980): 42–47. This is one of the touchstone papers on patronage.

186. Abecassis, *Islam and Human Development*, 29.

187. *The Alim*, ver. 6.0.11.1, (Silver Spring, MD: ISL Software Corp, 1986–1990), CD-ROM.

188. See Romans 6:3–4, 8–12.

189. For example, Colin Chapman states that "it is essential for Christians to realise that the Qur'an is to Muslims what Jesus is to Christians. It is a mistake to make a direct comparison between the role of Jesus in Christianity and the role of Muhammad in Islam." Colin Chapman, *Cross and Crescent: Responding to the Challenge of Islam* (Leicester, England: InterVarsity, 1995), 76.

190. Paul Hattaway, s.V. "Hui," *Operation China* (Colorado Springs, CO: Global Mapping International, 2002), CD-ROM.

191. This chapter is based on my PhD dissertation, "Receptor-Oriented Communication for Hui Muslims in China: With Special Reference to Church Planting" (Pasadena, CA: Fuller Theological Seminary, 2009).

192. Hattaway, "Hui."

193. Dru C. Gladney, *Ethnic Identity in China: The Making of a Muslim Minority Nationality*, Case Studies in Social Anthropology series, ed. George and Louise Spindler (Forth Worth, TX: Harcourt Brace College Publishers, 1998), 12.

194. Andrew G. Findlay, *The Crescent in North-West China* (London: China Inland Mission, 1921).

195. Muzhi Zho, 城市化: 中国现代化的主旋律 (*Urbanization: Theme of China's Modernization*) (Hunan, China: Hunan People's Publishing House, 2000), 10. Author's translation.

196. Robert L. Worden, et. al, *China: A Country Study* (Washington D.C.: Library of Congress, Federal Research Division, 1987), <http://memory.loc.gov/frd/cs/cntoc.html>.

197. Bob Hitching, *McDonalds, Minarets, and Modernity* (Kent, England: Spear, 1996).

198. William G. Flanagan, *Contemporary Urban Sociology* (Cambridge and New York: Cambridge University Press, 1993), 21.

199. Claude S. Fischer, *The Urban Experience*, 2nd ed. (San Diego: Harcourt Brace Jovanovich, 1984), 114.

200. Edwin Eames and Judith Granich Goode, *Anthropology of the City: An Introduction to Urban Anthropology* (Englewood Cliffs, NJ: Prentice-Hall, 1977).

201. Fischer, *Urban Experience*, 115, 120.

202. Martin King Whyte and William L. Parish, eds. *Urban Life in Contemporary China* (Chicago, IL: University of Chicago Press, 1984), 191.

203. Martin King Whyte, ed. *China's Revolutions and Intergenerational Relations* (Ann Arbor, MI: Center for Chinese Studies, University of Michigan, 2003), 85–111.

204. Whyte and Parish, *Urban Life*, 353–354.

205. Maris Boyd Gillette. *Between Mecca and Beijing: Modernization and Consumption among Urban Chinese Muslims* (Stanford, CA: Stanford University Press, 2000), 219.

206. Eames and Goode, *Anthropology of the City*, 160.

207. Ibid., 214.

208. Ibid.

209. Raphael Israeli, *Muslims in China: A Study in Cultural Confrontation* (Bangkok: Curzon and Humanities, 1980), 120.

210. For further details about Azerbaijan see <www.azerbaijan.az>.

211. The names of all respondents have been changed to protect their privacy. Unless noted, interviews took place in November 2004.

212. Most of the believers in Azerbaijan came to know and profess Christ in the late 1990s. Thus, at the time of my interviews with most of them, including BSN leaders, their faith was less than ten years old.

213. Some thoughts in this conclusion drawn from William Carr Peel and Walt Larimore, *Going Public with Your Faith: Becoming a Spiritual Influence at Work* (Grand Rapids: Zondervan, 2003), 210.

214. Some paragraphs of this essay appeared in "Contextualization without Syncretism," *International Journal of Frontier Missiology*, 23/3 (July 2006): 127–133 and "Contextualization, Indigenization, and Syncretism," in *Global Mission: Reflections and Case Studies in Local Theology for the Whole Church*, ed. Rose Dowsett (Pasadena: William Carey Library and WEA Mission Commission, 2011). I wish to acknowledge a number of helpful suggestions and revisions to the present paper from VJ Gresham and Doug and Anne Sampson.

215. In *Worldview for Christian Witness* (Pasadena: William Carey Library, 2008), 12, Charles Kraft describes worldview as "the totality of the culturally structured images and assumptions (including value and commitment or allegiance assumptions) in terms of which a people both perceive and respond to reality."

216. In Acts 22:3 and 23:4, Paul begins his message by identifying with the religious Jews and in particular with the Pharisees, while in general he begins his preaching to Jews and proselytes by citing OT passages. But when Paul preaches to Greeks at the Areopagus in Athens (Acts 17:22–31), he begins by praising their religious concerns and by affirming the principle that all ethnic groups should seek God because he created them all from one man (Acts 17:26–27), supporting his statements with relevant quotations from two Greek poets (v.28).

217. For a brief summary see Rick Brown, "Like Bright Sunlight: The Benefit of Communicating in Heart Language," *International Journal of Frontier Missiology*, 26,2 (April 2009): 85–88.

218. Eric Adams, Don Allen, and Bob Fish, "Seven Themes of Fruitfulness," *International Journal of Frontier Missiology*, 26,2 (April 2009): 75–81.

219. Ibid., 79. The article, with a chart summarizing these findings, can be viewed at <www.ijfm.org/26_2.htm>.

220. Larry Owens, "Syncretism and the Scriptures," *Evangelical Missions Quarterly*, 43,1 (January 2007): 74–80.

221. Paul Hiebert, "Critical Contextualization," *International Bulletin of Missionary Research*, 11,3 (July 1987): 104–112.

222. Darrell Whiteman "Contextualization: The Theory, The Gap, The Challenge," *International Bulletin of Missionary Research*, 21,1 (January 1997):2. Emphasis added.

223. Ibid.

224. For a thorough discussion of the biblical mandate for contextualization, see Dean Flemming, *Contextualization in the New Testament: Patterns for Theology and Mission* (Downers Grove: InterVarsity Press, 2005).

225. There are Scriptures that endorse kneeling, bowing to the ground, and raising hands in prayer, such as Psalm 95:6 — "Come, let us bow down in worship, let us kneel before the LORD our Maker" and Psalm 134:2 — "Lift up your hands in the sanctuary and praise the LORD." The Bible provides several models of prayer posture, but does not say they are necessary in order for prayers to be effective.

226. Roland Müller, *Honor and Shame: Unlocking the Door* (Philadelphia: Xlibris, 2000).

227. David W. Augsburger, *Conflict Mediation across Cultures: Pathways and Patterns* (Louisville, KY: Westminster/John Knox Press), 82.

228. Ibid., 124.

229. In 1996, the German missiologist Klaus Müller, put shame on an axis with prestige, and guilt on an axis with justice. Klaus Müller, "Elenktik: Die Lehre vom Scham- und Schuldorientierten Gewissen" (Elenctics: The Theory of Shame and Guilt Oriented Conscience), *Evangelikale Missiologie* 4 (1996), 98–110; see also Klaus Müller, *Das Gewissen in Kultur und Religion: Scham- und Schuldorientierung als empirisches Phänomen des Über-Ich / Ich-Ideal* (The Conscience in Culture and Religion: Shame and Guilt Orientation as an Empirical Phenomenon of the Superego/Ego Ideal) (Nuremberg, Germany: VTR, 2010). Ruth Lienhard adopted this model, arguing that "shame and guilt are but expressions of the more underlying core values of honor and justice." Ruth Lienhard, "Restoring Relationships: Theological Reflections on Shame and Honor among the Daba and Bana of Cameroon," PhD dissertation, School of Intercultural Studies, Fuller Theological Seminary, Pasadena, CA, 2000: 19.

230. Roland Müller, *The Messenger, the Message and the Community: Three Critical Issues for the Cross-Cultural Church Planter* (Istanbul, Turkey: Anadolu Ofset, 2006), 146.

231. R. Müller, *Honor and Shame*, 70.

232. Larry R. Burke, "Culture and Fruitful Practices in Muslim Ministry" (Narrative Review Fellowship, Fruitful Practices Research, 2008), 30. Available upon request from Fruitful Practice Research at info@fruitfulpractice.org.

233. *The Qur'an: Arabic Text and English Translation*, trans. M.H. Shakir (Elmhurst, N.Y.: Tahrike Tarsile Qur'an, 1999).

234. The full quotation states: "As Muslims, we do not accuse Adam and Eve of transmitting sin and evil to the whole of mankind. The two were absolved of their sin, and their descendants made immune from its effects. Sin is not original, hereditary, or inevitable . . . Muslims believe that man is fundamentally a good and dignified creature. He is not a fallen being." Badru D. Kateregga and David W. Shenk, *A Muslim and a Christian in Dialogue* (Scottdale, PA: Herald Press, 1997), 141.

235. Martin Lomen, "Benefits on the Shame-oriented Perspective for Theology and Missions" unpublished: 17. See also Martin Lomen, *Sünde und Scham im Biblischen und Islamischen Kontext: Eine Ethno-Hermeneutischer Beitrag zum Christlich-Islamischen Dialog* (Sin and Shame in Biblical and Islamic Context: An Ethno-hermeneutical Contribution to Christian-Islamic Dialog) (Nuremberg, Germany: VTR, 2003).

236. Lomen, "Benefits," 8.

237. R. Müller, *Honor and Shame*, 103.

238. Lomen, "Benefits," 8.

239. Ibid.

240. I offered a model for presenting the Gospel beginning with the theme of purity during the consultation at which chapters for this book were first presented, "That They Might See Him for Who He Is: Community, Shame, and Purity in the Muslim Context," Second Coming to Faith Consultation, (England, February 2010).

241. Lomen, "Benefits," 17.

242. Reinhold Straehler, "Coming to Faith in Christ: Case Studies of Muslims in Kenya," DTh dissertation, (Pretoria, University of South Africa, 2009), available at <http://uir.unisa.ac.za/bitstream/10500/3527/1/dissertation_straher_r.pdf>.

243. Andrew F. Walls, "Converts or Proselytes? The Crisis over Conversion in the Early Church," *International Bulletin of Missionary Research* 28,1 (January 2004): 2.

244. Millard J. Erickson, *Christian Theology*, (Grand Rapids: Baker), 935, 938; Wayne Grudem, *Systematic Theology: An Introduction to Biblical Doctrine* (Leicester, England: InterVarsity, 1994), 713.

245. Erickson, *Christian Theology*, 937.

246. Johannes Behm, s.V. "Metanoeo," in Gerhard Kittel and Gerhard Friedrich, trans. Geoffrey W. Bromiley, *Theological Dictionary of the New Testament*, Vol. 4, (Grand Rapids: Eerdmans, 1976).

247. Erickson, *Christian Theology*, 939.

248. James F. Engel, "The Road to Conversion: The Latest Research Insights," *Evangelical Missions Quarterly* 26,2 (April 1990): 184–193.

249. Viggo Søgaard, *Research in Church and Mission* (Pasadena: William Carey Library, 1996), 56–61.

250. Frank Gray and Ross James, *Radio Programming Roles: FEBC Perspectives* (La Mirada, CA: Far East Broadcasting Company, 1997): 50.

251. Paul G. Hiebert, *Anthropological Reflections on Missiological Issues* (Grand Rapids: Baker, 1994), 122–131.

252. Reinhold Straehler, "Conversions from Islam to Christianity in the Sudan," MTh dissertation (Pretoria, University of South Africa, 2005), available at <http://uir.unisa.ac.za/bitstream/handle/10500/2438/dissertation.pdf?sequence=1>.

253. Changes that take place during the process of conversion are catalyzed by significant factors in the form of causal and intervening conditions. These factors, together with a typology of different conversion processes, are described in details in Straehler 2009.

254. Timothy C. Tennent, "Followers of Jesus (Isa) in Islamic Mosques: A Closer Examination of C5 'High Spectrum' Contextualization," *International Journal of Frontier Missiology* 23,3 (July 2006): 113.

255. David Greenlee, *One Cross, One Way, Many Journeys: Thinking Again about Conversion* (Atlanta: Authentic, 2007), 10.

256. Paul. G. Hiebert, "Worldview Transformation," in *From the Straight Path to the Narrow Way: Journeys of Faith*, ed. David Greenlee (Waynesboro: Authentic and Secunderabad: OM Books India), 29.

257. Charles H. Kraft, *Christianity in Culture: A Dynamic Biblical Theologizing in Cross-cultural Perspective* (Maryknoll: Orbis, 1979), 243.

258. Michael Kimmelman, "At Louvre, Many Stop to Snap but Few Stay to Focus," *The New York Times*, August 2, 2009,<www.nytimes.com/2009/08/03/arts/design/03abroad.html>.

259. J. Dudley Woodberry, "A Global Perspective on Muslims Coming to Faith in Christ" in *From the Straight Path to the Narrow Way*, ed. David H. Greenlee (Waynesboro, GA: Authentic and Secunderabad: OM Books India: 2005), 11–22 and J. Dudley Woodberry, R. G. Shubin, and G. Marks, "Why Muslims Follow Jesus," *Christianity Today*, October 2007: 80–85.

260. Don Allen et al., "Descriptive List from Plowing to Harvest," in *From Seed to Fruit: Global Trends, Fruitful Practices, and Emerging Issues among Muslims*, 2nd. ed., ed. J. Dudley Woodberry (Pasadena: William Carey Library: 2010), 153–167, fleshed out with some true stories behind the descriptive list in *Where There is No Church: Postcards from Followers of Jesus in the Muslim World*, ed. E. J. Martin (n.p.: Fruitful Practice Research/Learning Together Press, 2010).

261. David Greenlee and Pam Wilson, "The Sowing of Witnessing" and Andrea Gray and Leith Gray, "Transforming Social Networks by Planting the Gospel" and "Attractional and Transformational Models of Planting" in Woodberry, *Seed to Fruit*, 93–94, 275–308.

262. Bob Fish and Richard Prinz, "The Effects of Language and Communication Choices," in Woodberry, *Seed to Fruit*, 263–272.

263. For simplicity, BMB will be used for all Muslims who follow Christ as Lord and Savior irrespective of what identity they choose.

264. Greenlee and Wilson, "Sowing of Witnessing," 101.

265. Eric Adams, Don Allen, and Bob Fish, "Seven Fruitful Branches" in Woodberry, *Seed to Fruit*, 178–179.

266. Warren Larson, *Islamic Ideology and Fundamentalism in Pakistan: Climate for Conversion to Christianity?* (Lanham, MD: University Press of America, 1998).

267. See Andrea and Leith Gray, "The Imperishable Seed: Toward Effective Sharing of Scripture" and Adams, Allen, and Fish, "Seven Fruitful Branches," 25–37, 177–178.

268. Allen *et al.*, "Descriptive List," 155, 157.

269. Adams, Allen, and Fish, "Seven Fruitful Branches," 174–175.

270. Nik Ripkin, "Recapturing the Role of Suffering," in Woodberry, *Seed to Fruit*, 357–365.

271. Adams, Allen, and Fish, "Seven Fruitful Branches," 179–180.

272. Greenlee and Wilson, "Sowing of Witnessing," 98–99.

273. Caleb Chul-Soo Kim, John Travis, and Anna Travis, "Relevant Responses to Popular Muslim Piety," in Woodberry, *Seed to Fruit*, 245–249.

274. Greenlee and Wilson, "Sowing of Witnessing," 99.

275. Greenlee and Wilson, "Sowing of Witnessing," 93–94; Adams, Allen, and Fish, "Seven Fruitful Branches," 175–176; Gray and Gray, "Transforming Social Networks," 275–308.

276. Kim, Travis, and Travis, "Relevant Responses," 239–249.

277. Joseph Henry Smith, "The Practice of Da'wah in North America and the Attraction of Islam," ThM in Missiology thesis, Fuller Theological Seminary, Pasadena, CA, 1995: 113–209.

278. Ripken, 357–365.

279. Allen et al., 156.

280. Starting with St Paul: "Jew with the Jews, Gentile with the Gentiles" (1 Corinthians 9: 20–21 and going on to all the main missionary figures of the past (such as Mateo Ricci, 1553–1610). In recent times, and more directly concerned with Islam, Cardinal Lavigerie (1825–1892) insisted so much on this theme that he forbade his missionaries to preach Christianity to Muslims as long as they were not so completely integrated into the Muslim society and its culture as to be totally accepted by the group as men of God and brothers.

281. One could mention the worker-priests, Cardijn and the Catholic Action movements, Fr. Peyriguère (1883–1959) in Morocco; Fr. Monchanin (1895–1957) and Fr. H. Le Saux (1910–1973) in India among Hindus.

282. This does not mean giving up Christ and becoming a Muslim, but it does mean 'living Christ,' using the language, categories, and gestures of that particular culture insofar as it is possible without betraying one or the other, Christ or this culture. To twist a Muslim text into a Christian one is a betrayal that must be avoided. On this, read M. L. Fitzgerald, "Christian Liturgy and Islamic Texts," in *Encounter* 30 (December 1976) and "Christian Liturgy in an Islamic Context," *Encounter* 48 (October 1978).

283. For further insights, see A. Merad, *Charles de Foucauld au regard de l'Islam* (Paris: Chalet, 1975); A. Peyriguere, *Le Temps de Nazareth* (Paris: Seuil, 1964); J. P. Lauby FSC, *Le Père Peyriguère, témoin du Christ et de l'Eglise*, ad Licentiam dissertation, Lateran

University, Rome, 1965; J. Loew, "Les trois temps de la mission," in *Comme s'il voyait l'invisible* (Paris: Cerf, 1964): 210–216.

284. This *dhimmi* status gradually forced the local churches into a ghetto mentality. Under the Ottomans, the Millet System perpetuated this situation with even more stringency.

285. See J. Corbon, *L'Eglise des Arabes* (Paris: Cerf 1977), 247, a study on the situation of churches in the Arab World, their past, their wounds, and present opportunities to find unity and purpose in a new presence in the Arab World, both Christian and Muslim. For new developments on that question, read: "La présence chrétienne en Orient: témoignage et mission," (lettre pastorale du Conseil des Patriarches catholiques d'Orient), in *Documentation Catholique*, 2052, June 21, 1992: 595–611; R. Khoury, "L'insertion de nos Eglises dans le monde de l'Islam arabe" in: *Documentation Catholique*, 2087, February 6, 1994: 140–143. See as well the new declaration of Latin bishops of the Arab world issued on October 10, 1997.

286. H. Kraemer, "Islamic Culture and Missionary Adequacy," *The Muslim World*, 50,4 (October 1960): 244–251. The extract given here is found on page 251. On the evolution of H. Kraemer (1905–1965) and of his concept of mission among Muslims, see A. Garon, WF, "Hendrik Kraemer and the Mission to Islam," PhD dissertation, Ottawa, 1979: 439. The conclusion of this study can be read in A. Garon, "Second Thoughts on the Mission to Islam — Dr. Kraemer," in: *Kerygma*, 13 (1979): 13–68.

287. There is no place here to describe the initiatives Lavigerie took concerning the evangelization of Africa, the protection of the Eastern Christians from Latin proselytism, his part in French politics or his leading role in the Anti-Slavery Campaign.

288. Note the coincidence with Charles de Foucauld's vocation.

289. This is in striking agreement with the principle of Thomas Aquinas and with the method used by Elias of Nisibis in his *Daf' alHamm*. When suggesting themes of dialogue, Lavigerie often quoted Hebrews 11:6, "Whoever comes to God must have faith that God exists and rewards those who seek him." He used as well the ideas expressed in Pope Gregory's Letter to al-Nasir in 1076. See Cardinal Lavigerie's pastoral letter of February 1, 1883 in *Oeuvres Choisies*, Vol. 2 (Paris: 1884): 471–479.

290. Lavigerie wanted every conversion to be tested through one or two years of spiritual formation (the Postulate) to make sure that the prospective convert was really under the influence of the Spirit and determined to go ahead. He was not given Christian dogmas but a moral training. If he persevered in his decision, he would then enter a two-year course of instruction. Then, and only then, would he be taught Christian dogma.

291. For instance, the prophets of Israel, Jesus himself, who condemns the Pharisees and the Sadducees for just these same reasons, Paul in his struggle against legalism and Jewish racial pride; more recently Lavigerie listed the same obstacles. Marchal only develops his arguments.

292. This pride was condemned by Jesus and the prophets in Judaism (for instance Jeremiah 7:1–15; Luke 13:23). It has been fought against by Christian pastors generation after generation, with such vigor at times that a 'Christian neurosis' of guilt feelings and

fear spread through large sections of the Christian people (without suppressing this pride which grows with guilt as a compensatory reflex). In Islam, certain texts of the Qur'an (3:110) have been seized upon by many to justify this attitude of pride.

293.   Even when God is not known explicitly, a similar attitude towards a certain cause or ideal prevents a man from becoming totally locked up in his own subjectivity and self-centeredness. (cf. "Lumen Gentium: Dogmatic Constitution on the Church," (Rome: Vatican II Council, November 21, 1964): 2:16.

294.   Many texts link this discovery of Jesus and his message with a previous attitude of conversion to God: John 7:17; 8:47; 18:37. Hence the probability that, in most cases, the Spirit will lead a person first to be converted to God before drawing this person to a conversion to Jesus. The probability is increased in Islam, since the focus of attention is primarily God and secondarily his prophets. But the Spirit of God moves in unpredictable ways and there is no knowing how he will lead any particular individual.

295.   With Charles de Foucauld and Marchal we have seen that this was not a tactical move, but really a mystique, the extension of Christ's incarnation through us to a new people.

296.   Marchal remarked that these were the themes of the Sermon on the Mount, those of the first week of the *Exercises* of Ignatius of Loyola.

297.   It is not a matter of calling Muslims to the practice of the *salat*; neither is it a matter of criticizing the *salat*. It means going beyond this to a deeper level, that of our attitude at the innermost center of ourselves: do we pray in truth? Without apparent link with Marchal, we find similarities with practical applications to a classroom situation in an article written by Marie, a missionary lay woman, on evangelization (understood in this way), *Le Christ au Monde*, 1981,3: 186–197; 1982,1: 11–26, 1982,2: 111–121.

298.   This may be conveyed through humble disinterested service (*diakonia*), but must be completed at times with a personal word of witness about the way in which Jesus answers our own prayers and comforts us in our difficulties. Although Marchal could not have mentioned it in his time, this presentation of Jesus' saving power manifested in our lives is made easier through the use of charismatic gifts, as they are granted and manifested so abundantly in the Church of our time.

299.   See the same idea in J. D. C. Anderson, "The Missionary Approach to Islam: Christian or 'Cultic'?" in *Missiology* 4 (July 1976): 285–300. Such cases of "conversion to Jesus" among Muslims are more frequent than is usually thought. Some people may come to see in Jesus much more than just a prophet, have a real and mutual relation with Him, and yet never perceive any call to leave Islam for Christianity. In a romanticized version, see a true story in G. Diallo, *La nuit du Destin* (Mulhouse, France: Salvator, 1969), 247.

300.   This and Marchal's extreme reserve explain why his works can be found now only in some libraries or archives, such as those of his Congregation, the White Fathers.

301.   At the same time, another pioneer of this new attitude to Islam, M. Asin y Palacios (1871–1944), a Spanish priest and an orientalist, studied the ways in which Christian and Muslim Mystics influenced one another at various periods of history. On

this scholar, one may consult: M. Borrmans, "Le dialogue islamo-chrétien des dix dernières années," special edition of *Pro Mundi Vita*, 74 (September, October 1978): 8; Y. Moubarac, *Recherches sur la Pensée Chrétienne et l'Islam dans les Temps Modernes* (Beirut: Univ. Libanaise, 1977), 291–337.

302.   Even local Christians (Copts, Arabs, or any other nation) who are not foreigners in their own country, know that they are strangers in the religious universe of their Muslim fellow countrymen and are sometimes treated as strangers politically, reminiscent of the *dhimmi* status.

303.   We touch already on the following paragraph. Let us note here that this idea should be compared with similar intuitions of other contemporaries: P. Teilhard de Chardin (1881–1955) and his "Mass on the World," in *The Heart of Matter* (London: Collins, 1978), 119–134; P. Couturier (1881–1953) and his idea of an "invisible monastery" of Christian Unity. At the service of this unity, Fr. Couturier had developed the same theme of mutual hospitality of all Christians in their prayers and liturgies. Cf. M. Villain, *L'Abbé Paul Couturier* (Tournai, Belgium: Casterman, 1957), 333–334; 363.

304.   One should study the form taken by the devotion to the Sacred Heart in the nineteenth century to understand certain expressions used by K. Huysmans (1848–1907), de Foucauld, and Massignon.

305.   This spirit of the *Badaliyya* brings about very concrete changes in our lives. For instance, the daily call to prayer so noisy in some countries needs no longer be a cause of impatience if used as a signal to assume our role of 'priestly people' and we begin to praise God and to present all these prayers to Him in a spirit of filial love. Restrictions on our freedom (food taboos, ban on liquor, Ramadan discipline) begin to make sense when they become the very bread of our Eucharist in union with Christ's passion.

306.   For further reading on Louis Massignon see L. Massignon, *Sur l'Islam* (Collections Confidences, L'Herne: Paris, 1995); L. Massignon *Les Trois Prières d'Abraham* (Paris: Cerf, 1997); D. Massignon, ed., *Louis Massignon et le Dialogue des Cultures* (Paris: Cerf, 1996); G. Basetti-Sani, *Louis Massignon, Christian Ecumenist* (Chicago: Franciscan Herald Press, 1974); G. Harpigny, *Islam et Christianisme selon Louis Massignon*, Homo Religiosus 6 (Louvain La Neuve, Belgium: Service d'Impression de l'Université Catholique: 1981); R. L. Moreau, "La Badaliyya et la Mission d'Aujourd'hui," *Parole et Mission*, (October 1966): 561–574; J. Keryell, ed., *Louis Massignon et ses Contemporains* (Paris: Karthala, 1997); J. Keryell, ed., *Louis Massignon au Cœur de Notre Temps* (Paris: Karthala, 1999).

307.   John Kiser, *The Monks of Tibhirine: Faith, Love, and Terror in Algeria* (New York: Saint Martin's Press, 2002), 244–246.

308.   Patrick Johnstone, *The Church is Bigger than You Think* (Fearn, Scotland: Christian Focus Publication and Gerrard's Cross, England: WEC, 1998), 73.

309.   This paper draws in part on my PhD dissertation, Jae Hyun Paik, "Bozkır Kültürü ile Türk ve Kore Kültürü Arasında Münasebetler" (The Relationship between Turkish

and Korean Cultures Based upon Nomadic Culture), Ankara, Hacettepe University, 1996.

310.   Ian Gillman and Hans-Joachim Klimkeit state that "the Jewish Christianity to be found in Palestine, Syria and Mesopotamia formed a resource of Christianity 'independent of and of equal importance with Latin and Greek Christianity' . . . Christianity has been interpreted in several ways . . . if Rome stressed the legal aspects of the new religion, and the Greeks developed an ontological interpretation of God and Christ, the Syriacs were not very interested in dogmatic strife, at least until Ephrem Syrus in the fourth century, and conceived their faith rather as a Way, a way of life." Ian Gillman and Hans-Joachim Klimkeit, *Christians in Asia before 1500* (Ann Arbor: University of Michigan Press, 1999), 22–25.

311.   Vasilli V. Barthold, *Mussulman Culture*, trans. Shahid Suhrawardy (Philadelphia: Porcupine Press, 1934), xxii–xxiii.

312.   Richard C. Foltz, *Religions on the Silk Road* (New York: St. Martin's Press, 1999), 63.

313.   Ibid., 64.

314.   Gillman and Klimmkeit, *Christians in Asia*, 15.

315.   In Persia, although Eastern Christians didn't take part in the Council due to persecution, they had the synod adopt the creeds and canons of Nicea (AD 325) and Constantinople (AD 381) in the presence of 26 bishops from different parts of Persia.

316.   Philip Jenkins, *The Lost History of Christianity: The Thousand Year Golden Age of the Church in the Middle East, Africa, and Asia – and How it Died* (New York: HarperOne, 2008), xi.

317.   "We believe in one God, the Father, who upholds everything, the Creator of all things that are seen and unseen. [We believe] in one Lord God, and in Jesus [Christ], the only son of God, [the firstborn] of all beings, who. . .in the beginning was not created but begotten by the Father; [true God] of the true God. . .by whose hand the [aeons] were fashioned and everything was created, he who for the sake of men and for our salvation descended from the heavens and clothed himself in a body by the Holy Spirit, and became man and entered the womb; who was born of Mary, the virgin, and [who] suffered agony and [was buried] and ascended and sits on the right and of the Father and is ready to come (again) to judge the dead and the living. And [we believe] in the Spirit of Truth, the Holy Spirit, who went forth from the Father, the Holy Spirit who gives life." Gillman and Kilkeit, *Christians in Asia*, 242–253.

318.   There were three Christian centers in this period: Jerusalem, Antioch (Antakya in modern Turkey), and Edessa (Urfa in modern Turkey). Antioch was the center for the West influenced by Hellenism, while Edessa for the East with the eastern background. This church appears to have more in common with the Jerusalem Church. Gillman and Kilkeit, *Christians in Asia*, 28.

319.   Andrew F. Walls, "Eusebius Tries Again: Reconceiving the Study of Christian History," *International Bulletin of Missionary Research* 24,3 (July 2000): 105.

320.   There was a reaction to excessive asceticism among Nestorians regarding celibacy which had its roots in Jewish Christianity: they permitted the marriage, not only

of priests, but also of bishops. Nor did they accept sacrament, marriage, unction, confirmation or a belief in purgatory, which differed from Latin Christians (Gillman and Kilkeit, *Christians in Asia*, 143).

321.   John Stewart, *Nestorian Missionary Enterprise* (Edinburgh: T and T Clark, 1928), 19.

322.   Ho Dong Kim, *Dongbang Gidoggyowa Dongseomunmyoung* [*The Church of the East and Civilizations of the East and the West*] (Seoul: Gachi Geulbang, 2002), 104.

323.   Barthold remarked: "The exceptional success of Christianity in the western frontier districts of the Sasanian Empire from the estuary of the Euphrates and Tigris up to Armenia and the Caucasus . . . By the time of Muslim conquest, these districts, with the exception of a few Jewish colonies, became purely Christian." Samuel Hugh Moffett, *A History of Christianity in Asia*, vol. 1, *Beginnings to 1500* (Maryknoll: Orbis Books, 1998), 115.

324.   Presently Iran and the southwestern part of Central Asia.

325.   Foltz, *Religions on the Silk Road*, 67.

326.   Moffett, *History of Christianity*, 138.

327.   Ibid.

328.   Gillman and Klimkeit, *Christians in Asia*, 150.

329.   Ibid.

330.   Ibid.

331.   Ibid., 149.

332.   The Patriarch was called "Father of Fathers," "Supreme Shepherd," and "Peter of our Days." "He had full jurisdictional powers, in loyalty to non-Christian rulers. It was he that convened and led synods, who consecrated bishops, even for more remote 'outward regions,' who established bishoprics." Gillman and Klimkeit, *Christians in Asia*, 238.

333.   He actually sent the first delegation of Nestorians to China during the Tang dynasty, and created the first metropolitan in India. Moffett, *History of Christianity*, 257.

334.   This monument is important for the study of Nestorians in China, revealing their belief and history from AD 635–781.

335.   Gillman and Klimkeit, *Christians in Asia*, 222.

336.   Aziz S Atiya, *History of Eastern Christianity* (Notre Dame: University of Notre Dame Press, 1968), 239–302, cited in Mark Dickens, "Nestorian Christianity in Central Asia," The Tarsakan Pages: Syriac Christianity in Central Asia, (2001) <www.oxuscom. com/Nestorian_Christianity_in_CA.pdf>.

337.   Foltz, *Religions on the Silk Road*, 62.

338.   Alphonse Mingana, "The Early Spread of Christianity in Central Asia and the Far East: A New Document," reprinted from *The Bulletin of the John Rylands Library*, 9,2 (1925): 15.

339.   Jenkins, *Lost History of Christianity*, 15.

340.   Ibid., 17.

341.   Mingana, "Early Spread of Christianity," 11–12.

342. Jenkins, *Lost History of Christianity*, 18–19.

343. James Dickie, "Allah and Eternity: Mosques, Madrasa and Tombs," in *Architecture of the Islamic World*, ed. George Michell (New York: Thames and Hudson, 1978), 40.

344. "Inbetweeners" are those who have settled in an insider's society, originally as outsiders but striving to become like insiders. In the early stage of settling in, they may come from different ethnic and religious backgrounds and thus be regarded as outsiders, but in the end, they are accepted by the insiders' community as being almost like them.

345. John Kim, "Muslim Villagers Coming to Faith in Christ: A Case Study and Model of Group Dynamics," in *From the Straight Path to the Narrow Way*, ed. David H. Greenlee (Waynesboro, GA: Authentic and Secunderabad: OM Books India, 2005), 239–253. Here, I again use "Anotoc" to refer to the main village of the people while "Bangunda" represents the name of their ethnic group.

346. The whole passage is: *Show us the straight way; The Way of those on whom thou hast bestowed Thy Grace, those whose (portion) is not wrath, and who go not astray.*

347. See Matthew 20:1–16 with reference to Ben Naja, *Releasing the Workers of the Eleventh Hour: The Global South and the Task Remaining* (Pasadena: William Carey Library, 2007).

348. Kim, "Muslim Villagers," 239–253.

349. For an example, see Andrea Gray and Leith Gray, "Fruitful Practices: What Does the Research Suggest? Paradigms and Praxis; Part II: Why Are Some Workers Changing Paradigms?" *International Journal of Frontier Missiology*, 26:2 (April 2009): 63–73.

350. Drawn from my PhD dissertation, Christine Shepherd, "The Influence of Savings-Based Micro-Credit on the Status and Role of Rural Bangladeshi Muslim Women," School of Intercultural Studies, Fuller Theological Seminary, Pasadena, CA, 2007.

351. Anonymous, excerpts from a presentation to the Asian Institute of Intercultural Studies (AIIS) Round Table, Pune, India, March 2009.

352. Although much of the information in this writing comes from my dissertation, for the sake of readability I have not specifically referenced each interview or informant.

353. David Abecassis, *Identity Islam and Human Development in Rural Bangladesh* (Dhaka, Bangladesh: University Press Limited, 1990), 40.

354. Therese Blanchet, *Meanings and Ritual of Birth in Rural Bangladesh* (Dhaka, Bangladesh: The University Press Limited, 1984), 28–29.

355. Jitka Kotalova, *Belonging to Others: Cultural Construction of Womanhood in a Village in Bangladesh* (Dhaka, Bangladesh: University Press Limited, 1993), 199.

356. Guiseppe Scattolin, "Women in Islamic Mysticism," *Encounter: Documents for Muslim-Christian Understanding*, Pontifical Council for Interreligious Dialogue, ed. Justa Lacunza Balda, 198 (October 1993): 3–26.

357. Santi Theresa Rozario, "Women's Solidarity: The Village Perspective" (CARE Bangladesh, 2005).

358. Loren Cunningham and David Joel Hamilton with Janice Rogers, *Why Not Women? A Fresh Look at Scripture on Women in Missions, Ministry, and Leadership* (Seattle, WA: Youth With a Mission Publishing, 2000), 71–93. See also Paul K. Jewett, *Man as Male*

and Female: A Study in Sexual Relationships from a Theological Point of View (Grand Rapids: Eerdmans, 1975), 9. Jewett finds that the argument for female subordination is incompatible with the biblical narratives of man's creation, the revelation which is given us in the life of Jesus, and Paul's fundamental statement of Christian liberty in the epistle to the Galatians.

359.   Thomas John Carlisle, *Eve and After: Old Testament Women in Portrait* (Grand Rapids: Eerdmans, 1984), 4. Reprinted by permission of the publisher; all rights reserved.

360.   Jewett, *Male and Female*, 94; italics in the original.

361.   Donald B. Kraybill, *The Upside-Down Kingdom* (Scottsdale, Penn.: Herald Press, 1990), 251.

362.   Mary Evans, *Woman in the Bible* (Carlisle, England: Paternoster, 1998), 44.

363.   Joachim Jeremias, *Jerusalem in the Time of Jesus: An Investigation into Economic and Social Conditions during the New Testament Period*, trans. F. H. Cave and C. H. Cave (Philadelphia, Penn.: Fortress Press, 1969), 376.

364.   Jewett, *Male and Female*, 102.

365.   Kraybill, *Upside-Down Kingdom*, 217.

366.   Joseph A. Grassi, *The Hidden Heroes of the Gospels: Female Counterparts of Jesus* (Collegeville, MN: The Liturgical Press, 1989), 134.

367.   Rebecca Lewis, missionary at one time to Morocco, discovered through her research that, although many young men returned to Islam, those that stayed in the faith oftentimes had believing mothers who had been won to faith years before by missionaries. Rebecca Lewis, "Underground Church Movements: The Surprising Role of Women's Networks," *International Journal of Frontier Missiology* 21,4 (October 2004): 45.

368.   "Verily the Muslims men and women, the believers men and women, the men and the women who are obedient, the men and women who are truthful, the men and the women who are patient, the men and women who are humble, the men and the women who give alms, the men and the women who fast, the men and women who guard their chastity and the men and the women who remember God much, God has prepared for them forgiveness and a great reward" (33:35). All quranic quotations are taken from *Translation of the Meanings of the Noble Qur'an in the English Language*, trans. Dr. Muhammad Taqi-ud-Din al-Hilali and Dr. Muhammad Muhsin Khan (Medinah, Saudi Arabia: King Fahd Complex for the Printing of the Holy Qur'an).

369.   The same word used within Islam for the prophetic vocation.

370.   Sarah Mullin, "Faith on Camelback: Reaching non-Arabic-Speaking Urban, Less-Educated Muslim Women," in *A Worldview Approach to Ministry Among Muslim Women*, ed. Cynthia A. Strong and Meg Page (Pasadena: William Carey Library, 2006), 81.

371.   Also Eleanor Abdella Doumato, *Getting God's Ear: Women, Islam and Healing in Saudi Arabia and the Gulf* (New York: Columbia University Press, 2000), 187.

372.   Ibid., 13.

373.   Saba Mahmood, *Politics of Piety: The Islamic Revival and the Feminist Subject* (Princeton and Oxford: Princeton University Press, 2005), 92.

374. Similarly Middle Eastern Orthodox (and some Protestant) women will not take communion at that time. There is some variation among Muslim writers about reading the Qur'an. Some suggest that there is no harm in a menstruating woman reciting a quranic verse, e.g. Abu Ameenah Bilal Philips, *Islamic Rules on Menstruation and Post-Natal Bleeding* (Kuala Lumpur: A.S. Noordeen, 1995), 16–17.

375. There is some disagreement about whether the breastfeeding should take place once, three, or five times before the child becomes *mahram* to the woman's children. The evidence of the woman who breastfed may also be taken as evidence. Shaykh Muhammad S al-Munajjid, "Islam: Question and Answer," n.d. <http://islamqa.com/en/ref/45620>.

376. Most Muslim writers require four *male* witnesses. Iranian law (Qisas Bill 1982, Article 91) requires four men, or three men and two women, and so on. However Asghar Ali Engineer cites Imam Sahfi'i that "in matters connected with women such as childbirth" women can bear witness without the testimony of a man being required. Ibn Taymiyyah also agreed that "if in a place of bathing only women are present and something punishable by *hadd* (rape, adultery, etc.) takes place then the case will be decided on grounds of women's testimony alone," in *The Rights of Women in Islam*, 3rd ed. (New Delhi: Sterling Publishers, 2004, 2008), 79.

377. This is known as the *khitma* or sealing of the Qur'an.

378. D'Souza records a similar practice among Shia women in south India, where the women track the number of times they call on Ali for help with the prayer beads: and then use seeds to mark a hundred and a thousand repetitions. "Devotional Practices among Shia Women in South India," in *Lived Islam in South Asia: adaptation, accommodation, and conflict*, ed. Imtiaz Ahmad, Helmut Reifeld and Konrad-Adenauer-Stiftung, Esha Beteille (New Delhi: Social Science Press, 2004), 191.

379. Also in the Gulf, for Muhammad or for other saints' days: Doumato, *Getting God's Ear*, 111–112.

380. Doumato, *Getting God's Ear*, 112ff; Mary Elaine Hegland, "Shi'a Women's Rituals in Northwest Pakistan: The Shortcomings and Significance of Resistance," *Anthropological Quarterly*, 76 (Summer 2003): 3; Rehana Ghadially, "A Hajari (Meal Tray) for Abbas Alam Dar: Women's Household Ritual in a South Asian Muslim Sect," *The Muslim World* 92,2 (2003): 309–322: Doumato, *Getting God's Ear*, 170–184; Janice Boddy, *Wombs and Alien Spirits: Women, Men and the Zar Cult in Northern Sudan* (Madison, WI: University of Wisconsin Press, 1989); Barbara M. Cooper, "Gender and Religion in Hausaland: Variations in Islamic Practice in Niger and Nigeria," in *Women in Muslim Societies: Diversity in Unity*, ed. Herbert L. Bodman and Nayereh Tohidi (Boulder, CO and London: Lynne Rienner, 1998), 21–37.

381. *Da'wa* means to call or invite. M. Canard notes with reference to Surah 14:44 that, in religious terms it is "the invitation, addressed to men (*sic*) by God and the prophets, to believe in the true religion, Islam." It determined the Muslim community's relationship to non-Muslims: "Those to whom the da'wa had not yet penetrated had to be invited to embrace Islam before fighting could take place." M. Canard, s.V. "Da'wa,"

in *Encyclopaedia of Islam*, Vol. 2, (Leiden: Brill, 1965). The contemporary piety move-ment relates *da'wa* not only to non-Muslims, but also to the duty of every practicing Muslim to urge fellow Muslims to correct Islamic practice.

382. Poorer women in Egypt had similar co-operative arrangements where each person in turn took the money collected for whatever their need was; however these usually weren't accompanied by meals.

383. Anne Jansen, "Building Community in a Muslim Background Believer Church: A Case Study among Uighur Women," in *Ministry to Muslim Women: Longing to Call Them Sisters*, ed. Fran Love and Jeleta Eckheart (Pasadena: William Carey Library, 2000), 192.

384. Mahmood, *Politics of Piety*, 58.

385. Maria Jaschok, and Jingjun Shui, *The History of Women's Mosques in Chinese Islam* (Richmond, England: Curzon Press, 2000).

386. Herbert L. Bodman, introduction to *Women in Muslim Societies: Diversity within Unity*, ed. Herbert L. Bodman and Nayereh Todhidi (Boulder, Colo. and London: Lynne Rienner Publishers, 1998), 12.

387. Cynthia Strong, "A Mystic Union: Reaching Sufi Women," in *A Worldview Approach to Ministry Among Muslim Women*, ed. Cynthia A. Strong and Meg Page (Pasadena: William Carey Library, 2006), 184.

388. It takes its name from its founder, Miss Munira al-Qubaysi.

389. "Home of Sheikh Moulana Nazim," n.d. <www.sheiknazim2.com/naqshbandiorder. html>.

390. Ibrahim Hamidi, "The Qubaysi Women's Islamic Movement," posted by Joshua Landis, May 16, 2006, <http://faculty-staff.ou.edu/L/Joshua.M.Landis-1/syriablog/archives/2006_05_01_faculty-staff_archive.htm>.

391. Yoginder Sikand, "Women and the Tablighi Jama'at," March 23, 2009, <sociol-ogy_of_islam@listserv.vt.edu>.

392. Jasmine R. Meydan, "Messiah Families: From a Movement of Individuals to the Establishment of Jesus-centered families in Bangladesh" (Unpublished, 2007), 57.

393. Doumato, *Getting God's Ear*, 128.

394. Hegland, "Shi'a Women's Rituals."

395. Doumato, *Getting God's Ear*, 225; Hegland, "Shi'a Women's Rituals"; and Ghadially, "A Hajari (Meal Tray) for Abbas Alam Dar." Similarly Sunday school teaching in Egypt offered young Christian village women an acceptable reason to leave their homes, and even go on summer conferences for training or with the children they taught.

396. Shahrbanou Tadjbakhsh, "Between Lenin and Allah: Women and Ideology in Ta-jikistan," in *Women in Muslim Societies: Diversity within Unity*, ed. Herbert L. Bodman and Nayereh Tohidi (Boulder, CO and London: Lynne Rienner Publishers, 1998), 174.

397. Cooper, "Gender and Religion in Hausaland," 27.

398. The latter exemplify female authority validated by a patriarchal structure — women can often wield great power, but they receive power though their relationship with a powerful male.

399. Also Hegland, "Shi'a Women's Rituals."

400. Doumato, *Getting God's Ear*, 128.

401. Tadjbakhsh, "Between Lenin and Allah," 174.

402. Cooper, "Gender and Religion in Hausaland," 26.

403. Ibid.

404. Ghadially, "A Hajari (Meal Tray) for Abbas Alam Dar," 309–322.

405. Doumato, *Getting God's Ear*, 177, 183.

406. Tadjbakhsh, "Between Lenin and Allah," 174.

407. Meydan, "Messiah Families," 68-70; Jaschok and Shui, *History of Women's Mosques*, 116.

408. See also Doumato, *Getting God's Ear*, on the effect of the Wahhabi revival on women's religious practices in the Gulf.

409. Cooper, "Gender and Religion in Hausaland," 27.

410. Jansen, "Building Community," 192.

411. Since every seeker has the potential of going on a journey towards spiritual maturity in Christ, it seemed fitting to lead them onwards and allow the Holy Spirit to continue the work of conviction and guidance. This recognizes that the point at which spiritual birth takes place varies with each individual. While spiritual birth or conversion may be an important moment, it is not the goal — spiritual maturity is.

412. Ruth J. Nicholls, "Catechisms and Chants, A Case for Using Liturgies in Ministry to Muslims," DMin thesis, Bible College of Victoria (now Melbourne School of Theology), Lilydale, Australia. The thesis including full-color sample liturgy plates is available at <http://postgrad.mst.edu.au/sites/postgrad.mst.edu.au/files/RNichollsThesis.pdf>.

413. The spiritual exercises of St Ignatius; the interior journey of Teresa of Avila, and the three ways of St John of the Cross are some examples.

414. James F. Engel and William A. Dyrness, *Changing the Mind of Missions: Where Have We Gone Wrong?* (Downers Grove, IL: InterVarsity Press, 2000), 101. I am aware of several forms of Engel's Spiritual Decision Process Model.

415. James Fowler, *Stages of Faith, The Psychology of Human Development and the Psychological Quest for Meaning* (Blackburn, Victoria: Dove, 1981).

416. Robert J. Clinton, *The Making of a Leader* (Colorado Springs, CO: NavPress, 1988).

417. Janet O. Hagberg and Robert A. Guelich, *The Critical Journey, Stages in the Life of Faith* (Salem, WI: Sheffield Publishing, 1989).

418. "Fruitful Practices: A Descriptive List," in *Where there was No Church: Postcards from Followers of Jesus in the Muslim World*, ed. E. J. Martin (n.p.: Fruitful Practice Research and Learning Together Press, 2010), 195–196.

419. S. Abul Ala Maududi, *Towards Understanding Islam*, trans. and ed. Khurshid Ahmad (Lahore: Idara Trajuman-ul-Quran, 1999), 895ff, 129ff.

420. *HarperCollins Dictionary of Religion,* ed. Jonathan Z. Smith, (New York: HarperSan-Francisco, 1996), 298; Frank H. Gorman, Jr., *The Ideology of Ritual, Space, Time and Status in the Priestly Theology* (Sheffield, England: JSOT Press, 1990), 14ff.

421. Paul G. Hiebert, R. Daniel Shaw, and Tite Tiénou, *Understanding Folk Religion* (Grand Rapids: Baker, 1999), 283.

422. Darrell Whiteman, introduction to A. H. Mathias Zahniser, *Symbol and Ceremony, Making Disciplines across Cultures* (Monrovia, CA: MARC, 1997), x.

423. Zahniser, *Symbol and Ceremony,* 2.

424. William G. Doty, *Mythology, the Study of Myths and Rituals* (Tuscaloosa, AL: University of Alabama Press, 1986), 104–105).

425. Donald K. Smith, *Creating Understanding* (Grand Rapids: Zondervan, 1992), 263.

426. Contra *The Documents of Vatican II,* ed. Walter M. Abbott, S. J. (New York, Corpus Books, 1996), 142. In this case the word 'liturgy' primarily refers to the Eucharistic Mass.

427. One of the reasons behind Thomas Cranmer's sixteenth century liturgical reforms was the need to provide adequate materials for the conduct of services where there was a lack of suitably trained leadership.

428. Dallas Willard, *The Spirit of the Disciplines* (San Francisco: Harper and Row, 1988), 158.

429. Hiebert, Shaw, and Tite Tiénou, *Understanding Folk Religion,* 283.

430. While "Light in Darkness" is a prose form, in translation a poetic form would possibly have a greater impact. Frequently, poetic forms lend themselves to repetition, important in Islamic liturgy and especially in the language in which I worked. The tile forming the background was cited at <www.historywiz.com/images/middle-east/mosaic-dado.jpg>.

431. This Affirmation of Faith, related to the truth that "God is Light," brings together a number of important Christian concepts. In some cases they challenge Islamic thinking but others such as God's light providing revelation and direction (cf. *Sura* I) find a resonance in Islam. The background is based on a Persian rug design and was cited at <www.nejad.com/consumer/Persia/19th-century-kerman.jpg>.

432. The Hebrew word used in the Bible is related to the Arabic *dhikr.*

433. For church growth rates see James Bultema, "Muslims Coming to Christ in Turkey," *International Journal of Frontier Missiology,* 27:1 (Spring 2010): 28. For population growth rates see the World Bank database at <http://data.worldbank.org/indicator/SP.POP.GROW?cid=GPD_2>. See also Jason Mandryk, s.V. "Turkey," *Operation World,* 7th ed. (Colorado Springs: Biblica, 2010).

434. Mustafa Numan Malkoç, *Günümüz Türkiye'sinde Protestanlık* (Istanbul: Marmara Üniversitesi Sosyal Bilimler Enstitüsü, 2006) gives brief histories of specific Protestant churches in Turkey.

435. For a fuller discussion of these three reasons, see Bultema, "Muslims Coming to Christ," 27–31.

436. In addition to analyzing dozens of conversion stories of Turks, I have collected and am analyzing narrations of approximately fifty Christian workers who have labored

or are laboring in Turkey. While my research is not yet completed, I have gleaned enough evidence to support this statement. My PhD dissertation on the Turkish Protestant Church should be completed by 2013 and published soon thereafter.

437.   Bultema, "Muslims Coming to Christ," 28.

438.   For more on assertive secularism in Turkey, see Ahmet T. Kuru, *Secularism and State Policies Toward Religion: The United States, France, and Turkey* (New York: Cambridge University Press, 2009), 161–235. Also highly recommended is Soner Cagaptay, *Islam, Secularism, and Nationalism in Modern Turkey* (New York: Routledge, 2006).

439.   Bultema, "Muslims Coming to Christ," 30–31. See narration summaries 3, 5, and 7.

440.   Cagaptay, 1.

441.   Although this fact is not expressed in Cosmades' account, my personal interview with Fatma Unutmuş on March 6, 2008 bears this out.

442.   See J. Dudley Woodberry's chapter in this volume, with reference to J. Dudley Woodberry, "A Global Perspective on Muslims Coming to Faith in Christ" in *From the Straight Path to the Narrow Way*, ed. David H. Greenlee (Waynesboro, GA: Authentic and Secunderabad: OM Books India: 2005), 11–22 and J. Dudley Woodberry, R. G. Shubin, and G. Marks, "Why Muslims Follow Jesus," *Christianity Today*, October 2007: 80–85.

443.   Bultema, "Muslims Coming to Christ," 28.

444.   Ibid. See also Woodberry, "Global Perspective" and "Why Muslims Follow Jesus."

445.   Davut Muratoğlu, *Neden Hıristiyan Oldular?* (Istanbul: Müjde Yayıncılık, 2002), 169–73.

446.   David Smith, "Conclusion: Looking Ahead," in Greenlee, *Straight Path*, 285–303.

INDEX